TheHumanThing

The Human Thing

The Speeches and Principles
of Thucydides' History

Marc Cogan

The University of Chicago Press • Chicago and London

MARC COGAN is assistant professor of humanities
at Wayne State University.

The University of Chicago Press, Chicago 60637
The University of Chicago Press, Ltd., London

85 84 83 82 81   5 4 3 2 1

Library of Congress Cataloging in Publication Data

Cogan, Marc.
  The human thing.

  Includes bibliographical references and index.
  1. Thucydides. De bello Peloponnesiaco.   2. Greece
—History—Peloponnesian War, 431–404 B.C.   I. Title.
DF229.T6C63   938'.05   80-24226
ISBN 0-226-11194-6

For David Grene

ἔνδοθεν ἀγάλματα ἔχοντι θεῶν

Contents

Acknowledgments

Writing a book is a long and involved process, I discovered, and along the way one receives precious help and encouragement from many people. It is impossible to thank them all; it is impossible to thank even some few adequately. I would, however, especially like to acknowledge my debt to the following persons.

Martin Ostwald and James Redfield, for advice and assistance during the earliest stages of this project.

My colleagues at Monteith College, who provided an atmosphere and community (now, alas, gone) in which it seemed both a reasonable and a serious activity to undertake writing this book. No one colleague and friend more completely embodies the values of that community than Martin Herman, with whom it has been both a pleasure and a privilege to work.

My wife, Sarah, for her strategic judgment and her political insights throughout the many revisions of this manuscript.

There are, in addition, three persons to whom I feel that special debt of the truly philosophic friendship whose bonds and whose aim are found in the search for wisdom. Their influence on this book is measureless; their value priceless.

Robert Berg, traces of whose thoughts and hand can be found in almost every word on these pages.

Douglas Mitchell, in whose ingenious and unique faculty seminar on the nature of history the conclusion of this book took shape.

David Grene, who is in a fundamental sense the only begetter of all this work, and to whom this book is dedicated.

Introduction

There are two parts to this book. The first (comprising chapters 1–4) is a commentary on the speeches of Thucydides' history as they figure in the initiation of events and an analysis of the interpretation of the Peloponnesian War that is structured by these speeches. The second (chapters 5–7), taking the results of the first part as its material, is an analysis of the practice of the history for the purpose of discovering the principles which informed the writing of the history, and which are necessarily embodied in it. The results of the second part complete the inquiries of the first in two senses. First, in the discovery of the principles which directed the composition of the history we discover the sources and rationale of the particular interpretation Thucydides has given to these events, and so our understanding of that interpretation is reinforced and improved. Second, in the isolation of the principles of the history we discover that principle of action which Thucydides believed was embodied in all actions—especially in the events of the Peloponnesian War as he understood it—and whose exposition, for him, guaranteed the eternal utility of his history (1.22.4).

This book, then, is not directly about the Peloponnesian War but about Thucydides' history of it. It assumes—whether this is true or not—that all assertions Thucydides makes as to the occurrence of events or the delivery of speeches are deliberate and are meant by the historian to be accepted as accurate. No attempt is here made to determine the veracity of Thucydides' account. This assumption is not made rashly or naïvely, and the resulting limitation of the scope of this inquiry is accepted deliberately. There is, simply, no other way to proceed if we are to determine properly *Thucydides'* interpretation of events. In the end, moreover, despite the initial avoidance of considering the relation of the history to actual historical fact, our historical understanding can only be improved. Our position as readers relative to Thucydides' history and to the events of the Peloponnesian War can be stated baldly: even if Thucydides were lying at every moment in his account of the war, we can determine *his* account only by considering those "facts" he has chosen to present to us, and no others. To consider other facts to correct (or attempt to correct) Thucydides' account might bring (or seem to bring) us a more accurate understanding of the Peloponnesian War; it could not, however, bring us a more accurate understanding of Thucydides' version of that war. And yet, in fact, Thucydides' history remains our most important source of information for this war, so that the proper understanding of that history must always be the first task to be completed in trying to understand the war. To examine Thucydides' history in its own terms is not, then, merely a literary exercise. We must consider the history as if it were a piece of documentary evidence concerning the war; and, as is the case with every document, it must be properly understood before it can be properly used. While the purpose of this inquiry is simply the interpretation of Thucydides' text—and questions of the veracity of the text are postponed as necessarily posterior to a determination of what precisely the text asserts—the ultimate aim of the inquiry is to render Thucydides' history more useful to historians and more fruitful for historical researches.

No sections of the history have been more controversial—in respect of the existence of the phenomena or the fidelity of Thucydides' record of them—than the speeches. It is in their regard that commentators and historians have most often questioned Thucydides' veracity, and have insisted that certain speeches were never given at all, or were never given in the form in which they appear in the history. Nonetheless, for our purposes the speeches, too, must be accepted not only as data Thucydides has presented to us, but especially as exactly what Thucydides claims they are: accurate accounts of actual speeches given on specific historical occasions.

Not to accept the speeches at face value would obscure Thucydides' interpretation of the war, for in that interpretation the speeches play their parts as speeches. This alone would compel us to deal with them as genuine speeches, since operationally it is only thus that we can securely recover Thucydides' view of this war, and understand what in fact the text of his history is saying. Again, this is no blind leap of faith or merely speculative hypothesis, for the alternative, denying the authenticity of the speeches (or Thucydides' accuracy in reporting them), has extensive and destructive consequences which I believe ultimately outweigh any benefits (for the understanding of either Thucydides or the Peloponnesian War) that might come from the apparent independence of such skepticism. These consequences, and the shaky grounds on which the denial of the speeches' authenticity rests, have been pointedly and compellingly examined by Donald Kagan;[1] but we can frame a brief statement of their destructiveness in a single formula. Inasmuch as Thucydides presents the speeches simply as speeches, and gives no indication that he has fabricated them in any material way, he has given to the speeches the same guarantee of their historicity that he has given to every other aspect of his history, every other event in his narrative. There is no way for us to question Thucydides' guarantee in the one instance and not in all the others. If we claim that Thucydides has tampered with the facts of the historical circumstances in the case of the speeches, we must also be prepared to admit that he has tampered with the facts on other occasions as well. If we believe Thucydides will invent speeches (yet attempt to pass them off as genuine events and declarations), what is to have prevented him from inventing events, battles, or the details of the progress of battles? To question the veracity of the speeches has the ultimate consequence of undermining—if not utterly destroying—the credibility of all of Thucydides' history.[2]

Such a nihilistic position is unacceptable. It is not merely practically unacceptable (in the sense that to destroy the credibility of this history would rob us of our most important source for the Peloponnesian War—a consequence from which we would instinctively shrink), there is no evidence to support it. Not only can we find no objective evidence to make us doubt Thucydides' essential reliability, every internal indication re-

inforces our belief in the fundamental veracity of his account.
Insofar as we believe the narrative essentially true, we must
believe the same about the speeches, for Thucydides himself
declares that he has treated them both with the same care.

Although it is usually overlooked by those attempting to
interpret Thucydides' specific statements about his treatment
of the speeches (1.22.1), the historian describes himself (in
1.22 considered as a whole) as utilizing what is essentially the
identical method—or criteria—in dealing with both speeches
and events.

> Now, what was said in speeches by either side, as it was
> about to go to war or when it was already in it, has been diffi-
> cult for me to remember exactly in terms of what precisely
> was spoken (both of what I heard myself or of what was re-
> ported to me by others). But as every individual would seem
> to me to have said pretty much what he had to concerning
> the circumstances at hand, so have I written it, staying as
> close as possible to the entire sense of what was actually
> spoken. And as far as the facts of what was done in the war
> are concerned, I did not think it fit to write what I learned
> from anyone who merely happened to be on the spot, nor
> merely what I thought seemed right. But both about those
> events I was witness to and those I learned of from others, as
> much as possible I scrutinized everyone [and his account]
> with a view to accuracy. Even so it was a difficult task to dis-
> cover [a true account] because participants in events did not
> agree with each other in their statements, but differed be-
> cause of their memories [being faulty] or because of their
> interests in the event. [1.22.1-3]

Of what is Thucydides attempting to advise us here? Directly, I think, of little more than that he has been as careful
and as accurate as possible in the acquisition and verification of
his information. Although he makes a distinction in this chapter between the speeches and the events in his narrative, the
distinction is merely one of the materials with which the historian has to deal. The key word in both halves of this chapter
is ἀκριβεία—"accuracy" or "precision." Throughout this

chapter Thucydides attempts to convince us of the trustworthiness of his account by demonstrating the difficulties he has overcome in dealing with both sorts of material. On the one hand, he says, it is hard to recollect speeches exactly. On the other, even first-hand reports of events are incomplete or biased. In both cases the historian's responsibilities do not end with the collection of raw data, but begin there. The historian must sift the data, scrutinize it to purge it of error or bias, and then analyze it to fill lacunae and to discover significance.

The points that he makes, and the historical problems that he reveals in this chapter, are not in themselves sophisticated or detailed. But Thucydides is merely informing us (presumably arguing against those who believe that history is a simple kind of story-telling) that the recording of words spoken and of actions performed is never simple or straightforward, and that in the collection and analysis of data he has been aware of these problems and has been as careful as possible. There can be no grounds, in this statement, for concluding that he here apologizes for inventing the speeches. Thucydides does not apologize for the inclusion of the speeches, he apologizes for any errors of fact. The problem with the speeches is accuracy, not historicity. If one were inventing speeches and their occasions, one would not trouble about the exactness of the record of what was spoken. This becomes a matter of concern only when one is trying to record faithfully actual words spoken on specific occasions. Thucydides' display of concern here is our proof that he intends us to accept the factuality and accuracy of his reports of the speeches in the history.

Despite these arguments, the historicity of these speeches—either their occasions or the words reported on them—has most often been denied. Accompanying the denial almost inevitably is a complementary manner of interpreting the words Thucydides has presented in the speeches, a manner that throughout this inquiry I call "epideictic" from its resemblance to epideictic rhetoric insofar as it is more concerned with the presentation and embellishment than the establishment or proof of facts or disputed facts. Freed of their original contents by the denial of their historicity, the speeches become, first, free inventions by the historian (in part or as a

whole) and, then, opportunities for the historian to make pro-
nouncements on events which, if concealed behind the masks
of other speakers, are nonetheless direct expressions of his own
opinions. By denying the historicity of the speeches, the
speeches become Thucydides' own exhibition (*epideixis*) of
causes and principles, abstracted from particular historical
circumstances, enunciated in universal formulations.

The desirability of such direct and general statements by the
historian is apparent, and no doubt explains the currency of
epideictic interpretations and perhaps even the denial of the
authenticity of the reported speeches. These sorts of statements
would provide us with direct evidence of Thucydides' interpretation of the events of this war and of the nature of action in
general. Yet, desirable as this would be, the price is too high,
for the epideictic interpretation not only necessarily attacks
Thucydides' utility (by undermining his veracity)—an effect
surely not desired by these commentators—it fundamentally
misunderstands Thucydides' practice and the sense in which
he is indeed valuable as an interpreter of this war and of action.

Political situations are irreducibly concrete and particular.
Individual political decisions grow out of particular circumstances and depend, for their actualization into the unique
decisions they become, on equally particular thoughts and
statements that respond to the given circumstances. The job of
the historian is to recover and explain events precisely in their
particularity. The epideictic interpretation, by suggesting that
Thucydides utilizes the speeches to propose general political
analyses, not only suggests he has failed in his duty as a historian, it also deflects us from inquiry into, and therefore from
ever discovering, what particular information about a given
situation Thucydides may indeed have been attempting to
convey. But it is in performing this historian's duty, and recognizing the particularity of politics—rather than in abstract
political formulations—that Thucydides truly becomes a great
political scientist.

In fact, the epideictic interpretation is not even necessary for
the purpose which evoked it, the discovery of Thucydides'
interpretation of events. While a direct statement by him
would no doubt be the best evidence of his intentions, we can

find perfectly adequate and clear, if indirect, evidence of his intentions in the practices he follows in the history. As H.-P. Stahl has written:

> Mere narration of any set of historical facts already implies a subjective element (because presentation includes judgment, evaluation, selection, arrangement, in short: interpretation)—to recognize, I say, the inherent subjective character of any historical narration at the same time allows us, in this field too, to rediscover and appreciate more fully the categories which Thucydides applied for selecting and presenting events.[3]

Nowhere is Thucydides' selectivity more accessible to us than in the speeches he records, and for this reason they provide the most direct route to the understanding of his interpretation of the war. That is, it would be difficult for us to evaluate Thucydides' principles of selection with respect to the events of the war without knowing what events (if any) he omitted, or that he gave different priorities to events than would have been given by other observers. In the absence of truly satisfactory alternate accounts of this war, a judgment on this must always be speculative or incomplete. But with respect to the speeches we are in quite a different position. It is no exaggeration to say that thousands of public political speeches must have been given throughout Greece during the course of this war. Of these thousands Thucydides has recorded twenty-seven. Without even knowing what other speeches were given that he has omitted, we can be confident in concluding that the twenty-seven selected were to Thucydides the most vital representatives of those processes and forces which he felt were the true meaning of the war, and in exhibition and explanation of which he composed his history.

Not only does the vast field of speeches from which Thucydides selected his few render the authenticity of the speeches more credible (for with so many to choose from it should have been possible for Thucydides to find actual speeches presenting the facts or attitudes he wished to exhibit, and therefore not to need to invent his own);[4] the high degree of selectivity ensures that an interpretation of the information contained in these speeches and of the reasons for the inclusion of these particular speeches will speak directly to the principles of selectivity by which Thucydides operated in the composition of the history.

If our goal is to understand these principles and Thucydides' intentions, our inquiry must begin, as Kagan has made clear,[5] not by asking what Thucydides meant to say by writing such a speech, but by asking what the purposes of the speaker were in giving it. Only by first having determined this can we be in a position to ask what Thucydides' intention may have been in recording this speech and these purposes. At that point it becomes possible for us to determine what account of the war is constructed by the record of these occasions and declarations; at that point it becomes possible to discover the general truths of action Thucydides has felt would be conveyed, not by any abstract statement separated from specific occasions and actions, but by the representation of those concrete actions and statements in which they operate and through which they are manifested.

The procedures by which this inquiry has been carried out are essentially straightforward. In part 1 the speeches are examined individually to recover the information about specific situations they were meant to convey, and then examined in their relations to one another in order to determine the general structure they give to Thucydides' account of the war. This general structure is necessarily the form of Thucydides' interpretation of the war. In part 2 the examination shifts to the kinds of evidence Thucydides has presented and the kinds of explanation he has given in order to characterize the nature of action and the corresponding nature of historical explanations of action as he conceived them and as these conceptions informed and directed his practices in the history.

In chapters 1–3 some special attention is paid to certain speeches that Thucydides has recorded despite their apparent material inconsequentiality. These include speeches which seem to result in no action (Pericles' Funeral Oration, the speeches at Camarina), speeches whose actions are of no material magnitude (the debates at Plataea and Melos), and one whole class of speeches—those which lose in debates—of no instrumental force whatever. These "inconsequential" speeches are the most difficult cases to deal with in understanding Thucydides' principles of selection. Nonetheless, he clearly believed them crucial to our understanding of the war, and if we can recover what they exhibit about their occasions in the war, we are a long way toward recovering those facts Thucydides considered significant to an explanation of the war.

In chapter 4 attention is paid to certain "irregularities" in Thucydides arrangement of the speeches. With so few speeches recorded, we might expect them to be spread with reasonable regularity throughout the history. They are not. All of the debates of the history—moments of political decision which receive the greatest emphasis Thucydides can provide by virtue of their being represented by *two* speeches—occur in three "clusters," each cluster occurring within a single calendar year. The clustering is clearly deliberate, and by it Thucydides exhibits three moments in the war worthy of, and requiring, the most extensive presentation of motives, intentions, and designs. In understanding the significance of these three moments we recover the structure Thucydides saw in the war and represented in the structure of his narrative.

Chapters 5–7 examine one final peculiarity of Thucydides' practice in the recording of speeches: his presentation of the speeches not as excerpts but as whole (if abridged) speeches. The practice is, of course, foreign to contemporary historical practice, but, we must recognize, novel in Thucydides' time as well. In understanding his purposes in attempting to replicate the complex experience of political oratory on particular occasions, we can discover Thucydides' conceptions of the nature of action that required this form of presentation of the moments of deliberation.

The ultimate utility of his history, according to Thucydides himself, lay in its presentation of a universal principle which was the cause, and explanation, of human events. His history, he says, will be useful because the same actions or ones much like them will occur again, $\kappa\alpha\tau\grave{\alpha}\ \tau\grave{o}\ \mathring{\alpha}\nu\theta\rho\mathring{\omega}\pi\iota\nu o\nu$—in accordance with "the human thing." As the significance of the history (in Thucydides' terms) and its utility depend on this, so must our goal be the understanding of that "human thing" which was for Thucydides both the principle of the history he wrote and the principle of all human action.

Part One
Commentary

The Speeches, 433–428 B.C.

Before we can begin a consideration of the meaning of the speeches in Thucydides' history, we must confront a peculiarity of the historian's practice in presenting speeches. There are twenty-six political speeches and one dialogue in Thucydides' history. Nine of the speeches appear by themselves, the remaining seventeen and the dialogue as parts of political debates occurring on eight different occasions. These, then, are seventeen moments at which Thucydides believed that an understanding of the Peloponnesian War required the exhibition of the public statements of policy or of the rationales for policy. Since his history covers approximately twenty-two years, this does not seem an unreasonable number of occasions that might be seen as important enough, or complicated enough, to need the extra information, and the special sort of information, that political addresses can provide for the perception of motivations behind and meanings attributed to the events as they occurred.

But of these seventeen occasions, eight are represented not only by speeches, but by debates. On these occasions Thucydides has not only reported those speeches which were approved by the various political bodies and whose policies were therefore put into effect, he has also reported speeches which were failures, their policies and justifications rejected by the same political bodies. The successful speeches are precisely those political addresses that can explain the motives of a given policy. They were the instruments by which the policy was promulgated. For the unsuccessful speeches no such claim can be made, and no such direct explanation of their inclusion can be found. Yet on eight occasions Thucydides has included these unsuccessful speeches. Since his practice is clearly deliberate, we must at least find a hypothesis to account for his decision sometimes to record single speeches and sometimes debates. And, given that Thucydides' first decision in recording a political moment is whether to include only the winning speech or a losing speech as well, any proper understanding of the meaning of the speeches must begin from this primary datum (in Thucydides' history): whether the speeches appear in isolation or as positions in a debate.

The appearance of a debate on an occasion certainly draws special attention and gives special emphasis to the occasion, just as the appearance of even a single speech at a moment in the history gives added emphasis to its occasion. At the least, we can say that recording a debate seems to give the greatest weight to a moment of action, and brings the moment of debate into the sharpest light that Thucydides can provide in his history. On these occasions Thucydides has wanted the event to stand out in the boldest relief, and to be accompanied by the most elaborate explanation. Occasions marked by single speeches would then constitute a second rank, since they, too, stand out from the general narrative of the history, though not with the emphasis of debates.

But in addition to the emphasis that the recording of two pieces of political oratory can provide, embodied in the very structure of debate is political information which is essentially recoverable in no other way, and which is often crucial to the understanding of an action or an event. A single speech provides only the statement of a policy and its supporting arguments. On some occasions, however, the decision to pursue a policy takes shape as a fundamental choice between radically different and competing alternative positions to a controversial issue. For these occasions, a proper understanding of the policy may well require an awareness (at the least) of the alternatives among which the choice was made and of the issue that was joined, and which gave structure to the deliberation and the eventual decision. No single speech, not even the successful speech, can make the issue of a debate clear, since it is only in the opposition of arguments that issues are constituted and can be perceived. It is in the conflict of arguments in debate that issues are created and made manifest, and it is to provide information about issues that Thucydides sometimes makes use of the record of debates rather than simply single speeches.

While it has often been said in the literature on Thucydides that the debates present issues, this has usually been given the wrong emphasis. "Issues" have been taken to mean "general issues," and the interpretation of the speeches has become epideictic, looking to the speeches for the atemporal exhibition of philosophical conflicts or dilemmas. Such interpretations seem to make Thucydides a writer of political or philosophical tracts rather than a historian, and they overlook the real significance of issues in action, thereby also overlooking the historical use to which issues (in this adversarial or rhetorical sense) can be put.

Debates in a history can present particular issues—that is, issues locked solidly into a particular moment and situation— as well as general ones. In the actual deliberations of political bodies it is exactly the particular issues that are debated. This presentation of particular issues allows for a very special location of events and of the policies which cause them. If one merely asks, "What caused a particular action?" and looks to speeches as the instrumentalities by which action is caused, there can be no purpose in recording any but the winning speech in a debate. Any losing speech, perforce, did not cause the action. But if we wish to move beyond this bald question toward a more profound understanding of cause, and toward the discrimination of policy decisions as deliberate choices, and as events which are novel and consequential, we will require a context against and in which (as background and as source) to perceive the event. That is, choices as initiating actions of change and movement can be perceived only by reference to some fixed point which renders the movement apparent. Further, we recognize that no choice is ever entirely free or unconditioned. To understand the meaning of an event, we must also understand the real limits within which choice and action were, or were felt to be, possible.

We must, in at least these two senses, be able to locate events in their contexts. It is this need which explains the representation of political debate by Thucydides (including the "inconsequential" losing speeches), for the representation of issues by debates performs this locative function. Since no single speech can do this (inasmuch as its context must be supplied from outside), this suggests a general principle with respect to the recording of speeches. On those occasions when some radical new policy is enunciated or a radical break with past policies occurs—any time when an event occurs for which we have no preparation nor a context in which to judge its significance, a single speech will be insufficient for making the event truly apparent, and for exhibiting its meaning. Not all events, of course, are the results of radical departures and changes; but for those which are, unless we understand the context of these events (so that we can evaluate how great the change is), our understanding of them will be diminished. Pairs of speeches, however, in their presentation of issues, simultaneously present contexts. The issue, indeed, is the embodiment of the context, the nexus of needs and possibilities, and in the speeches to an issue the context can be made apparent. The fact that a given speech in a debate lost makes it inconsequential in terms of explaining what a chosen policy was. But in terms of the historian's job of clarifying the meaning of the policy that was chosen, the losing speech is not inconsequential at all. For the losing speech, in conjunction with the winning one, helps define the parameters of the debate and supplies a context within which the direction and meaning of the victorious policy can be understood.

The speaker who gave a losing speech had hopes that it would win. However, it did not. What this provides for us as readers is a structure in which the losing speech embodies the outer, but near, limits of the political situation. Outer, because its policy was rejected; near, because the speaker felt his policy had a chance of being accepted. As two points determine a line, so two speeches enable us to determine the location of a political event. We can make an estimate of the political consciousness of the audience to a debate, and we can estimate the direction in which this consciousness was tending and the significance it would give to the event. We know what the audience accepted, and we know what it did not. On any given issue (represented in debate), then, we can determine what the *range* of alternatives was that the audience thought conceivable at that time. If the losing speech proposes action in accord with an older policy, we can see the new policy as a conscious change from previous procedure. If the winning speech, on the other hand, proposes action according to older principles, we can see the conscious decision to continue that older policy even in new circumstances.

Debates enable us to understand events through their self-contained creation of a context in which we can perceive deliberate movement in a meaningful direction. Their greatest usefulness would, therefore, be on occasions for which we have no other context or background to aid us in making these perceptions. If a context can be supplied, either from the narrative or from other, earlier speeches, then presumably a debate would not be necessary in the writing of the history. In this case, a single speech would suffice, for we would be able to judge its significance by its relation to this externally provided context. The appropriate places for debates, then, would be at the beginnings of new actions or new policies—places for which no context could as yet have been provided. In this light, it stands to reason that Thucydides would begin his history of the Peloponnesian War (as he does, with only the briefest prior narrative exposition) with a debate, to create a context in which we can understand the meaning of the first event that led to the war.

We are in a position, now, to formulate a general hypothesis about Thucydides' practice in employing debates or single speeches. The debates are used for the introduction and explanation of events which constitute the first appearance of attitudes or principles or policies, or the appearance of radical departures from earlier policies. Single speeches (even though —with the exception of one occasion—all of the single speeches must themselves have been part of debates) are used where their import would be clear by reference to the surrounding narrative or to earlier debates, either because the single speeches involve executions or extensions of policies represented in earlier debates, or because the significance of the changes of policy in the single speeches is perceivable by comparison to the policies represented in debate.

The Debate over the Corcyrean Alliance (1.32–44), 433 B.C.

Thucydides begins his history of the Peloponnesian War with an account of an incident at Epidamnus, and with this debate, which is its consequence. It is a striking and surprising way to begin, for just before he starts his narrative of the events at Epidamnus, he makes his assertion (1.23.5–6) that the incidents of Epidamnus and Potidaea were merely "alleged causes" of the war, while the truest cause was the growth of Athenian power and the fear this created in Sparta. We might expect that the historian would begin his history with an account of the truest cause. He does not, even though the growth of Athenian power antedates the events at Epidamnus. We might at least expect a description of the state of Greek international relations as a context in which to put this first event. Thucydides does not even give us this. Rather, after the briefest of explanations (a mere seven chapters) of the early development of events at Epidamnus, Thucydides presents us with this debate. In essence, the first sight that the historian gives us of the war is through these speeches. We will later be given a considerable amount of information concerning the existing relations between the major Greek powers, but this much is clear: whatever final meaning we come to attribute to his terms, "allegation" ($\alpha i \tau i \alpha$) and "truest cause" ($\pi \rho \delta \phi \alpha \sigma \iota s$), Thucydides has wanted us to begin our understanding of the Peloponnesian War with this pair of speeches alone. And he has wanted us to come to these speeches cold, without benefit of any other clarification of the circumstances or issues involved than that provided by the speeches themselves.

The circumstances which led to this debate (1.24–31) are the following. Some time at least a year (and probably more) before 435 B.C.,[1] the democratic faction in the city of Epidamnus expelled the oligarchic faction. The oligarchs, having made an alliance with neighboring barbarians, made war on the democrats in the city. The democrats sent to Corcyra, which had founded the city, for help, but were refused. They then sent to

Corinth (itself the metropolis of Corcyra), and received a promise of aid. The Corcyreans, angered by Corinthian intervention, took the side of the expelled Epidamnian oligarchs, and laid siege to the city of Epidamnus. The Corinthians sent a fleet in support, but were defeated by the Corcyreans at the battle of Leucimne in 435. For about two years following this defeat, the Corinthians made preparations for an attack on Corcyra. It was these preparations which brought the Corcyreans to Athens in 433 to ask for an alliance, and the Corinthians to argue against it. This is the extent of the explanation Thucydides gives us before he plunges us into the first debate.

The speech of the Corcyreans, asking for an alliance, is simple and straightforward. Their arguments for the utility of such an alliance depend entirely on the assertion that a war between Athens and the Peloponnesian League (of which Corinth was a member) is inevitable. The assertion comes early in their speech:

> And as for the war (because of which we may prove useful): if anyone of you does not believe that there will be war, he is mistaken in his judgment, and does not perceive that the Spartans (through fear of you) are making preparations for war, and that the Corinthians, who are influential with them and enemies to you, are subduing us first as a preparation for making an attempt on you. [1.33.3]

The Corcyreans assert that enmity between Athens and the Peloponnesian League already exists, and try to support the assertion by key words that echo through the entire speech: "and what more grievous to your enemies [πολέμιοι]" (1.33.2); "and the Corinthians, influential with them, and enemies [ἔχθροι] to you" (1.33.3); "he lives out his life safest who has fewest regrets for the favors he has done his opponents [ἐναντίοι]" (1.34.3); "those [the Corinthians] who are your enemies [ἔχθροι]" (1.35.4); "we can exhibit much profit [in this alliance], and the greatest is that the same persons [the Corinthians] have been enemies [πολέμιοι] to us both (which is the clearest grounds for trust) and not weak ones" (1.35.5); and "the war [πόλεμος] which is to come and is only that far from being actually present" (1.36.1).

The word "enemy" rings through the whole speech, and it

is the power it had and the response it got which eventually decided matters in this debate. Thucydides leaves us in no doubt on this. At 1.44.2 he asserts the motive of the Athenians in aiding the Corcyreans: "For it seemed to them that there was going to be war with the Peloponnesians. . . ."

This is the first speech we read in Thucydides, and its effect on us is great, especially since the judgments of the Corcyreans seem to fit not only with the judgments of the Athenians, but with that of Thucydides as well (1.23.6). In this light, the Corinthian speech seems a strangely ineffective one. Yet it was not a weak speech.

The speech of the Corinthian delegates is at once an appeal and, in effect, an ultimatum. They cannot ask for a favorable decision by the Athenian assembly on the basis of existing friendship between Athens and Corinth. Such an assertion would have been false, and as such, rhetorically stupid. Rather, they freely admit the existence of their fear and suspicion toward Athens. In effect, they make the Athenian decision on this question of alliance the test of these fears and suspicions. It is a rhetorical and political move which is desperate and perhaps even reckless, for it (like all ultimatums) left the Corinthians no room to maneuver if the Athenians decided unfavorably. On margin, however, I believe we should view their concern, and even their offer of future friendship as at some level genuine.

For whatever reasons, good or bad, serious or unworthy, the Corinthians were both desperately bent upon defeating the Corcyreans and desperately uncertain of how Athens stood in relation to themselves. Their desperation made them overreact, as we would say, and force the issue: peace or war, which is it to be? I do not believe that this forcing was an attempt to threaten the Athenians, to wring the first of many concessions from them (as later Pericles will accuse the Peloponnesians, justly, on the occasion of other ultimatums). I believe the Corinthians were willing to risk everything simply to clarify the situation (for, indeed, if the Athenians did think of themselves as enemies to Corinth, it would come to that risk eventually in any case), and I believe, guardedly, that if the Athenians had decided in their favor the Corinthians would have been forced to take that seriously as a sign of good intentions.

Since the Corinthians are explicit in making the *decision* in this case the test of their relations with Athens, we must recognize that the actual justice or injustice of the statements and claims they make is irrelevant to our understanding of the significance of this debate and to our perception of the political processes occurring at the outbreak of the war which Thucydides embodies in the debate.[2] Similarly, the actual terms of the Thirty Years' Peace (under which Athens and Corinth were nominal allies, and to which the Corinthians appeal) are also irrelevant. The debate is not about the treaty. The treaty was merely a field from which to select rhetorical points for use in the speeches. We will see this in the way the Corinthians make use of the treaty, and we can see it in Thucydides' refusal to clarify the actual terms of the treaty. If it were important for us to know the actual terms, can we doubt he would have summarized them for us?

What is it, then, about the Corinthian speech that is relevant to our understanding of this event? One thing only: the Corinthians draw a line, and, essentially, issue an ultimatum to the Athenians. In effect they say: If you decide in our favor, you act appropriately as the "allies" you are at least in name, and you remove a great deal of the suspicion we have of you; if you decide against us, you confirm our worst suspicions, and that means war, for we must then act in the spirit you announce by your decision.

This ultimatum is made explicit in the Corinthian speech almost from its beginning. The Corinthians begin by attacking the character of the Corcyreans (1.37 and 1.38), accusing them, neither temperately nor especially accurately, of all manner of injustice. But in chapter 1.39, the attack on the Corcyreans takes on a new quality, and becomes a warning to the Athenians:

> They have come here, not simply because they have failed there [at Epidamnus], but because they estimate that you will—not make an alliance with them—but commit injustice with them, and will accept them [into alliance] inasmuch as you are at variance with us. . . . [And they should

not have come] when you—who had no share in their crimes
—shall get an equal share of the blame as far as we are concerned. [1.39.2-3]

From this warning, veiled slightly in the guise of criticism of
the Corcyreans, the Corinthians proceed to more direct warn-
ings. Chapter 1.40 contains the first reference to the terms of
the Thirty Years' Peace. The Corinthians allege that the cities
which were not members of any alliance at the time of the
treaty (ἄγραφοι πόλεις) could not enter an alliance if it were
for the sake of injuring other parties to the peace. The way in
which they make this allegation is so peculiar and periphrastic
that it must lead us to believe no such qualification existed in
the terms of the treaty. But the Corinthians do not raise this
point as a *legal* point, they raise it as a political one. By claiming this qualification (using, as I said, the treaty as a source for
rhetorical material) the Corinthians are able to move to the
first statement of the stakes of this decision. This follows so
quickly on the introduction of the treaty that it must surely be
where the weight of this argument is intended to lie.

[This clause, i.e., on the enrollment of the unaligned cities,
was intended] for those who will not bring war instead of
peace to the cities which receive them into alliance. [1.40.2]

The speech is so composed that the clause ends with the
phrase "war instead of peace (πόλεμον ἀντ' εἰρήνης
ποιήσει)—that is, with what the Corinthians feel is the entire
issue of the debate. So that there could be no doubt in the
minds of the Athenians, the Corinthians expand on this and
issue the ultimatum. Again, the Greek is brutally clear. No
periphrasis is used in this statement; no ambiguity is possible:

. . . bring war instead of peace. This is what you would indeed suffer if you are not persuaded by us. For you would
not only become their allies, but our enemies (instead of the
"treaty allies" you now are). For we would be compelled,
should you go along with them, to take our revenge on
them, and not except you. [1.40.2-3]

The Corinthians then move to the treaty a second time for a
new set of arguments. At this point the qualities of the speech

as both ultimatum and appeal become joined, never again to be separated. The Corinthians say: We allowed you to punish Samos when it revolted from you; you should allow us to punish Corcyra in the same way. Once again, the "legal" reasoning is faulty, for Corcyra was not at all in the same legal relation to Corinth as Samos was to Athens. But surely the Corinthians were as aware of this as we are. The treaty argument, bad as it was in a legal sense, was brought forward in order to enable the Corinthians to introduce the one exemplary case of their own aid to Athens. The language of the speech reflects this, too, for as the Corinthians begin the next stage of their speech (chapter 41), the Samian case is first called a "legal ground" ($\delta\iota\kappa\alpha\dot{\iota}\omega\mu\alpha$) but then, immediately, a "claim on the Athenians' gratitude" ($\pi\alpha\rho\alpha\dot{\iota}\nu\epsilon\sigma\iota\varsigma$ $\kappa\alpha\dot{\iota}$ $\dot{\alpha}\xi\dot{\iota}\omega\sigma\iota\varsigma$ $\chi\dot{\alpha}\rho\iota\tau\sigma\varsigma$).

This marks the next turning of the speech. To the notion that Athens owes Corinth an authentic favor (in addition to its formal treaty obligations, whatever they were), the Corinthians add the notion that this moment is the critical moment (the $\kappa\alpha\iota\rho\dot{\sigma}\varsigma$) both for the repayment of the favor and the determination of the hostility or friendship of the Athenians.

> We have this claim on your gratitude which, we say, demands its repayment to us now, since we are neither enemies so that we would naturally [want to] harm each other nor friends so that we would have dealings with each other [i.e., we are calling in this debt since we cannot count on your helping us simply as friends]. [1.41.1]

The Corinthians then mention Samos again, and Aegina, another instance of their aid. Again, the importance of this moment is stressed:

> [We helped you in those moments when men think nothing more important than victory. . . . And in such moments] men consider the man who supports them their friend, even if he was an enemy before, and the one who opposes them their enemy, even if he had in fact been a friend. [1.41.3]

Warning is given of the stakes once more, coupled with an appeal:

Whether or not a war is coming[3] . . . is still shrouded in ob-
scurity, and it is not worth acquiring our hatred (which will
immediately be anything but obscure, and which will not be
to come [but will be present]) for its sake. Rather, it would
be wise to remove our existing suspicion (that we have on
account of Megara). The latest favor (even if it is small), if it
comes at the critical moment, can remove a great grievance.
[1.42.2–3]

I believe the appeal was genuine, at least at the moment it
was given, even though it is impossible to say that a favorable
Athenian decision would have avoided the war. The Corinthians (and presumably, all of the Peloponnesians) were very
much afraid of Athens, and the Athenians knew this. Would
Corinthian gratitude endure? would it seriously alter the
already existing fear and suspicion? Perhaps not. And yet I
believe that the Corinthians were not simply threatening
Athens. I believe that the Corinthians—reasonably or un-
reasonably—felt this moment was a true καιρός, a true moment of crisis or decision. This is embodied in the vehemence
of their feelings toward Corcyra, and in the clear hatred Athens
will incur if it aids the Corcyreans. But if this is so, then
perhaps we must also take seriously the relief (not to insist
upon "gratitude") the Corinthians would feel if, at this critical moment, Athens did not aid Corcyra.

This is, in any case, the spirit in which the Corinthians finish
their speech. They ask for repayment of the favor they had
done the Athenians and they reiterate—so that there be no
possible doubt—the combined appeal and ultimatum:

Having had the benefit of our vote, do not injure us with
yours, but give back an equal return, recognizing that this
is that critical moment in which he is our greatest friend who
supports us, and our greatest enemy who opposes us.
[1.43.2]

At the conclusion of this debate opinion in the Athenian
assembly was about evenly divided between the cases. On the
second day of deliberation, the Athenians concluded a "defensive" alliance (an ἐπιμαχία, in which one party would aid
the other only if it were attacked) rather than a "full" alliance

(a ξυμμαχία, under which Athens would support Corcyra even if it were the aggressor) with the Corcyreans. Some commentators (de Ste. Croix the latest among them) have asserted that this distinction indicates Athens' moderate and unaggressive response to this situation. But to believe that the Athenian decision was anything else than, first, a conscious admission of their understanding that relations between Athens and Corinth were hostile and, second, a clear declaration to the Corinthians that this was how they understood relations between the cities is unrealistic for four reasons.

First, the defensive alliance was almost certainly simply the compromise proposal which ended the deadlock in the assembly. Unable to agree, the first day, to a full alliance with the Corcyreans, the proposal of a defensive alliance, on the second, secured the necessary votes to come to a decision.[4] Second, Thucydides alludes to this political maneuvering at 1.44.1, where he says that the Athenians were unwilling to conclude a full alliance,

> For if the Corcyreans ordered them to sail with them against Corinth, then the Peace with the Peloponnesians would be broken by them.

The "by them" (the Athenians, surely) is critical, for what Thucydides is saying is that the Athenians did not want to be responsible for breaking the Peace. This is probably what caused the deadlock in the assembly, and made it necessary for those who favored alliance with Corcyra to look for a compromise. But Thucydides is not saying that the Athenians were fundamentally unwilling that the Peace be broken. They simply did not want it to be their responsibility.

The third ground for regarding the decision of the assembly as authentically hostile is the terms of the defensive alliance itself.

> They made a defensive alliance, to come to each other's aid if anyone came against Corcyra or against Athens or its allies. [1.44.1]

But no fleet or army was poised to attack Athens. Rather, it was Corcyra that was on the very brink of attack. The distinction between a defensive and a full alliance breaks down if one knows that the defensive alliance will be invoked almost immediately after its constitution.

The final ground is also the most authoritative: the Corinthians unequivocally denied the possibility of any such distinction. *Any* Athenian aid to Corcyra, as they stated again and again, would be interpreted as a hostile act. The Corinthians left the Athenians only two "friendly" alternatives (1.40.4): remain neutral or assist us. In the face of this clear statement, the Athenians necessarily knew that their grant of aid to Corcyra (defensive or full alliance) would be taken as an equally clear declaration of their intentions by the Corinthians.[5]

Why has Thucydides begun his history of the war with this decision? And why has he felt that this decision required a debate (two speeches rather than one) for its exposition? Our hypothesis suggests that a debate would be used for the first appearance of a policy or attitude, and the initial indecision of the Athenian assembly also suggests such a moment. The two deliberations, the closeness of the vote, the compromise proposal all indicate the last moment, as it were, of equilibrium between war and peace in Athenian minds; and the final decision indicates the tipping of the scale.

But why should the choice of this moment require two speeches for the exposition of its significance? Let us imagine that Thucydides had only reported one speech, the winning one. If the Corcyrean speech were the only one Thucydides had recorded from this debate, we would have a perception of the outbreak of the war very different from that which we have from reading both speeches (and, evidently, therefore, from the one Thucydides meant to convey). Had Thucydides only represented this winning speech, we would have to draw the following conclusions: the Corinthians and the Peloponnesians were unalterably and actively hostile to Athens; the coming war, to which the Corcyreans appeal, was almost an accomplished fact; the Athenians, therefore, had no choice but to accept the alliance with Corcyra. These are assertions the Corcyreans make, and the Athenian decision in favor of Corcyra would seem to confirm these claims.

In fact, if we knew only what the Corcyreans asserted about the political situation in Greece, we would be in some doubt as to why Thucydides had chosen to record a debate on this occasion. If things were simply as the Corcyreans asserted, what was there to decide? Seen through the Corcyrean speech alone, this moment would lose all momentousness, and we would receive a very simple notion of the necessity of the war. Seen through the Corcyrean speech, the alliance would be merely another small, necessary step in an apparently unbroken progression of hostility. This occasion would disappear as a decisive moment in the Peloponnesian War. It would most emphatically not be the most suitable moment at which to begin the history of that war. Seen through the Corcyrean speech, the beginning of the history ought to be found somewhere in the events of the Pentacontaetia, at the very moment the hostility first began. To begin the history with the Epidamnian affair would appear an arbitrary choice.

That Thucydides saw the Epidamnian affair, and the alliance of Athens and Corcyra, as anything but an arbitrary point at which to begin his history becomes clear from his recording of the Corinthian, the losing, speech. That he saw the Corcyrean alliance as the decisive act that set events in motion that led to the Peloponnesian War is revealed in the same way. What the Corinthians said at Athens—even though their speech was finally unpersuasive—gives us the context which restores (or recreates) the momentousness of this occasion, and which indicates the crucial role this debate played in the outbreak of the war.

This debate begins the history because it is the first decisive moment in events which properly relate to the Peloponnesian War. A line was drawn, and the meaning of this line was made clear and unambiguous: if the Athenians crossed it, the Corinthians would regard them as enemies and act accordingly. The Athenians knew this, but nevertheless crossed the line. The debate on the Corcyrean alliance and the events which follow appropriately begin the history of the Peloponnesian War because they are the occasion of the *first unequivocally hostile act* between participants in the war.

Both "unequivocal" and "act" have their own proper importance in this statement. The Epidamnian episode takes place at a moment of equilibrium: Athens and the Peloponnese were neither clear friends nor clear enemies. Suspicion and fear existed on both sides, but no particular action by either side could be interpreted as a clear sign of hostility. When the Corinthians issue their ultimatum, the way is prepared for the giving and the receipt of such a sign. Further, the sign, when it came, was also an act: an alliance and the sea battle at Sybota (involving Athenian and Corinthian ships) which was its consequence. It is the consequences of this action which lead to other acts and new consequences which bring about the breaking of the Peace.

This event, however, which Thucydides calls an "alleged cause" ($αἰτία$), was not the "true cause" ($πρόφασις$) of the war, but stands, in one respect, in a dependent relation to the true cause (the fear the Peloponnesians had of Athens' continued growth). This event would not have occurred without the preexistence of the $πρόφασις$. The Corinthians would not have been likely to have issued so serious an ultimatum had they not already been afraid of Athens. The Athenians would most likely not have felt the need for the Corcyrean fleet (to acquire which they had to defy the ultimatum and accept the consequences of that act) had they not perceived the already existing fear among the Peloponnesians, and felt it prudent to be prepared to meet whatever actions the Peloponnesians might take in response to that fear.

But the "allegations" are not mere pretexts for starting the war, nor are they mere diplomatic charges. While the allegations depend on the true cause, they are also *actualizations* of the true cause, and are necessary elements in bringing the war into existence. One may be afraid of another party, but if one is at peace with him, catalytic events must occur before one feels compelled or even justified to act on that fear. Further, fear is fundamentally an individual emotion, and events of a certain sort must occur for this individual motivation to be translated into a collective motive and to result in the actions of a nation. These are authentic human and political processes, and ones which Thucydides felt it important to exhibit. The $αἰτίαι$, he says at 1.23.5, broke the Peace. They were not the real cause of the war, but they were what broke the Peace. They were the first actualizations (or manifestations) of the πρό-φασις, and they were the true catalysts of the processes which led to war.[6]

The debate about the Corcyrean alliance (and the decision of the assembly) was the first of these catalysts, and begins the history. It is worth repeating that we are able to perceive this event (as distinct from some hypothetical moment during the Pentecontaetia) as the first moment of change from peace to war only because Thucydides recorded the Corinthian speech as well as the Corcyrean. Without this losing speech we would be unable to perceive any change, and we would be unable to see the political process of *two* nations going to war. For it is two nations, not merely one, that we see engaged in a process that leads to war. The Athenians do not start the war by accepting an alliance with Corcyra. This act only leads to war because the Corinthians have insisted that they will view such an act as hostile. The Corinthians do not start the war by being afraid of Athens. This attitude is significant only because, at a *particular* moment, the Athenians inform the Corinthians that this attitude is the correct one to have. Both nations have to act, and it requires the action of both to render the decision, when it comes, the critical decision which finally moved the parties out of a gray area of suspicion and uncertainty into a definite state of active hostility.

What happens next? The speeches and decisions of political bodies not only exhibit the changing and shaping of judgments and beliefs, they also result in actions, and these actions have further consequences. The conclusion of the alliance with Corcyra is followed by the naval battle at Sybota in 433, the first military confrontation of Athens with a Peloponnesian city. That such a confrontation occurred compelled the parties to take further measures. Αἰτία suggests αἰτία.

With both sides simply acting defensively, the Athenians and Corinthians precipitate the second of the αἰτίαι. The Athenians, worried about the security and trustworthiness of one of their imperial cities, Potidaea, which, since it had been founded by Corinth, seemed potentially dangerous, demanded hostages from it and the destruction of its walls. That these were defensive measures is reflected in the Greek at 1.57.1 and 1.57.6: προπαρεσκευάζοντο ("arranged as precautions") and προκαταλαμβανειν ("to prevent the revolt").[7] The Potidaeans attempted to get Athens to lighten the demands, and failing in that, asked the Peloponnesians for aid. The Corinthians supported this, but did nothing active until the Athenian fleet arrived at Potidaea. Then Corinth did send an expedition, but while we might have expected them to have done so out of a desire for revenge on Athens,[8] Thucydides says clearly that they acted from fear: "being frightened about the place [Potidaea], and believing that the danger touched them closely" (1.60.1).

The result of these defensive measures is the second military confrontation between Athens and Corinth, the second of the allegations, the siege of Potidaea (433). Thucydides has not marked this αἰτία with a debate or even a speech. No policy has changed; the second allegation is a direct consequence of the policies decided in the first debate, and can be understood in its terms. Such a chain of actions and consequences—αἰτίαι —could have gone on longer, though presumably not indefinitely. For the war to enter a new stage, a further change is required: Corinth's private war with Athens must be generalized. This brings us directly to the next set of debates.

The Lacedaemonian Congress (1.68–86), 432 B.C.

From the end of the debate at Athens concerning the Corcyrean alliance, Thucydides proceeds with his narrative. Chapters 45–55 contain his description of military preparations and the sea battle at Sybota; chapters 56–65 his description of the events at Potidaea. Both of these events, we have seen, are consequences of the Corcyrean debate, one immediate, one at one remove. Then, with one brief chapter of introduction, Thucydides again plunges us into the world of political debate and deliberation. Again, he does so without giving us any background information. The speeches must speak for themselves.

Having been defeated, or at least balked, on two occasions by the Athenians, the Corinthians arranged the convocation of this Spartan congress, bringing with them the other members of the Peloponnesian League and delegates from cities which claimed to have been injured by Athens. The purpose was to enlist the Spartans in these hostilities by claiming that Athens' actions had violated the Thirty Years' Peace. From Thucydides' comments at 1.79 and 1.88 it is clear that the Spartans were much more decided in their opinions than the Athenians were at the time of the Corcyrean debate. Nor do we find the same closeness of votes that indicates the moment opinion changes from one view to another. Yet, even if we do not find here the same kind of dramatic shift of opinion that is represented in the first debate of the history, the movement of the Spartans to open hostility against the Athenians is one whose importance is so great that it requires a context in which it can be evaluated. We can examine the speeches on this occasion to clarify the way in which the Peloponnesians went to war, and to establish the range of choices which were, or which they felt were, open to them.

The speeches that Thucydides records from this congress constitute two debates: one between Corinthian and Athenian speakers for and against Spartan action; another between two Spartan speakers deliberating whether or not to take action. As distinct from the deliberation at Athens, here Thucydides apparently felt that the significance of this decision could not be entirely understood from the two speeches of the interested parties. The Spartan deliberation itself had to be represented in order to arrive at the proper interpretation of the event. The success of the Corinthian speech brings about the next critical stage in the history, a state of war between Athens and the Peloponnese as a whole. The actual declaration of war at the second Spartan congress was, by comparison, a mere formality, and the Corinthian speech on its occasion is really much less about whether war should be declared than how it should be prosecuted. But although the Corinthian speech here appropriately marks this new stage, it is worth noting that the losing Athenian speech, by providing a particular context for the Corinthian, makes the stage appear as a distinct stage, and opens up our interpretation of it. Similarly, it is important to see how Archidamus' losing speech in the

Spartan deliberation throws a new light on the way in which the Spartans went to war.

The rhetorical task the Corinthian speakers at the Spartan congress undertook was to secure the military involvement of the entire Peloponnesian League in their dispute with Athens. Until the decision of this conference, the hostility between Athens and Corinth could have remained a private dispute rather than the beginning of a general war.[9] At the congress, the Corinthians attempted to convince the Spartans that the Athenian threat was already general, and therefore League involvement, too, should be general and overt. The point of which the Corinthians were trying to convince the Spartans, and so secure the general support they desired, is found early in their speech:

> What need is there to speak at length? You see some enslaved, you see they are plotting it for others (and not least for our allies), and you see that they have been prepared for a long time, should they ever come to war. [1.68.3]

They make a bald claim that nothing, except the interposition of another force, will limit Athenian domination:

> We know in what way, and we know that, the Athenians are advancing little by little against their neighbors. Believing that they do so undetected because you are unaware of it, they are less bold; but when they know that you see it, and overlook it, then they will press on strongly. [1.69.3]

The claim is per se neither true nor persuasive. It, and the statement that "[the Athenians] are plotting [slavery] for others" (1.68.3) depend for their persuasiveness on a determination of what Athenian intentions in fact are. And in the Corinthian argument the determination of Athenian intentions depends on a certain interpretation of the Athenian character.[10] If the Athenians can be shown to possess an illimitably ambitious character, then the particular actions that the Athenians have taken against the Corinthians can be persuasively said (given the size of the Athenian empire) to be mere particular instances of a more general threat that either already encompasses or will shortly encompass the whole of the

Peloponnese. It is in this manner that the Corinthians attempt to make their case for Peloponnesian involvement, and the primary support for their argument is the celebrated chapter (1.70) comparing the Spartan and Athenian characters.

This chapter is a famous piece of Thucydides' history, yet while a rhetorical masterpiece, in another respect it is usually overrated. As a useful characterization of the Athenians it is, though pointed, strangely insubstantial. A far more concrete and striking picture of Athenian ambition and self-confidence (or perhaps arrogance) can be found in the statements Athenian speakers themselves make—as in the speech of the Athenians at this congress (1.73–78) or Pericles' speech at 1.140–44. Both the pointedness and the insubstantiality of the Corinthian characterization have the same source. The speech is designed to serve a particular rhetorical purpose, and that purpose is not necessarily best served by the most accurate characterization. Rather, the purpose is best served by a characterization of a certain sort, whatever the relation between that picture and a truly accurate one. The characterization given by the Corinthians is a masterpiece of rhetorical maximization: working from two formal oppositions made into rhetorical *topoi* (old/new and active/passive), they invent two opposite characters appropriate to a situation of aggression and defense. They call one of these characters "Athenian" and the other "Spartan," but in truth they are merely the "overreacher" and the "sluggard."[11] The pointedness comes from the perfection of the opposition of these types, but that same perfection robs the portraits of the concreteness which would make them truly portraits of Athens and Sparta.

The two portraits gain apparent concreteness, mutually, by their opposition to each other. Probed, however, their insubstantiality emerges. That the characters described are the result of the desire to construct perfect opposites can be seen at several moments, sometimes because the descriptions do not quite fit with the actual actions of either the Athenians or the Spartans, sometimes because the descriptions, in their formal perfection, slide over underlying realities, sometimes because, in their rhetorical elegance, the descriptions make little sense at all as description—except in the all-important rhetorical sense of coloring the audience's response to one or the other nation.[12]

Nevertheless, even if we must minimize the fidelity of these portraits, we can see chapter 70 as the brilliant rhetorical stroke that it is. By it, the Corinthians construct an argument for general war that they could have justified in no other way. Indeed, the extreme abstractness of this argument is a peculiar touch, but rhetorically deliberate. In their speech they hardly mention the actual military activities of the Athenians at Corcyra and Potidaea. They were aware that to a Spartan audience, given Sparta's habitual wariness of foreign military involvements, these events would appear too far off to constitute any imminent threat. This is one audience not likely to be moved, in this instance, by concreteness. It is a rhetorical situation that demands an argument in which, even if abstractly, it may appear that the Spartans themselves are already injured. What the Corinthians accomplish, with chapter 70, is to create a picture of the Athenians which, when coupled with the mere existence of the empire, will demonstrate that the expansion of the empire to include the domination of the Peloponnese is not mere speculation, but a present danger.[13]

The picture of the Athenians that the Corinthians construct is shot through with three points: the Athenians are unique, they are ambitious, and they are unlimited in their desires. Throughout chapter 70 the characteristics of *excess* are compiled. "Bold beyond their strength" ($\pi \alpha \rho \grave{\alpha} \ \delta \acute{\upsilon} \nu \alpha \mu \iota \nu \ \tau o \lambda \mu \eta$-$\tau \alpha \acute{\iota}$) and "willing to run risks beyond reason" ($\pi \alpha \rho \grave{\alpha} \ \gamma \nu \acute{\omega} \mu \eta \nu$ $\kappa \iota \nu \delta \upsilon \nu \epsilon \upsilon \tau \alpha \acute{\iota}$) at 1.70.3; "unhesitant" ($\mathring{\alpha} o \kappa \nu o \iota$), "advancing farthest" ($\mathring{\epsilon} \pi \grave{\iota} \ \underline{\pi \lambda \epsilon \hat{\iota} \sigma \tau o \nu} \ \mathring{\epsilon} \xi \acute{\epsilon} \rho \chi o \nu \tau \alpha \iota$) at 1.70.5; "indifferent to their present possessions, but eager for more" ($\mathring{\alpha} \ \delta$' $\mathring{\alpha} \nu \ \mathring{\epsilon} \pi \epsilon \lambda \theta \acute{o} \nu \tau \epsilon \varsigma \ \kappa \tau \acute{\eta} \sigma \omega \nu \tau \alpha \iota, \ \mathring{o} \lambda \acute{\iota} \gamma \alpha \ \pi \rho \grave{o} \varsigma \ \tau \grave{\alpha} \ \mu \acute{\epsilon} \lambda \lambda o \nu \tau \alpha$ $\tau \upsilon \chi \epsilon \hat{\iota} \nu \ \pi \rho \acute{\alpha} \xi \alpha \nu \tau \epsilon \varsigma$) at 1.70.7. All three characteristics are brought together in a single sentence near the end of this chapter:

> For equally they (and they alone) have and hope for their designs because they are so quick to attempt their designs. [1.70.7]

The picture of the Athenians the Corinthians painted was exactly the one they had to in order to obtain the Spartan assistance they needed. It is a picture which produces fear, and, when complemented by the mention of the empire, produces the immediate and intense fear of imminent domination. It is also a picture that it is essential for them to present if their final threat—to desert the Spartans and go elsewhere for help (1.71.4)—was to have any force. Turning away from Sparta would be frightening to the Spartans only if they already had something to be frightened of so that they would see losing the Corinthians as something dangerous. But this, too, depends on a determination of Athenian intentions, and, therefore, of Athenian character. If Athens' character is as the Corinthians described it—if its ambition is limitless—then, given the material resources Athens possesses in the empire, the domination of the Peloponnese is a plausible Athenian goal and a sensible object of Spartan fear.[14] But the "if" clause is crucial, for there are other ways of describing the character of the Athenians, and therefore other ways of regarding the empire. In fact, the empire had not been expanding in the period preceding the Peloponnesian War, and Athens had added no new colonial possessions since the Thirty Years' Peace (of 445 B.C.).[15] Hypothetically, then, it would be possible to regard the empire as static and basically peaceful, and therefore as no threat to the Peloponnese at all. It is just such a picture that the Athenian speakers try to convey, by suggesting that their character is radically different from the portrait drawn by the Corinthians.

Much has been written about the speech of the Athenians, but little about its particular relevance to this debate. That it is a defense of Athenian policy has, of course, been noted. But the oddness of the defense has not been sufficiently explained. The Athenians did not respond to charges that might have been made about their actions against Corinth, or Potidaea, or Megara, or Aegina. Instead, they defended their imperial policy, and the acquisition of the empire, even though the empire *qua* empire was not the source of the particular acts and grievances that led to this congress.

This apparent dislocation of defense and charge might seem to point in the direction of an epideictic interpretation: that is, that Thucydides has here taken the opportunity to acquaint us, in general, with Athenian attitudes toward their empire, and has composed a speech of a generality and import beyond that of the specific Athenian defense. The truth is otherwise. In fact, this Athenian account of the acquisition of the empire, and even its brutally candid explanation of the motives which drove them to it are *specific* answers to the particular speech the Corinthians gave in asking for Spartan involvement. The Corinthians had put their emphasis, not on specific acts and grievances (which in themselves would not persuasively necessitate Spartan action), but on the character of the Athenians. In their turn, the Athenians too are silent about specific recent acts, and concentrate all of their arguments to rebut the Corinthian description of their character. It is as material supporting this rebuttal that Athenian statements about their empire acquire their relevance.

The Corinthians portrayed the Athenians as a restlessly active nation with unlimited desires, and the Athenians attempted to counter these arguments in two ways. To the notion of their constant activity the Athenians oppose their own account of the acquisition of the empire (1.73–76). The Corinthians claimed their *nature* made them active, but the Athenian account lays the blame for their activity (which in itself is undeniable) on *accident* and *necessity* rather than any innate impulsion. Athens had to oppose the Persian empire because Persia initiated the war and because safety required it (1.73–74). Athens came to possess its own empire first through fear of the remains of Persian power, and then because it was asked to assume the leadership of the allies. It retained the empire, again, through fear for its safety at the hands of the imperial cities, and later at Spartan hands (1.75). The Corinthians claimed Athenians act as they do out of the pleasure it gives their unique personalities; the Athenians reply that it gives them no pleasure, and that they do it for reasons which, far from being unique, are *common to all men:* fear, honor, and profit (1.75.3).

The possible rhetorical loss from claiming that all men (that is, including the Spartans—and this said to a Spartan audience) act from fear, honor, and profit is balanced by the possible gain of destroying one of the bases of the Corinthian argument. If all men act from these motives, and all Athenian actions can be reduced to the operation of these forces, then the Athenians have no special, uncommon character, and, therefore, pose no special threat. This will go part way toward undermining the Corinthian portrait.

Then, in chapters 1.76 and 1.77, the Athenians make their defense against the most serious of the Corinthian attacks, the picture of an Athens possessed of unlimited desires. This is the most serious resource of the Corinthian case because it is this alone which makes the Athenian empire a source of direct Spartan anxiety. Only if Athenian ambitions are unlimited does the empire threaten Sparta; otherwise, it is a danger merely for smaller cities, and the record of Spartan assistance for other cities, when it is itself unthreatened, is quite bad. The Athenians, therefore, argue that they are in fact moderate in their desires, and support their argument by describing their imperial administration in some detail (1.77).[16]

The imperial cities, they say, complain of injustices at court, but fail to recognize that although Athens could dispense with justice altogether in their cases and rule by force, yet it chooses to be bound by the rule of law. This is the key point, for by this example the Athenian speakers hope to demonstrate that, far from having unlimited ambitions, Athens has *unexpectedly* imposed limits on itself in dealings with its allies over whom it has complete control, and so, *a fortiori,* has them in its relations to other states more nearly its equals. If it will be bound by law with its allies, it must surely respect the law in the cases of independent, large states. The Athenians then conclude with an offer—either genuine or as another example of their acceptance of limits—to submit all current disputes to arbitration.

The Athenian speech failed to persuade the Spartan assembly, and, apparently, had little chance at all to be persuasive there. This was not just the result of the arguments used. Thucydides' statements (at 1.79 and 1.88) indicate that the vast majority of Spartans decisively and unequivocally rejected the Athenian arguments, and suggest the existence of a complex substratum of emotion which influenced the course of this debate. The speeches, in addition to their primary purpose of exhibiting the issues and arguments which figured in the debate, also reveal the unmistakable traces of this critical, extrarational aspect of this deliberative situation.

The contrast in the styles and emotional tones of these two speeches is striking and informative. The cool, reasonable, almost nonchalant and philosophical speech of the Athenians is at the same time a demonstration of their clear belief that the war was far from inevitable and an exhibition of exactly those characteristics that evoked the Peloponnesian fears which rendered the war indeed inevitable. The highly charged rhetoric of the Corinthian speech—especially the topical tour de force of chapter 1.70—exhibits the pent-up fury and frustration of those who had to deal with the Athenians, and illuminates the feeling of pressure and fear which led to the outbreak of the war.

The overwhelming impression of the Athenian speech is of even-mindedness and leisurely deliberation. It was, unfortunately, delivered on an occasion when its audience felt that leisure was a luxury it could ill afford. Gracefully turning, at one moment, to universal principles of political action and, at another, to the influence of immediate circumstances and concrete events, it may be exemplary to us, but was surely infuriating to the Spartans. The Athenians can even allow themselves the opportunity to make ironic—and rhetorically pointless—observations on human behavior (1.77.4) and casually insulting reflections on the morals of the audience they were attempting to persuade (1.76.1 and 77.6).

The effect is a devastating portrayal of the Athenians as self-confident to the point of arrogance, immune to pressure, certain that they were in control of everything. Of course they were under no pressure. It was precisely that Athens had so far taken all the initiative itself which had put the Peloponnesians under pressure. The flood of rhetorical tropes in chapter 70 of the Corinthian speech is testimony to that pressure and revelatory of the Peloponnesian stress under which the debate was held. With this Athenian speech coming on the heels of the Corinthian, it can come as small surprise to us that the outcome of the deliberation was what it was.[17]

Nonetheless, despite the Spartan predisposition to war, and despite the psychological factors which underlay and reinforced their disposition, a conscious decision was taken at the congress. And for our understanding of the decision as a decision, the Athenian speech is crucial. The record of the *two* speeches puts both into relief.

As in the case of the debate about the Corcyrean alliance, the reporting of a single speech alone would be insufficient to explain the action that is taking place. Although the Athenian speech results in no action, it serves a critical expository purpose. Without it, we would be forced to believe the Corinthian interpretation of the Athenian empire and of the future. If we did that, we would be unable to see this congress as a distinct and deliberate event.

If the Corinthian interpretation is accepted unquestioned, then the Spartans had no choice here: they must fight or expect to be subjugated in turn. But two observations must be made. First, although this is what the Corinthians hoped to convince the Spartans was the case, it was not necessarily true. The Athenian speech, which argued the opposite, shows us that there was at least room for another interpretation. Second, if we were without the Athenian speech, and so were compelled to believe that the Corinthian argument was simply true, then the momentousness of the congress would vanish, just as the momentousness of the Athenian alliance with Corcyra would vanish without the Corinthian speech at Athens. Like that alliance, this congress, too, would become merely another small step in a long progression of events which began with the building of the Long Walls at Athens almost immediately after the Persian War.[18]

By including the Athenian speech with is alternate interpretation (unsuccessful though it is), Thucydides considerably liberalizes our own interpretation of the necessity of the war. Consciously or not, the Spartans *chose* to accept the Corinthian picture of the empire. The two speeches exhibit a deliberate reinterpretation of the political situation by means of which the Athenian-Corinthian conflict was generalized into one involving all parties to both blocs. Further, they do this while at the same time exhibiting the compelling—and undeliberated—passions which made the reinterpretation possible, reasonable, and, in a sense, necessary. Thucydides says that Spartan fear necessitated the war, but insofar as we can see the Athenian account as a possible representation of the empire, we can also understand what Thucydides meant by saying it was Spartan *fear* of the empire, and not the empire itself, which was the truest cause of the war. We will not, at least, believe that the empire per se (nor any other institutions or oppositions per se) necessitated the war. Necessary the war may have been, but not in the simple sense the Corinthians alleged.

The two Spartan speeches that follow (Archidamus', 1.80-85, and Sthenelaidas', 1.86) enable us to complete our understanding of how Sparta declared war, by exhibiting Spartan attitudes toward Athens and Spartan expectations of the war to come. The rhetoric of both speeches is characteristically Spartan: Archidamus' caution, Sthenelaidas' unreflecting appeal to honor. But in this conflict of two appeals to different aspects of Spartan tradition, we can perceive an important change in Spartan attitudes and responses. The success of Sthenelaidas' appeal shows us the direction and content of the change. But, again, it is Archidamus' losing speech which is the key to our understanding of this moment. For we can only see the change as a change in seeing that Sthenelaidas' appeal denies a tradition to which Archidamus had appealed.

Sthenelaidas' terse argument has all the traits of Spartan rhetoric taken to the extreme of caricature. Short, inelegant, bull-headed, and founded solidly on matters of justice and injustice. The Athenians have committed injustices against Spartan allies, and Sparta must end this injustice. ''For others there is much money and ships and horses, but for us there are good allies, who must not be betrayed to the Athenians'' (1.86.3). In place of the elegant Corinthian proof by character that Athens' desires are unlimited, Sthenelaidas substitutes a crude enthymeme: the Athenians may have acted properly in the Persian War, but since then have done injuries to our allies; consequently, they have gone from good to bad, and we can therefore assume they will increasingly do evil to our confederates and to us (1.86.1). But although without the sophistication of the Corinthians, Sthenelaidas makes the same point they do: Athenian growth must be stopped (1.86.5), and it must be stopped immediately (1.86.3).

If Sthenelaidas' speech is characteristically Spartan in its "Laconic" style, Archidamus' is characteristically Spartan in its caution. Archidamus argues for a delay in the declaration of war along two main lines. On the one hand, he asserts that Sparta is militarily unprepared to make war on Athens (1.80–81), and the result of a prematurely begun war will be injurious to Sparta's material position and its honor (1.82.5–6). On the other hand, to justify the delay, he urges that such caution and consideration for the successful and honorable course is the traditional way in which Sparta has always gone to war (1.83–84). He begins his peroration, emphasizing the traditional sources of his policy: "Let us not give up these practices which our fathers bequeathed to us and which we ourselves have always profitably kept" (1.85.1).

Archidamus urges a strategic caution and a conservatism of response which we have come to recognize elsewhere (as in Herodotus) as habitually Spartan.[19] Further, he claims that this caution has its roots in peculiarly Spartan virtues of modesty and obedience. But the very deftness with which Archidamus touches on all the traditional slogans of Spartan politics, when seen in the light of the failure of this speech, reveals two striking facets of this Spartan decision.

First of all, Archidamus has been left unpersuaded by the two key points of the Corinthian argument: the uniqueness of the Athenian threat and the consequent necessity of an immediate reaction to it.[20] But neither is he unconscious or unmoved by the presence of the Athenian empire. At 1.82.1 Archidamus betrays the fact that he, too, fears Athens, and expects that there must one day be war between it and Sparta. Yet he sees neither uniqueness nor urgency in this threat. Rather, even as he suggests strategic innovations, Archidamus speaks of the war with a confidence that implies a belief that at bottom this war will be much the same as all other wars. He believes that the initiation of hostilities is entirely within Sparta's choice (as to time), and that the prosecution of the war will follow the same pattern as against any other city. Moreover, he does not see the Athenian threat as especially pressing, for he recommends a delay of no less than two years. Archidamus' coolness serves an important expository purpose. By recording it, Thucydides moderates our response to the Corinthian arguments. These had claimed that the Athenian actions per se necessitated an immediate declaration of war. Archidamus, by furnishing a different (and less urgent) interpretation of these same events, demonstrates that this is not so. The events themselves, at least, do not necessitate the war.

But this leads us to the second striking facet of this deliberation: that, despite the consonance of Archidamus' proposals with habitual Spartan responses, the Spartan assembly rejected Archidamus' policy and decided for war. In almost all cases, the Spartans would prefer to act as Archidamus suggests, but, evidently, not in this case. And the surprising readiness (testified to by the overwhelming support for Sthenelaidas' motion) with which the Spartans adopted the Corinthian interpretation of the urgency and seriousness of their situation betrays an attitude toward Athens unusual to this nation regularly the slowest of all to come into action.[21]

From this Spartan debate, then, we can draw this further piece of information about the outbreak of the war. At least in regard to Athens, the Spartan character has changed. A nation usually slow to move, on this occasion something has urgently driven them to decisiveness. Archidamus represents the past here, but the majority of Spartans have already arrived at a new state of mind. We should be curious about the cause of this change, and at this point in the history (and for the first time) the story of the growth of the Athenian empire—the Pentecontaetia—becomes relevant as an explanation of the origin of the Spartan fear which made them break with their habitual pattern of action.[22] In addition, we can see that the Spartans had a special attitude toward this war. Archidamus offered them a war of the traditional sort, rather harder than most, but no different in kind, whose purposes were simply rectification of injuries, victory, and honor. But in distinction to this possible policy, Sthenelaidas and the majority of the Spartans opted for another, new policy. Athens posed a new and special sort of threat, and the war had a special purpose: not merely the punishment of specific acts, but the ending of the expansion (or even the existence) of the Athenian empire, and so the ending of the possibility of further injury.

In these four speeches we have been able to discover the particular and definite choices, reasons, and purposes with which the war was begun. The next speeches we consider exhibit the strategies and expectations which were the product of these decisions.

The Corinthian Speech at the Second Spartan Congress
   (1.120–24), 432/31 B.C.
Pericles' First Speech (1.140–44), 432/31 B.C.

I have chosen to consider these two speeches together because the elaborations they give of the political situation are complementary.[23] Both speeches have the same rhetorical purpose and both provide us with similar sorts of information. Both speeches are addressed to assemblies at the very moment of the decision to go to war, and since in both cases the ground for that decision had been prepared by prior events and speeches, neither spends much time in arguing in favor of war. Rather, both expand upon the chances of success and the ways in which success will be achieved. For the reader, the two speeches complete the picture of the reasons for which these cities went to war, and present the strategic policies and the expectations according to which each side fought this opening phase of the war.

The Corinthian speech was delivered at a second congress at Sparta, on the occasion of the declaration of war by the Peloponnesian League as a whole, for which purpose the congress had been called. Having previously convinced the Spartans that the Peace was dissolved, the Corinthians here attempt to convince the rest of the alliance, and the success of their speech completes the progression of events from peace to war on the Peloponnesian side.

Believing, no doubt correctly, that the decision of the Spartans made a declaration of war at this congress a foregone conclusion, most of the Corinthian speech is concerned with the Peloponnesian strategy for the war.[24] Even while doing this the Corinthians complete our picture of Peloponnesian atti-

tudes at the start of the war by reiterating the immensity of the
Athenian threat as they conceive it. They represent the threat
as general by both a concrete and an abstract argument. First of
all (1.120), to convince the remainder of the allies of the need
for full league participation in the war, they enlarge the sphere
over which Athenian actions are said to have effect.

> Those of us who have had dealings with the Athenians need
> no instructions that it is necessary to be on guard against
> them. But those who are living more inland, and not in a
> sea-route, must understand that, if they do not aid those by
> the sea, they shall have more difficulty in exporting their
> produce (and in turn more difficulty in importing what the
> sea provides); and they must not be bad judges of what is
> being discussed (on the grounds that it does not concern
> them); but they must expect that should they sacrifice the
> interests of the people on the coast, the danger may come
> even to them, and so they are now deliberating no less about
> their own affairs. [1.120.2]

According to the Corinthians, the extent of Athenian control,
if allowed to grow unchecked, is potentially limitless. Should
Athens come to control the coastal cities, the only ones immediately threatened militarily, it could then indirectly, and
bloodlessly, subjugate the remaining inland cities by its control of trade. By this argument the Corinthians can exhibit an
apparently ever greater Athenian danger.

In addition to this concrete argument, the Corinthians
make a rhetorical generalization of the Athenian danger every
bit as effective in this situation as was their picture of the
Athenian character that they used previously at Sparta.

Coining the phrase—or perhaps merely exploiting it for the
first time—they label Athens a "tyrant city" (1.122.3 and
1.124.3). This phrase has a curious history of its own, which we
will trace in chapter 4, but its utility here is quite straightforward. It provides both a justification for this war and a statement of war aims apparently concrete, yet conveniently flexible and extendable. The way in which this justifies the war is
twofold. First, it provides an analogical foundation for the
Peloponnesian characterization of Athens and the fear that

Athens produces. Inasmuch as it would be understood as a political commonplace that tyrants are unlimited in their desires and ambitions, it is that much easier to accept the alleged limitlessness of Athenian designs (as depicted in the Corinthian characterization of Athens at the first Spartan congress) if Athens is labeled a tyrant city. And as the uncontrolled character of tyrants would naturally be feared, so, too, should Athens'. Second, the phrase creates a pious rationale for beginning the war:

> Whence we may appear either to suffer justly or to allow this [Athenian domination] because of cowardice (and thus appear worse than our fathers). Our fathers freed Greece, but freedom we cannot even secure for ourselves. Rather, we let a tyrant city be established, though we think it proper to put down tyrants in *a* city. [1.122.3]

Making use of this slogan, the Peloponnesians can believe they are pursuing the war in the same reforming spirit and with the same high motives as their ancestors.

Insofar as the entity that the Peloponnesians were fighting, the Athenian empire or Athenian imperialism, was vague, so had to be their war aims, and the slogan also provided what appears to be a concrete (but is actually an appropriately vague) definition of what they hoped to accomplish:

> And holding that this tyrant city which has been established in Greece is established over all alike, so that it rules some already and intends [to rule over] the rest, let us attack it and bring it to terms, and let us live safely ourselves for the future and free the Greeks who are now enslaved. [1.124.3]

But while this is formally solid, the bringing to terms of the tyrant and the liberation of Greece could conceivably range from the capture or liberation of certain Athenian dependents to the complete destruction of Athenian military potential, as prevailing opinion or emotion should suggest, and existing circumstances allow.

The strategies that the Corinthians propose (in chapters 1.121 and 122), and the Peloponnesian expectations these imply, are no departure from traditional patterns. The Peloponnesians will rely primarily on their greater manpower, and will raise money among themselves and particularly from the treasuries at Delphi and Olympia.[25] What is most important is that they act together, for thus they will be too strong for Athens, though separately they are each too weak. All in all, the Corinthians foresee a war fought in the traditional manner, and probably a rather short one. They count on the belief in a Peloponnesian victory (to be produced in the minds of onlookers by their greater numbers) to encourage the foreign sailors serving with the Athenians to defect to the Peloponnesian side, simultaneously strengthening their own, and weakening the Athenian, fleet. They will, as they always have, besiege Attica, and will exploit the opportunities of imperial revolt as they come.[26]

This is how we see the Peloponnesians, then, at the very moment that they go to war. Although they believed the magnitude of the Athenian threat was unprecedented, they still expected that the war would be ordinary in its manner and duration.

Pericles' first speech has a rhetorical purpose similar to that of the second Corinthian speech. It occurred during an extended Athenian debate on the whole question of war and peace which followed the final set of Peloponnesian demands, and Pericles' intention is to convince the Athenians to take the last step from peace to war. He is introduced to us as the foremost politician in Athens (1.139), and as it is his advice which the Athenians followed, his speech can presumably stand for the attitudes of the city as a whole. It is on this occasion that the Athenians do make their final decision for war, and through Pericles' speech we can complete our picture of the way in which, and the expectations with which, they went to war. Pericles' speech ends book 1, and with the opening chapters of book 2 the Peloponnesian War actively begins.

Pericles completes the picture of Athens' attitudes to this war that was begun in the speech of the Athenian envoys at the first Spartan congress. Even the envoys' portrayal of Athens as quiet rather than expansionist is reinforced, though this was not a major purpose of Pericles' speech.[27] The picture that is completed here is one of Athens entering the war in an entirely defensive mode, and of what Athenian expectations of that posture were.

What we must recognize in Pericles' speech, and what is most peculiar and most revelatory of Athens' orientation at the beginning of the war, is that Pericles proposed *no war aims.* This, at least, is the picture of Pericles quite deliberately and consistently given by Thucydides in both the speeches reported and the summary of Pericles' policies in his "obituary" (2.65. 5–13). As far as this Thucydidean Pericles is concerned, the totality of Athenian intentions at the beginning of the war was to be mere endurance.[28] Having been attacked, the Athenians should attempt nothing more than to outlast their opponents, and to come out of the war as they were when it began. All of Pericles' strategy and arguments are directed to this end. This must be stressed, for the Athenians' certainty that they were best served by doing this (and that they were capable of doing it) underwent a complete reversal during the war, which we can observe occurring from this moment to the end of the history. There is a total opposition between the calmness with which Pericles here explains that victory is certain as long as Athens did not "enlarge the empire... and add gratuitous dangers" (1.144.1) and the frantic activity of Alcibiades' statement in 415 that "a city, if it remains quiet, will wear itself away on itself just like anything else" (6.18.6).

Pericles' speech is quite simple. He begins by saying that war should be declared even though it seems the Peloponnesians are asking very small concessions for the continuation of the peace (1.140–41). He argues that a concession here will lead to concessions later, and eventually to obedience in all matters. The Peloponnesians ask these concessions, he says, to see if Athens will obey under the mere threat of war. Therefore, he concludes, the proper demonstration of Athenian resolution is to reject the offers (or ultimatums) and declare war:

Decide right now whether we shall obey before any damage is done, or whether—as seems best to me—we shall make war so that we will not yield either on great or slight pretexts, and so that we may hold what we possess without fear. For both a great and small claim of equals on their neighbors before judgment is imposed leads to the same slavery. [1.141.1]

An argument of this nature must always be suspect, but here seems more justified than it often is. Pericles supports his description of the offers as ultimatums and his perceptions of Peloponnesian intentions as actually hostile by asserting that Athens had already offered to have all disputes arbitrated, but that this was refused by the Peloponnesians.[29] The most telling argument in Pericles' favor, of course, is that if the Peloponnesians were indeed serious in their requests, they should certainly have forborne to declare war before making them.

Having made this point (and briefly, too, believing the Athenians already convinced that war was necessary), Pericles moves on to his strategy and expectations. As distinct from the Corinthians, he believes it likely the war will be a long one, and Athens' best hope its superior capacity for endurance. The Peloponnesians, since they have no free capital, will be able to prosecute the war only fitfully, and it will therefore stretch out in length (1.141). Without money, moreover, they will not be able to maintain a fleet for any long period of time. Since naval superiority can only be obtained by lengthy practice, they will never have an effective naval force (1.142); and because their chance of success in this will be so small, they will never convince the foreign sailors in the Athenian fleet to change sides (1.143.1–2). Further, and most important, this naval superiority makes Athens impregnable. Even if Attica is destroyed, the Athenians will have all the rest of their empire—which only they can reach—as a resource. Athens is as entirely defensible as if it were an island (1.143.5).

Pericles' tactics for the war, similarly, are designed merely to outlast the Peloponnesians until they give the war up either as too costly or as hopeless of success. Athens must not even engage the main Peloponnesian force in a direct battle. This would risk a useless defeat, and that defeat might cost Athens its empire, on which the security of its endurance depends. The Athenians can annoy the Peloponnese with their fleet, which is undefeatable, at safe moments of their own choice. But this is all they can do (1.143). Most importantly, they must avoid the temptation to extend the empire, and must avoid any superfluous campaigns (1.144).

This almost wholly passive strategy is one which was extremely difficult to follow once the war began (as Pericles himself foresaw at 1.140.1), and, indeed, was eventually abandoned. But it was with this strategy that Athens began the war, and as long as Pericles controlled the city, this remained the Athenian strategy, as we shall see in the next section.

Pericles' Funeral Oration (2.35–46), 431 B.C.
Pericles' Third Speech (2.60–64), 430 B.C.

I will treat these two speeches together, for, as different as their occasions and styles are, they are both given for the same purpose. Pericles' strategy for the war would be a difficult one for any state to follow, let alone an active state like Athens.[30] To remain apparently passive in the face of the hardships and losses which must be suffered once war is actually begun demands tremendous resources of will and morale. Both of these speeches were given on occasions when it was likely that the Athenians' morale might have weakened, and the war, or at least Pericles' strategy for it, have been abandoned. On both occasions Pericles spoke not only to strengthen their determination to pursue the war, but also to convince them to continue to follow his cautious and difficult strategy. On the one hand these speeches explain to us how it was that the Athenians continued the war when they might easily have stopped; on the other hand they provide us with a picture of the psychological and political resources on which the Athenians drew to maintain this determination.

I am not going to do justice to the many things the Funeral Oration can tell us about Pericles and about Athens. What I shall do is to stress its *political* point (without denying that it is more than merely political), to indicate its place as a political speech in the chain of political events we have been tracing. The general situation in which the speech is set is this: the end of the first year of war, the burial of the first year's casualties, with no gains to show for them, rather only losses. These circumstances alone would make this a moment for taking stock, an occasion of doubt that with so little accomplished the war were worth prosecuting. But in addition to this general context Thucydides has given us a specific one which helps to explain why, on this occasion, Pericles gave this extraordinary speech in praise of the city, and why he felt that the speech, beyond being fit for the occasion, would be "profitable to the whole company (citizens and foreigners) to hear" (2.36.4).

The most serious loss Athens incurred in the first year of the war, and the hardest to bear, was the destruction of its outlying fields and villages. In the pursuit of Pericles' strategy of minimal direct engagement with the Peloponnesian forces, the inhabitants of these Athenian country districts had to watch the destruction of their possessions while they waited restless and in great discomfort within the city walls. In his first speech Pericles had tried to convince the Athenians to ignore such a loss when it came. But though later the routine invasions of Attica would be received routinely, this first invasion and the sudden loss of these possessions were taken badly in Athens, especially by those whose farms and homes were destroyed.

Archidamus, the commander of the Peloponnesian forces, tried to exploit the situation in two ways: first, he hoped to draw the Athenians into an engagement:

> For he hoped that the Athenians, at the peak of their
> strength in young men and prepared for war as never before,
> would come out against him and would not allow their land
> to be wasted. [2.20.2]

Second, hoped the destruction of the country districts would lead to division in the city between the country-dwellers and native Athenians:

> And also it did not seem likely that the Acharnians (being a
> large part of the city) . . . would allow the destruction of their
> property, but rather would urge everyone into battle. . . .
> For the Acharnians, having been deprived of their own
> property, would not be so eager to run risks for the sake of
> others', and division would enter their decisions. [2.20.4]

That this strategy had a profound effect Thucydides makes clear both indirectly, in an unexpected piece of urban archaeology to explain the sacrifice entailed in the movement of the country population into Athens (2.15),[31] and directly in his narrative at 2.21:

> But when they saw the army around Acharnia (sixty stades distant from the city), they made out that it was no longer to be borne . . . and when their territory was wasted in full view, . . . this appeared a terrible thing, and it seemed to everyone —and most of all to the young—that they should not allow it, but should go out and fight. And assembling in little groups, they were in great contention, some urging attack, and others not allowing it. . . . And the Acharnians, considering among themselves that they were not the smallest part of the Athenians, and since it was their territory being wasted, proposed the attack most vigorously. And the city was in every manner of excitement, and they were angry with Pericles . . . and said reproachfully that he was the general but would not lead them out, and they held him responsible for everything they were suffering. [2.21.2–3]

It is against this background of discontent with his policy, and discontent primarily occasioned by the loss of homes and property, that Pericles gave his Funeral Oration. With this in mind we can recognize both the usefulness (in Pericles' terms) of what he says, and the appropriateness of this speech to this occasion. Inasmuch as the Athenians were uneasy about their material losses, the speech was especially apt in that in it Pericles constructed a vision of an Athens that existed quite apart from any specific possessions, and to whose defense he could appeal in the face of any material losses; it was useful because, as the Athenians responded to the evocation of this new sense of what Athens was, Pericles could convince them of the utility of his passive strategy despite the loss of the countryside and the towns.

The Funeral Oration is, of course, well known, and I will not examine it in detail. But it is important to notice that all of Pericles' statements tend toward one point: that Athens is unique in Greece and in Greek history, that its greatness is not to be judged as is the greatness of other cities, and that its strength, greatness, and prosperity do not reside (as in other cities) in its material wealth or monuments, but in singular qualities of habit, intellect, and will. The city is what it is because of its settled habits ($\dot{\epsilon}\pi\iota\tau\dot{\eta}\delta\epsilon\upsilon\sigma\iota\varsigma$), its political institutions ($\pi o\lambda\iota\tau\epsilon\dot{\iota}a$), and its national character ($\tau\rho\dot{o}\pi o\iota$) (2.36.4). Its memory will endure because of its (nonmaterial) monuments of good and evil (2.41). The memory of its soldiers' greatness endures not in stone, but in "an unwritten memorial which will live with everyone more in thought than in any works" (2.43.3). The city is a way of life and a certain manner of activity, and in his famous demand Pericles asks the Athenians to become lovers of their city, not by looking to its physical magnificence or their own prosperity, but by "contemplating the power [$\delta\dot{\upsilon}\nu a\mu\iota\varsigma$] of the city daily in its reality" (2.43.1).

What Pericles attempts, successfully, in this speech is to show the Athenians that the city they are defending exists in the kind of life they lead, not in any of its material possessions. It is an attempt to convince them that the material losses they have received (and will continue to receive) and the hardships they endure are insignificant in comparison with the unique lives the city allows them to lead. And, if he can convince them of this, he can make them minimize the loss of the countryside and so minimize the effect that loss would otherwise have in their deliberations. By revealing a city that exists wherever the Athenians may be, Pericles can convince the Athenians both to continue the war and to continue it on his terms (for in the city of his speech what is essential has not yet been threatened) at a time when their passions might move them either to end the war or to abandon his strategy and run into danger merely for the repossession of some land.[32]

The occasion of Pericles' third (and last) speech, in 430 B.C., was another at which one might easily expect Athens to abandon the war. In addition to the unsettling circumstances which preceded the Funeral Oration (real losses, but no real gains to offset them), the plague had struck Athens. With no apparent change in the state of the war, and with terrible loss of life from the plague, the Athenians did in fact sue for peace (2.59). Against this background of compelling reasons for surrender, we again need an explanation of why and how they continued the war so contrary to reason or expectation. It is this explanation that Pericles' third speech provides.

The speech is more anxious in tone than either of his others, but indeed the danger was greater to Athens at this moment than at any other until the end of the war. Pericles uses phrases that later (in book 6) are echoed by other Athenians: the choice is between continuing the war or being subject (2.61.1), to lose the empire involves not only simple loss but retribution from the imperial cities as well (2.63), Athens holds the empire as a tyranny (he first of the Athenians, according to Thucydides, used this slogan about his own city), ''for quietness is not secure unless ranged with activity'' (2.63.3). But what distinguishes these statements of Pericles' from those of Alcibiades and Euphemus is that, on the one hand, they are very nearly true at this moment (but not at all objectively true in the latter cases), and that, on the other hand, even in these fears of the second year of war there still seems to be some room for freedom of choice or maneuver that is believed wholly lacking when these fears reappear fifteen years later. Pericles, at least, is convinced that there is a quiet life for the sake of which one engages in war; for Alcibiades and Euphemus there is no quiet at all, merely struggle.

Moreover, in addition to the fears which Pericles evokes to urge the Athenians to continue, the speech also includes a calm certainty that even now Athens cannot be defeated. When Pericles calls attention to the fact that not only does Athens control half of the usable world, but the better half at that (2.62), it is at once a boast, an argument for the possibility of the city's survival, and a demonstration that the only strategy left to the Athenians is also the one he had always supported. It is, indeed, their best strategy. For Pericles (and Athens at this time) the empire is still seen as a luxury and an immense resource. It is what Athenians can draw on to survive this crisis, it is what they will repossess and enjoy when the war is over, and it is what will guarantee the quality of life which they are fighting to preserve. Only its loss, not its possession, is something to be feared, and to call attention to it is both to provide the symbol of the comfortable life that makes the war worth fighting and to show the grounds for hope that it can be won.[33]

With these fears and hopes Pericles persuaded the Athenians to continue the war when one could reasonably expect them to try to end it. Though all they could do in those circumstances was to endure, he reminded them that his strategy for victory had never required any more than endurance. In this speech he not only extended Athenian resistance beyond expectation, he also reinforced his strategy. The importance of this strategy to our historian is explicitly stated in Thucydides' obituary for Pericles which immediately follows this speech:

> For he said that by their remaining quiet and attending to their navy and not adding to the empire during the war nor running any risks with the city they would prevail. But they did just the opposite in all these things. [2.65.7]

> Whence many other errors were committed, as is likely with a great city which possesses an empire, including the Sicilian expedition. [2.65.11]

> So much of a margin of correctness had Pericles from what he himself saw, that the city might have easily overcome the Peloponnesians in the war. [2.65.13]

These two speeches of Pericles in book 2 explain to us how the Athenians continued the war when we would reasonably expect them to quit. With Pericles' death, however, the most important proponent and defender of the passive strategy was removed. From that moment, despite a preponderance of successes, Athenian policy began to evolve from that with which they began the war (whose exposition is here completed) to one that led to fear and failure.

The Mytilenean Speech at Olympia (3.9–14), 428 B.C.

This speech, addressed to the Peloponnesian League then meeting at Olympia, is the last single speech recorded by Thucydides before the next set of debates of the history. With the next debates we discover a significant transformation in the thinking and the policies of the participants in the war. This single speech in itself exhibits no such dramatic change; yet, in the elaboration and extension of existing policy which it presents, it creates material and rhetorical conditions that prepare the ground for the important developments of 427.

The occasion of this speech, early in the fourth year of the war, is the first serious revolt of a large and important Athenian ally, and its attempt to enlist the assistance of the Peloponnesians in the revolt. At the beginning of the summer of this year, the entire island of Lesbos (the largest of the islands off the coast of Asia Minor that were members of the Athenian empire), with the exception of one city, revolted against Athenian control. The revolt was led by the city of Mytilene, the largest city on the island, and had been planned, according to Thucydides (3.2), from a moment even before the war had begun, though postponed because the Peloponnesians had not been willing to support it. Mytilene was, apparently, one of the strongest members of the empire, having retained its own fleet (with which it fulfilled its obligations to Athens, rather than, as in the case of the smaller cities, having lapsed into the position of giving up its navy and paying tribute to Athens [2.9]), as well as a large measure of political independence from Athens.[34] Although they would have preferred to wait for a more propitious moment, once news of the intended revolt was confirmed at Athens, the Lesbians began their revolt immediately, and sent to the Peloponnesian League for support.

The success of this appeal and its supporting arguments marks a stage in the development of Peloponnesian strategies and attitudes toward Athens. About the Mytileneans themselves the speech is not so revealing. It is in fact the only speech given in the history by a subject of the Athenian empire, and so offers our only glimpse of what it felt like to be in that dependent relation. The value of the account is probably somewhat reduced both by Mytilenean tailoring of it to fit the preconceptions of their audience, and by the Mytileneans' own jaundiced view of their position in the empire. Nonetheless, there is no good reason not to think that their statements reflect something very much like the experience of the smaller cities in the empire. For the Athenians, the empire is a great and dangerous enterprise which makes possible a special kind of life. For the allies, it is merely dangerous.

> Balanced fear is the only surety in alliances. For he who wishes to transgress at all is turned away from it by not having any advantage so that he could attack. [3.11.2]

> And bound by fear rather than friendship, we were allies. And to whomever safety would first give boldness, those would be the first to make the transgression. [3.12.1]

Of greater relevance to our concerns in plotting the unfolding of events in the war, however, are two Mytilenean arguments that touch directly on the development of the conflict between the Athenians and the Peloponnesians. The first argument exhibits an adjustment of the strategy with which the Peloponnesians pursued the war; the second exhibits to us a stage in the changing attitudes of the blocs to each other. Both were to have important consequences.

The first Mytilenean argument of significance to us is their final argument for the utility (to the Peloponnesians) of aid to Lesbos, and its influence on the war was felt immediately and concretely:

> Lesbos seems far off, but it will provide a nearby benefit. For the war will not be in Attica, as one might think, but will be where Attica draws its benefits. And this is the revenue of the allied monies—which will be even greater, if they subdue us. Nor will anyone else revolt.... But by being forward in your aid, you shall gain the addition of a city with a great navy (which is exactly what you most need), and you shall more easily overthrow the Athenians by stealing away their allies (for everyone will come over more boldly).... [3.13.5-.7]

As lukewarm as Sparta's aid to Mytilene was to be, the acceptance of this argument marked an important shift in Peloponnesian strategy.

As we saw in the Corinthian speech at the second Spartan congress, the Peloponnesians began the war with what was essentially their traditional strategy. They were to rely on superior forces and success in land engagements to secure victory. Whatever they might gain through the revolt of Athens' allies would be good fortune. Archidamus had earlier advised actively pursuing the revolt of the allies, but was not supported in the measures that would have been necessary to accomplish this. The Corinthian speech lowered this goal considerably, and in fact, up to this point in the war no effort at all had been made by the Peloponnesians to detach cities from the Athenian empire. Pericles' counterstrategy had been designed specifically to fight this conventional sort of war, to deprive the Peloponnesians of opportunities to exploit their strength by avoiding land battles, and to maintain a secure control over the allies which were Athens' most important resource. Up to this point, the counterstrategy had proved successful. With the decision to support Mytilene, however, the Peloponnesians exchanged their earlier strategy for one which, though at first its novelty made them uneasy (see the excessive timidity of the Spartan fleet commander in Ionia, 3.29–33), offered them their only serious chance of success.

At this moment the Peloponnesians take their first step toward an active policy of encouraging the revolt of Athens' allies. They are still some distance from that goal, but their gradual expansion of this policy changed the entire face of the war. The Peloponnesians were finally able to utilize their resources in a way that would have a serious effect on the Athenians, and pursuit of this policy applied the first significant military pressure to the Athenians. From the Athenian perspective, this pressure forced Athens for the first time to reconsider the general strategy with which it fought the war; from the Peloponnesian, it suggested further exploitation of these possibilities, leading, eventually, to the initiation of Brasidas' campaign in the north.[35] In the end, it was the success of this latter campaign that brought the first part of the war to a close.

The second Mytilenean argument of interest to us, though not as immediately important as the first, embodies a political (rather than military) development of tremendous long-term significance in the war. To convince the Peloponnesians of the justice of their revolt from Athens, the Mytileneans suggested a principle of international relations which, though it might have been used previously for descriptive purposes, was unprecedented as a basis for political prescription:

> For [we know] that no friendship among individuals nor any community among cities is secure in any respect, unless they share toward one another what is thought of as virtue, and especially unless they be alike in customs [καὶ τἆλλα ὁμοιότροποι εἶεν]. For it is in divergence of settled views that differences of action are founded. [3.10.1]

Although the Mytileneans do not give any particular content to the word *homoiotropoi* ("alike in customs"), the rhetorical and psychological implications of the statement are clear: if the Peloponnesians are *homoiotropoi* with most other Greeks (including the Mytileneans, who therefore feel confident in coming to them), then the Athenians must be *heterotropoi* ("of dissimilar custom"). No previous description of the Athenians or of the grounds of enmity between Athens and the Peloponnese has been this radical.

The Corinthians claimed Athens had a character different from Sparta, and claimed it exercised its power like a tyrant. But neither of these characterizations implied that Athens was fundamentally different from any other Greek city, nor did either imply that there were natural divisions of the Greek world which led or could lead to unchangeable and natural political groupings. The Mytilenean formulation does move in this direction, and does suggest the existence of static hostile alliances.

If we posit the Athenian statement in Herodotus (8.144) that *all* Greeks are *homoiotropoi*[36] as a hypothetical starting point, we can trace in Thucydides' narrative a process of reconsideration of Greek relations and Greek identity which becomes both more abstract and more intransigent as it responds to the pressures created by the developing conflict of the Athenians and the Peloponnesians. The end point of this process is embodied in two complementary descriptions of separation: of Athens set apart from the rest of Greece as radically and dangerously as the Persians were (the Theban formulation in the Plataean debate, 3.53–67; 427 B.C.), and of Athens at war with the Peloponnesian alliance as the actualization of an eternal and irreconcilable racial hatred between Dorians and Ionians (the formulation made at Camarina, 6.67–87; 415/14 B.C.).

The formulation that the Mytileneans made here lay well between the two extremes (of Greek identity in Herodotus, of Greek fragmentation late in this war), but can be seen as a part of the road that lies between the two termini. The Mytilenean characterization of the relations within an alliance as dependent on mutual fear (in chapters 3.11 and 3.12) was entirely consonant with the interpretation of international relations expressed so far in the war. Moreover, the Mytileneans were far from the abstractness of the later interpretations. They claimed neither that the Athenians were un-Greek, nor that *homoiotropoi* meant anything as restricted as Dorian or Ionian. Nor did they claim that *homoiotropoi* was politically definite, such as similarity of form of government, despite the fact that they were oligarchs addressing other oligarchs. Yet the psychological effect of using the similarity of custom as a political principle was compelling and ominous.

Once the opposition of the two powers could be summarized in this simple—but absolute—way,[37] the rhetorical ground was prepared for seeing the hostility of the two blocs as natural, and what is more, like all things natural, unalterable. Though by no means the end of this process, the Mytilenean argument, accepted apparently by the Peloponnesians, was a stage along the way in the reinterpretation of the grounds of the war that led to a final interpretation of the war in which the positions of the parties were irreconcilable.

2 The Speeches, 427–416 B.C.

The revolt of Mytilene had consequences beyond the immediate military situation. It was instrumental in generating an Athenian response that radically altered the shape of the war as the Athenians fought it, and stands, then, at the beginning of a significantly different phase of the Peloponnesian War. On the Peloponnesian side, too, this fifth year of the war brought profound revisions to explanations and justifications of it, and, consequently, to its execution. As we might expect, Thucydides constructs his explanation of these changes through the means of debate.

The Debate over Mytilene (3.37–48), 427 B.C.

The reduction of the revolt in Lesbos took approximately a year, despite the ineffectiveness of Peloponnesian aid to the island, aid which consisted of the dispatch of a single Spartan commander to organize the resistance, and, too late, of a Peloponnesian fleet. In 427 the Mytileneans surrendered unconditionally to the Athenian commander, an Athenian garrison was admitted, and hostages were sent to Athens pending a decision on the fate of the island. On the first day of debate, the Athenians, angered that the island had revolted even though it had been well treated in comparison with the other allies, voted to put to death all Mytilenean males of military age, and to enslave all the women and children. By the next day, according to Thucydides (3.36.4–5), the Athenians re-

50

gretted the harshness of the decree, and, irregularly, held a second debate to reconsider their verdict. It is this second day's debate that Thucydides has recorded.

The specific question of the debate, namely, What policy should Athens take toward the revolt of Mytilene? had, as it turns out, a much more extensive significance than might have at first been expected. The initial question attracted a more general formulation—According to what policy should Athens regulate its relations with all its subject states?—and this, in turn, eventually suggested the application of the principle, once discovered, to all of Athens' foreign relations, even those outside the membership of the empire. Initially, however, whether Athens needed a formal and deliberate imperial policy at all was itself open to question. It is doubtful that such a policy had been of any great concern to the Athenians before this moment in the fifth year of the war. Until this moment Athens had virtually no need for a consistent and articulated set of relations with its allies, for from the beginning of the war until this time the possibility of a general threat to its imperial status neither existed nor was felt to exist. On the one hand, because the greater number of its allies were islanders and because of the supremacy of its navy, Athens' empire was almost unapproachable by any other power than itself. On the other hand, where defections or revolts did occur, either in Asia Minor or in the north of Greece, they could be dealt with individually and as special cases. We can see confirmation of Athenian confidence in the stability of the empire in Pericles' third speech (2.62, in the second year of war), where, despite the gravity of the situation in Attica, he neither questions the ability of Athens to hold the empire if it wills nor considers as imminent the threat of any general uprising.

With Mytilene's revolt, however, Athenian complacency was destroyed. The revolt itself was unexpected, and occurred in a large and independent island, one well treated and therefore presumably with most reason to be loyal. Further, as a consequence of the revolt, the Peloponnesian fleet made its first appearance among the Athenian-controlled islands and cities in Ionia. The coincidence of these events created a new anxiety among the Athenians: that they could no longer take the quiet submission and support of the empire for granted. To the simple external threat the Peloponnesians had posed was added a new "internal" danger in the shape of the possible treachery of the empire. Pericles had been able to assume Athens' continued possession of the empire, and to use this to guarantee Athens' future safety in the war. But if disloyalty threatened their possession of the empire, it therefore also seemed to threaten Athens' security directly. This sudden change in the nature of the dangers of the war moved the Athenians toward an examination of the nature of their actions and intentions in the war, and brought to the question of the fate of Mytilene a broader significance, felt by both speakers in this debate. Whatever the differences of the measures they proposed, both Cleon and Diodotus realized that they were arguing much more than an individual case, and were, at the least, proposing policy that Athens was to follow in dealing with all its allies.

This debate, then, occurs at a moment of crisis in Athenian imperial policy, and its result in fact marks a significant change in that policy and in Athenian foreign policy generally. In a sense it is to be expected that, as the empire was at the center of Athenian war policy as a whole, the enunciation of imperial policies of a certain sort would influence deliberation on all matters. The principles articulated and chosen in the debate effect a serious change in the direction of the war.[1] A debate (rather than a single speech) is used to help us perceive the direction of the change, and Thucydides again signals the moment of equilibrium that precedes it (as in the debate about Epidamnus) in his narrative statements about the debate. At 3.36.6 Cleon is introduced as the politician with the most influence in Athens at the time, so that we recognize that his defeat would itself be an event of some note and would indicate a dramatic and significant moment of decision. Further, at 3.36.5-6, Thucydides informs us that the debate occurred during an extraordinary second session of the assembly called to reconsider the result of the first day's deliberation. Describing the outcome of this second debate (at 3.49.1), Thucydides says that the votes on either side of the question were virtually equal. Through signs such as these he suggests that in this debate we find almost the precise moment at which opinion in Athens shifted from one interpretation of imperial policy to another.

As we approach the debate it is important for us to notice that Cleon's response to the revolt of Mytilene is a thoroughly conservative one. If we compare his speech in the debate on the Mytileneans (3.37–40) to previous statements concerning the empire and international relations made by Athenians prior to this moment (the Athenian speech at the first Spartan congress and Pericles' three speeches), we can discover a complete consonance of the principles which are assumed to govern the actions of, and relations between, states. There is, indeed, a marked difference in tone between Cleon's speech and those earlier statements, and in the violence of Cleon's style we can see traces of both the violence of his character (according to Thucydides, 3.36.6) and the stresses and frustrations which five years of war and three of plague have created. But underlying the differences of style and temperament is an articulable identity of principle, and in this debate on Mytilene Cleon's positions provide us with our fixed point of reference (or the context) against which we can see the victory of Diodotus' speech as a distinct change in Athenian policy.[2]

The Athenian speakers at Sparta cited two principles of international relations: that states act as they do from fear, honor, and profit (1.75.3), and that the weaker is always subject to the stronger (1.76.2). We may characterize these principles as wholly materialistic in that they attribute no efficacy or relevance to the policies or thought of particular states. Rather, they explain all actions of states and the international relations that those actions imply by factors that are solely dependent upon the material aspect of states: essentially, their size, the possibilities size allows, and the automatic reactions, therefore, of states to the other states they encounter. All states, without exception, were said to act according to these principles, and all states could, therefore, be treated in the same way, as these principles demanded. Cleon's argument for the execution of the entire male population of Mytilene is founded on nothing else than these principles and the relations they describe.

His argument is a very simple one. Athens holds control of its allies like a tyrant (here, of course, he echoes Pericles, and we can see a further link—whether genuine or merely an artifice exploited by Cleon—to the past policy), by force or the fear of force alone (3.37). Any of the imperial cities, if it feels it can succeed, or that it would be profitable even to try, will revolt from Athens (3.39). In order, therefore, to preclude any further revolts, a terrible example must be made of Mytilene, so that the fear of failure can outweigh any hopes of profit from the attempt in the minds of the rest of the allies (3.40). There are two assumptions which underlie this argument. First, that the only bonds in the empire or between states generally are complementary threats and fear.[3] Second, and crucial to the dynamics of this debate, that the only significant agents with which one deals are states *as a whole.* The two assumptions depend on one another, and on the two previously mentioned principles, for if states are considered materialistically, then the interests that states have are a result solely of their material circumstances. Inasmuch as for any given state the material circumstances are a constant regardless of its political make-up or divisions, if states are thought of only in these terms, as nothing more than their size or wealth, then one can think of their interests or actions only as those of the state as a whole, as interests or actions proper to a body of a given size and with a certain wealth (much as in classical physics the body is identified by its mass and considered as a unit without parts and without reference to its composition). In these terms it is impossible or irrelevant to distinguish (as, by contrast, Diodotus does) different interests that may be held by different classes within the state. States with the possibility of power, the Athenians up to this moment would assert, will want to exercise that power, and that they will has no relation to the political composition of the state. So, finally, the only relations that exist among states are those seen in the exercise of power: either control or servitude, dominating or being dominated.

This line of reasoning suggests a further consequence: that a deliberate policy for dealing with other states in unnecessary. Seen in light of these principles, all attacks on one are of the same sort, an attempt to control one. All, therefore, are to be met in the same way: by surrender if the attacker is stronger, by his destruction if weaker. A state, therefore, needs no articulated policy because it has no choice about how to respond; all its actions must be automatic reactions to external threats. This is the point of Cleon's attack on the Athenian assembly for holding a second debate (3.37.1–2). Debate, he says, is unnecessary, since there can be only one meaning to the Mytilenean attack, and therefore the Athenian response is predetermined. Although Cleon's speech is intended by him as a pattern for all further relations with the allies, his proposal is that Athens needs no definite *policy* to deal with the allies. Simple reaction, in force, will serve as an imperial policy, as it does generally in all interactions with other states.[4]

Diodotus, who opposes Cleon in this debate, holds many beliefs in common with him (or at least claims that he does), both about the nature of the occasion and about the nature of states. With Cleon, he believes that the debate on Mytilene has more than immediate significance; it will decide imperial policy for other cases as well. He, too, believes that human nature is incorrigible and prone to crime, that cities as well as people are wont to commit violence upon one another if they think they can gain an advantage by doing so. He, too, believes that pity and mercy should play no part in the deliberations, and that the sole criterion should be the profitability of the decided policy for Athens. But where Cleon sees a simple solution according to well-known and recognized principles, Diodotus sees that the very beliefs that he holds in common with Cleon render the established principles and policies ineffective and even counterproductive.

The keystone of Diodotus' argument is the elegant sophistic (3.45–46) about love and hope. Having agreed with Cleon that human nature is aggressive and incorrigible, Diodotus uses the sophistic to deny that fear can ever prevent the operation of this nature. Fear has been used to deter crime for ages, the argument runs, but even the fear of death is rendered ineffective as a bar to crime by the action of love, hope, and fortune. This will be as true of states as of men, and the result of the execution of the Mytileneans will be to make other rebelling allies more intransigent in their rebellion rather than to keep them from it. Having suggested the futility of Cleon's solution, and having brought the deliberation to an impasse, Diodotus resolves the problem by transforming a simple political distinction into a prescriptive principle for international policy in a way that had not previously been done by the Athenians.[5]

When Diodotus insists (3.47.1–2) that the Athenians must distinguish between the interests and sympathies of the oligarchs and the interests and sympathies of the *demos* in subject states, he employs a distinction of no great subtlety or novelty. It is hard to think of a single Greek city in which citizens would not recognize that there were, broadly conceived, two classes with differing and opposed interests. Moreover, the Athenians themselves had on occasion recognized and made use of this distinction as a means of—as we would say—"pacification" of rebelling allies. At Erythrae and Samos (and possibly elsewhere) the Athenians dictated the institution of democracies following the surrender of these cities.[6] Underlying this action was the Athenian assumption that democracies would be less inclined, or less obsessed with the desire, to rebel from the empire.

That the Athenians had recognized this distinction previously should not, however, blind us to the fact that Diodotus' proposal of the distinction as a deliberate policy clearly does mark an innovation. We can see this from three different perspectives. First, earlier Athenian establishment of democracies in allied cities was hardly a matter of policy.[7] Any firm evidence we have of such establishments shows that they follow the quelling of a revolt. They are measures decided after the fact, and, apparently, only in cases of serious and determined rebellion. Diodotus, insofar as he is proposing policy not only for dealing with Mytilene but the allies generally, is offering a principle to direct action toward the allies and other states "before the fact"—that is, as an actual and uniform policy to maximize allied sympathy and cooperation, not merely a case by case expedient to return rebellious allies to Athenian control. No such consistent policy of encouraging allied loyalty through support for democratic factions in the cities had ever existed before, as we can see, on the one hand, from other occasions at which the Athenians did not establish democracies in recaptured cities,[8] and, on the other hand, from Athenian indifference to the ideological position of its allies *before* a revolt or the framing of an alliance.[9]

The second perspective from which we can see the novelty of Diodotus' proposal, and, indeed, the perspective in which it acquires its greatest significance for our purposes, is the range of its application. Though his speech on this occasion is addressed in the first instance only to imperial affairs, the principle Diodotus enunciates is one of much wider and more fruitful applicability. If support for democrats in the allied cities would bind them closer to Athens, should not support for democrats in other independent cities make possible the binding of those cities, also, to Athens? However widespread we might decide Athenian support of democracies inside the empire was before 427, up to this point in the war we can see no use of this principle to direct Athenian policy toward cities *not* in the empire. Rather, in the one case especially relevant to this fifth year of the war, we see that Athenian relations to Corcyra before this moment were decided solely on material, not ideological, grounds. Diodotus' transformation of a "domestic" political distinction into an abstract principle, however, made possible the extension or "externalization" of this principle beyond the bounds of the empire, and from this time forward we see Athenian relations to other cities (even outside the empire) profoundly shaped by this political or ideological interpretation. Not only is this extraimperial application of Diodotus' principle an innovation, it is precisely this aspect of its novelty which is most important to Thucydides. The occasions at which Thucydides draws attention to the political (or ideological) basis of actions in the war—*staseis* that encourage Athenian intervention, or instances in which the form of government makes a difference to the alignment of states in alliances—are predominantly those involving Athens with cities outside its empire.[10] In this, of course, Thucydides is consistent with his general interests in the history: deemphasizing, for the most part, questions of internal imperial administration, and concentrating on policies and actions that affect the independent participants in the war.

Finally, the third—and, for the purposes of this inquiry,

decisive—perspective from which we may see the novelty of Diodotus' proposal is that of Thucydides' narrative itself. Even were we ultimately to conclude that Diodotus' proposal was *not* a policy innovation at Athens in 427,[11] we would nonetheless have to conclude that it is presented to us as one by Thucydides. The distinction of the political positions of factions inside a state is one not only not made by any previous Athenian speakers in this history (the Athenian speakers at Sparta, Pericles, Cleon), it is one that is specifically irrelevant to the materialistic principles of foreign relations enunciated by them.[12] As we come to Diodotus' speech in this debate we have been prepared in such a way that the statement of the distinction as something significant to Athenian foreign policy indeed seems an innovation, and the proposal of both a new direction for Athenian action and, eventually, a new interpretation of the nature of the war to justify it. Whatever one's personal judgment as to the actual events of the Peloponnesian War, that Thucydides meant to emphasize this occasion as a moment of change in Athenian policy seems quite clear from the way in which he has composed his narrative. It is in what he perceived (and has presented to us) as the novelty of Diodotus' use of the distinction as a basis for international politics that Thucydides sees the beginning of an important change in the nature of the war.

As the first step of this change, when he uses the distinction, Diodotus is able to present an acceptable solution to the Mytilenean problem and to exhibit the possibility of a new kind of bond within the empire to replace the allegedly ineffective ones of fear. The distinction makes relevant a fact which Cleon ignored completely (perhaps from malice, perhaps because it was meaningless in the system described by his principles), and which justifies sparing the lives of the majority of the Mytileneans. When the oligarchs finally had to arm the Mytilenean populace, the people immediately delivered the city to the Athenian commander (3.47.3 in this speech, 3.27.3 in Thucydides' narrative). Diodotus generalizes this into an imperial policy: the allies can be kept close to Athens by cultivating the political sympathies which exist between the democratic factions of the subject cities and Athens. If human nature cannot be reformed, this, at least, is to him an appropriate canalization of the existing energies.[13] It is this policy that, in revising their earlier decision on Mytilene, the Athenians accept.

But the consequences of Diodotus' use of the political distinction do not end with this first step, and the effects of this debate on Athenian war policy were extensive and weighty. The debate marks a moment of radical change in the direction and imputed significance of the war. Traditionally, this has not been felt to be so, partly because Diodotus has often been taken as the representative of earlier Athenian policies (so that the debate appears to offer no change), partly because the long-term material insignificance of Mytilene obscures the wider importance of the moment. In fact, almost the whole of the third book of Thucydides' history is occupied by his accounts of three events in the fifth year of the war (the revolt of Mytilene, the reduction of Plataea, the *stasis* at Corcyra) which have in common, so it might seem at first, only their material inconsequentiality. Nonetheless, Thucydides treats them with a care and an emphasis reserved for only a very few events in the entire course of the war as he recorded it.[14] If the three events are of no material consequence, we must conclude that Thucydides saw in them some nonmaterial consequence or significance, and it is this nonmaterial significance which in fact binds the events of the third book, and these debates, together.

Other readers of Thucydides who have been struck by the lack of material importance in these three actions have tended, in explaining Thucydides' reasons for their inclusion and for the emphasis given them, toward two epideictic interpretations, two separate, moral demonstrations: either (1) that the events of book 3 show the increasing brutalization of the Greeks during the course of this war, a brutalization which will reach its deepest point with the execution of the Melians in book 5;[15] or (2) that the paired debates at Athens and Plataea show the different treatments accorded conquered foes by Athens and Sparta, a difference which shows the temperance of the Athenians and the cruelty of the Spartans.[16] Such moral explanations will not, unfortunately, bear scrutiny in light of other events in the history.

The actions of Athens and Sparta in book 3 are unlikely to

provide us with new evidence of brutality since there is nothing especially new about the brutality exhibited in them. On the Spartan side we can always find evidence of a kind of gratuitous brutality: at 2.67.4 Thucydides mentions (without any special emphasis) that since the beginning of the war the Spartans would kill any sailors they captured at sea, whether they were actually Athenian allies or were neutral; at 3.32.1–2 it requires a special argument to keep Alcidas, the Spartan commander, from executing captives of nations he was putatively in process of liberating from Athens. On the Athenian side, too, we can find evidence of a consistent level of violence: at 2.67.4 the brutality of the Spartans is used to excuse a set of illegal executions by the Athenians; the so-called low point of Athenian brutality (Melos) is antedated by an identical slaughter at Scione six years before (5.32.1) which receives no comment from Thucydides; it is worth noting that execution is not actually considered in the Melian Dialogue; it is probably the case that no more men were killed at Melos and Scione than were killed in the "less brutal" executions at Mytilene; and it is worth remembering that almost half of the Athenians who deliberated about Mytilene were in favor of executing the *entire* male population of that city. It is extremely difficult to demonstrate any progression of brutalization; rather, violence appears to remain at a uniform level throughout the war (although it may be fair to say that as the war progresses the rationalizations of the violence become more perfunctory).

Neither can we find a moral lesson by seeing the debates at Athens and Plataea as exemplary of the differing attitudes of Athens and Sparta toward the enemies they capture. In the first place, of course, Mytilene and Plataea do not stand in anything like the same relation to their respective conquerors, and so the comparison could hardly be considered adequate. More significantly, in neither case does the decision stand as much of an example: the Spartans never find themselves in a similar position in the remainder of Thucydides' history, and so never act this way again; and, while the Athenians do find themselves dealing with allies that rebel often enough, their responses in fact are always different from their response here, which cannot, then, be considered exemplary.[17] Finally, when this comparison is made, it is usually to demonstrate the greater temperance, if not decency, of the Athenians. But while it is true that there is something ugly about the way in which the Plataeans are condemned, it is necessary to remember that the "temperate" or "decent" Athenian solution killed probably as many as five times the number of men killed by the Spartan decision, and that this temperate solution was passed by only a few votes.

In error in both of these interpretations is the assumption that, since the two debates do not result in actions of *material* significance, the debates are examples of general attitudes rather than events in their own right. The exemplary interpretations separate the events of the fifth year not only from each other, but from any specific temporal location at all. Surely it would be better to return these events to their context in the war, and to consider them in their relation to one another. Thucydides felt these events were of prime importance, as we can judge from the treatment he has given them. Inasmuch as they stand together almost without interruption, we may consider that their importance (and the reasons for their inclusion and emphasis) can be found in the light that they throw on one another.

The nonmaterial significance the episode with Mytilene has lies in the shift of Athenian policy—and deliberation about policy—which occurs in this debate. Cleon's response to the revolt at Mytilene, and the principles which governed the response were, we saw, firmly linked to the Athenian past. The materialistic interpretation of international politics implied by these principles was the interpretation current in Athens (and probably elsewhere) throughout the first five years of the war. Diodotus breaks with this interpretation and these principles, and advances as the new principle of Athenian international politics the alliance of the democracy in Athens with the democratic factions of the subject cities, and, by extension, of all cities. The radical departure that this marks is the introduction of ideology[18] as a principle of international relations. Since action depends on policy, and policy on more fundamental patterns of interpretation, the acceptance of a new principle of interpretation by the Athenians gives this debate an importance far greater than its immediate material consequences.

From this moment all Athenian alliances were with democracies or democratic factions alone, and all captures of cities by the Athenians involved a change in the form of government (the latter is also true of cities captured by the Peloponnesians). At the beginning of the Peloponnesian War the nature of the governments of allied cities appears to have been simply irrelevant. Although Corcyra had some form of popular government in 433, it supported the exiled oligarchs from Epidamnus (1.24.5-7 and 1.26.3-4), and Athens was quite willing to help Corcyra aid the oligarchs. Moreover, before Corcyra approached the Athenians, it had approached Sparta, and indeed had received some moral support there (1.28.1), yet even this in no way affected Athenian attitudes toward an alliance with Corcyra. Mytilene, too, was most likely in the hands of its oligarchs at the time of its rebellion in 428, and that it was also an oligarchy in 432 is strongly implied by the statement (3.2.1) that the city was interested in revolution even before the outbreak of the war.[19] Yet Lesbian ships (certainly primarily Mytilenean) were allowed to serve with the Athenian navy until the rebellion actually took place (3.3.4). There was not, apparently, up to the fifth year of the war, any notion of an ideological ''security risk.''[20]

From the moment of Diodotus' speech, however, Athenian foreign relations took a decidedly ideological turn. Athenian involvement in the *stasis* at Corcyra was on the democratic side; Megara, which had been attacked ineffectually twice a year from the beginning of the war, was almost taken with the help of the Megarian democrats (4.66-74); the Boeotian campaign resulted from the initiative of Boeotian democrats (4.76.2). During Brasidas' campaign in Thrace, events depended almost entirely on politics: Thucydides tells us (4.78. 2-3) that the Thessalian *demos* would have prevented Brasidas' march north, but did not have the power to do so under their constitution; Brasidas was called into cities by the oligarchs (Torone, 4.110.1; Mende, 4.123.2); aid was given to Athens by the *demos* at Mende (4.130.4-5).

Further and perhaps definitive evidence for the importance

of ideological concerns at this stage of the war can be found in the complicated chains of events surrounding the shifting alliances of nations during the Peace of Nicias. At 5.31.6 (in 421) it is stated that Boeotia and Megara did not join the Argive alliance specifically because of the possible conflict of interest between oligarchic governments on the one hand and democratic governments on the other. At 5.47 (in 420) the quadruple alliance, Athens-Argos-Elis-Mantinea, is concluded, apparently with great enthusiasm from the Argives, who broke off negotiations with Sparta in order to take advantage of the Athenian offer (5.44.1). Among the reasons given for Argive preference for an alliance with Athens is that Athens, like Argos at this moment, was governed by a democracy (and the existence of democracies in all four cities of the quadruple alliance is testified to by 5.47.9). Finally, confirmation of the interrelation of ideology and international politics during the Peace is found in the following sequence: at 5.76 (418/17) the Argive oligarchs conclude a peace with Sparta as the first step to the overthrow of the democracy; at 5.78–79 the oligarchs break off Argos' alliance with Elis, Mantinea, and Athens, and conclude an alliance with Sparta; at 5.81.2 the democracy in Argos is put down with Spartan help, and the Argive oligarchs, in concert with Sparta, establish a new oligarchy in Sicyon; at 5.82.2 (in 417), however, a counter-revolution returns the democrats to power in Argos, and leads to Athenian aid and the renewal of the Argive alliance with Athens (5.82.5).[21]

In addition to influencing the nature of alliances, the introduction of ideology also changed the character of the conflict, for the proclamation at Athens of an ideological justification for friendship and military aid created the opportunity for an expansion of the war in new directions. Previously, the initiative for bringing the war to a new theater had lain with the great powers, Athens or Sparta. New cities were attacked as either of these powers deemed fit. But the introduction of ideological alliances dramatically enlarged the number of cities which could take the initiative, and at the same time opened the way to more dramatic shifts in the military situation.

On the one hand, political parties in smaller cities could take the initiative in bringing the war to their regions. A democratic or oligarchic faction, bent on the seizure of power, could invite the intervention of the appropriate great power. The *stasis* in Corcyra is the most complete and striking example that Thucydides gives of this new phenomenon, but the pattern of Athenian intervention on the democratic side and Peloponnesian on the oligarchic was, he insists, to be repeated throughout Greece, as we can see in the narrative from this point. With it came an extension of the war in area and cruelty, and, also, a reinforcement of the intensity of these ideological beliefs and conflicts.

On the other hand, the introduction of ideological alliances created the opportunity for more decisive events in areas the war had already touched. Previously, the capture of cities depended solely on military superiority, and in the first five years of war the results were less than dramatic. But from this point the appearance of an army before a city might precipitate overt political warfare, and the betrayal of the city to the army by the appropriate political faction. Military successes became more frequent in this phase of the war as military power was augmented by ideological support, as, for example, in the case of Megara (4.66–74).[22]

Of course, changes like this do not occur instantaneously. That Cleon specifically denies the application of the distinction between the interests of the oligarchs and the *demos* (3.39.6) indicates that the distinction was in use by other persons besides Diodotus, and that Cleon expected it to be used in the debate. What we see in the debate is not the invention of the distinction, but the acceptance of its applicability and its authorization for public use. Although the materialist interpretation held public authority throughout the first five years of war, an increasing dependence upon ideological interpretations must have begun appearing in Athens for this moment to have occurred at all. Diodotus' speech does not mark the first moment at which an ideological interpretation was used; rather, it marks the first moment at which ideology was used as a principle publicly and at the "policy level." With this speech the ideological interpretation was made accessible as a source for the formation of policy.

It is clear that Thucydides felt this fifth year of war to be particularly significant. Mytilene, Plataea, and the *stasis* at Corcyra all occur within it, the first two given emphasis by their debates, the third by its great wealth of detailed description and by Thucydides' personal intrusion into the narrative to explain the phenomenon. Mytilene was the occasion of an Athenian redefinition of the meaning of the war, for if Diodotus' arguments led to a reconstruction of policy which placed Athens unequivocally on the side of democracies, so too did the policy push the Athenians toward an interpretation of the war as essentially one of democracies against oligarchies. Similarly, Plataea was the occasion of a Peloponnesian reconsideration of the meaning of the war, as we shall see in the next part of this chapter. If the Peloponnesian redefinition was not so entirely based on politics as was the Athenian, it was nevertheless ideological, and complementary to the Athenian. Corcyra provided the proof of the vitality of these ideological forces, and exhibited the strength and reality of the effects these abstract forces could create.

The Debate at Plataea (3.53–67), 427 B.C.

At almost the same moment that the Athenians were dealing with the revolt at Lesbos, an event occurred in mainland Greece which Thucydides felt was important enough not only to narrate, but to record speeches for as well. The town of Plataea, an independent Athenian ally (not a member of the empire) in Boeotia near the border with Attica, surrendered as the result of a Peloponnesian siege which had begun in the third year of the war (429 B.C.). Plataea was a town of some interest to Thucydides. It had, at the time of the Persian War, been one of only two Boeotian cities to remain loyal to the Greek cause. The rest of Boeotia (and notably its largest city, Thebes) had abandoned the Greeks and "Medized"—or, as we would say, collaborated with the Persians.

In the period before the Peloponnesian War, Plataea was one of two democracies in otherwise oligarchic Boeotia, and the only Boeotian ally of Athens that Thucydides mentions. The Theban attack on Plataea in the spring of 431 B.C. was taken as the formal outbreak of hostilities in the war (2.2.1;

7.18.2). This initial attack was repulsed, but in 429 the Peloponnesians returned in force and besieged the town. Thucydides gives considerable detail about this siege in books 2 and 3, demonstrating evident admiration for the courage and resourcefulness of the Plataeans in frustrating what was on occasion the entire Peloponnesian army. Finally, however, at the brink of starvation, the remaining defenders of the town surrendered. The noncombatant population had been evacuated, and many of the defenders had escaped through the Peloponnesian lines in the last days before the surrender. In all, about two hundred men surrendered to the Peloponnesians, and, following a brutally brief trial in front of Spartan judges—of which the debate recorded here is a part—were executed.

Despite Thucydides' interest in the Plataeans, the inclusion of a debate here is nevertheless surprising for several reasons. The fall of Plataea was itself of minor military importance. Its loss did not deprive Athens of opportunities for action against Boeotia (in fact, the largest Athenian campaign in Boeotia was undertaken after the loss of Plataea); the addition of its territory to the Peloponnesian League did not result in any increase of activity against Athens from Boeotia. The surrender itself showed nothing unusual. Even the execution of all the Plataean prisoners, as unprecedented as it was at this time, and as relatively large a number as they were to a town the size of Plataea, was hardly an affair of the magnitude that it might appear from Thucydides' treatment of it in the history. (The Athenians had, after all, executed over a thousand persons [3.50.1], not two hundred, at the conclusion of the Mytilenean debate—and that was a moderate settlement!)

Beyond the material insignificance of this surrender, the political situation itself obscures the point of recording the speeches. Sparta was deeply involved in this affair only for the sake of the Thebans, and the virulent hatred between Thebes and Plataea antedated even the Persian War. The real concerns of the situation, therefore, had little to do with the Peloponnesian War per se. The Spartans killed the Plataeans because the Thebans wanted them to, and the Thebans wanted this because of old hatreds, not because of any particular attitude toward this present conflict.

As we look to the unfolding of this debate, however, we observe an unexpected event. Insofar as we recognize the underlying Theban hatreds that drive this trial (and the Spartan cooperation with the Thebans in them), we quite naturally expect that the execution of the captured Plataeans is the inevitable and foregone conclusion to this affair. We expect that the process that was to lead to it would be merely perfunctory, and simple in its train of events. At first, the Spartan judges were clearly favorable to the Theban request for the execution of all the Plataeans, and demonstrated this by the question they asked the Plataeans by way of trial (3.52.4: "Whether they had done any good to the Spartans and their allies in this war"), a question which allowed the Plataeans no opportunity for defense. And yet the eventual execution did not issue directly from these prejudgments. The chain of events was not a simple, it was a complex chain.

Originally, the Thebans were not going to speak on this occasion at all. After the Plataean speech, however, the Thebans were suddenly afraid that the Plataeans might have been successful in persuading the Spartans to show mercy. It is only at this point that the Thebans, too, asked for an opportunity to speak.[23] What the Thebans said at this moment was what they felt would sway the Spartans back from any softening, and their arguments were evidently successful. The Spartan judges show no mercy, and decide for the execution of the Plataeans. But that the Plataean speech was nearly successful alters our perception of this event, and directs our attention to the arguments the Thebans made in this debate (and away from the ancient animosities existing between Thebes and Plataea) as the cause of the condemnation. That is, had the Spartans executed the Plataeans without wavering, we could only look to the old hatreds for an explanation of the executions. But because the Spartans did waver (or seemed to sufficiently to frighten the Thebans), we know that in addition to the ancient hatreds something further was required to harden their opinions against the Plataeans. The Plataean speech apparently made some headway against the ancient hatreds. The new factor that caused the Spartans to overcome their hesitation must be found in the Theban. But at this point we see the execution of the Plataeans not as an automatic effect of ancient Theban animosity, but as a Spartan choice—a choice justified in the minds of the judges by the arguments they heard in the Theban speech.

The effective Plataean argument in this debate was surely simply their direct appeal for mercy, based on their actions during the Persian War (3.54, 56–59).[24] The most affecting part of this is their supplication on the graves of the Spartans killed at Plataea during the Persian War:

> Consider: Pausanias buried them, believing them placed in friendly land and amongst friendly men. But if you kill us, and make this Plataean land Theban, what else shall you do but leave your own fathers and relatives, stripped of the honors they now have, in a hostile land and amongst their murderers? Moreover, you will enslave this land in which the Greeks were freed, you will make desolate the temples of those gods to whom they prayed to conquer the Medes, and you will take the patrial sacrifices from those who built and dedicated them. [3.58.5]

This appeal depended on Spartan memory of the actions committed against the Hellenic cause by the Thebans. That is, it depended on a memory of Theban "Medism"—a charge which the Plataeans never made in name (the omission is of importance in understanding the Theban argument, below) but introduced early in their speech and returned to (after intervening arguments) no fewer than four more times[25]—and a willingness to consider Medism or fidelity to the Hellenic side the primary criteria for evaluating the moral character of nations. That this memory and judgment still exercised some hold on the Spartans can be seen in the effect the Plataean speech had on the judges. Unexpectedly, the Spartans were moved by the Plataean argument. But in the end, the Spartans ignored this appeal. What the Theban speech accomplished was the substitution of a new criterion for the moral evaluation of states, a new model of international character that enabled the Spartans to overcome their hesitation. The construction of a new model for (or description of) international relations is the issue of the debate, and its completion makes this debate significant in understanding the more general change of the war.

The Thebans delivered a brutal speech. It was angry, full of hatred for the Plataeans, and poorly reasoned as well (the argument considered in note 24 is not the only example of self-contradiction in the Theban speech). For all that, it was successful. In general, the argument of the Theban speech is: however badly we may have acted during the Persian War, the Plataeans have now acted much worse. If the Thebans could convince the Spartans of this, then it would be possible to claim that it was appropriate for the Spartans to show the Plataeans no mercy. And the Thebans did convince the Spartan judges, by the use of a rhetorical invention to suggest the existence of an entirely new standard by which to judge the actions of states. They made use of the moral indignation encapsulated in the familiar term, "Medism" ($\mu\eta\delta\iota\sigma\mu\delta s$), by inventing the concept of "Atticism" ($\dot{\alpha}\tau\tau\iota\kappa\iota\sigma\mu\delta s$), parallel in construction to it, and useful as a sloganistic shorthand to refer to a form of international behavior so hateful that it seemed reasonable to liken it to Medism.

The Thebans said in effect: the Plataeans may not have Medized, we admit, but they have Atticized, and that is worse. This is a cruel rhetorical trope, for by a mere verbal similarity the Thebans insisted that actions of vastly different qualities and magnitudes were in fact identical. Yet it was a singularly effective argument. It suggested that all the indignation against the Thebans to which the Plataeans appealed should now be reflected back upon the Plataeans. It had, for the Peloponnesians, an attractive appropriateness, representing (by the parallelism with Medism) both the felt immensity of the Athenian threat and the perceived limitlessness of Athenian ambitions. It presented a schematic model of the world which both reflected (in some sense) the realities of the political oppositions that then existed, and touched on Spartan attitudes of the alienness of Athens and of the worthiness of Sparta's motives in the war. Athenian hegemony, which might have been thought of fairly conventionally, was by this rhetorical invention attached to the vivid notion of treachery to Hellenism. Most importantly, as a slogan "Atticism" had the political effectiveness necessary for its acceptance, both at this moment and as an extended source of judgment throughout the war. As is always the case, the effectiveness of the slogan cannot be attributed merely to its verbal ingenuity. Rather, it is effective because it touches, and enables to be expressed, some deeper conviction or emotion. In this respect the slogan is more the emblem of an already existing state of mind than its creator, and yet it is the office of this slogan—as of all others—to make it possible to appeal to, and make active that underlying opinion or attitude. What is especially significant to us is that the attitude for which Atticism became the emblem is one new to the Peloponnesians in the war.

I believe that Thucydides has suggested that this debate at Plataea was the occasion of the invention of this slogan. This speech is the earliest appearance in the language of both Atticism and its verb, Atticize, but we can also see the novelty of the words in other indications. The words are used three more times in Thucydides (4.133.1; 8.38.3; 8.87.1), and then later by Xenophon.[26] Of the Thucydidean uses, three observations should be made. First, they are never used by the Athenians or their allies. They were not praise-words or even neutral, identifying words, they were words which denoted a crime. Nevertheless, it seems that the words were current among the Peloponnesians and their supporters. They were used by the Thebans, the Spartan faction in Chios, and (in the usage at 8.87.1) presumably by the Peloponnesians generally. (Thucydides, in using one of the words himself at 8.87.1, is echoing the popular explanation of Tissaphernes' actions circulating among the Peloponnesians in Asia Minor.) Second, in using the words in their three later citations, Thucydides gives no explanation of them, nor does he give them any special emphasis. In his off-hand and matter-of-fact use of the words we can find evidence of their acceptability as political slogans. Third, we can even trace in their appearances the outlines of the political history of the words. They are used for the first time in this speech for the rhetorical purpose of maximizing the criminality of Plataean resistance, and as a way of providing the Spartan judges with a justification for the execution of the Plataeans. Having found success once with the word, Atticism, the Thebans used it again later (4.133.1) against the Thespians. This time they alleged that Atticism was a crime in fact (not merely *like* a crime): ἐπικαλέσαντες ἀττικισμόν, "laying Atticism to their charge" (or, perhaps, "alleging Atticism as their crime"). When used in Chios (8.38.3) the word has indeed received the status of a formal crime.[27] And when Thucydides uses the word "Atticize" of Tissaphernes (8.87.1), the word sounds midway between a crime and a description. Eventually, the terms could be used wholly descriptively, as in Xenophon: "In every city some Laconized and others Atticized" (*Hell.* 6.3.14, 371 B.C.).

In addition to this history of the usage of these terms, I believe we can see stylistic grounds for thinking the Theban speech marks their first appearance. The Plataeans never used the term Medism in their speech. Their omission makes the word's sudden appearance in the Theban speech all the more striking. It is not a word one would expect a nation to be willing to use of itself. The Thebans at this debate were not only willing to use it, they were eager to. They pounced on the word (though the Plataean speech spared them its use) precisely because it allowed them to make use of their coinage, Atticism.

If the Athenians had to rethink their rationale for the war after five years of fighting, it is not unlikely that the Peloponnesians, too, at some point would have had to do so. I believe that Thucydides is here marking the formulation of that new rationalization, with which the Peloponnesians fought the war from this time forward. The argument to which the Spartan judges responded—the assertion that Athenian behavior in fact followed a pattern so feared and so criminal as best to be summarized by a slogan that reminded the hearers of the terrors of Medism—was, in its own way, as ideological an argument as Diodotus' at Athens. It is not specifically political, as was Diodotus', but oligarchs are especially prone to use nonpolitical slogans even in political situations.[28] Yet the slogan, Atticism, as the symbol of a specific perception of the Athenian danger, was as abstract and extensive a formulation of international action as was Diodotus'.

The Peloponnesians began the war against the growth of Athenian power and against imperialism. Difficult as it may have been to define what exactly the limits of such a war might be, there was, at least, a concrete object against which they were fighting. But in this new interpretation—the Peloponnesian ideologizing of the war—the object against which they believed they were fighting became much more diffuse, something which required a more general expression, like Atticism. The enemy was now the Athenian manner of life, its ideas (these two elements strikingly represented in the institution of democracy), and the fear that these ideas composed a system that was incorrigibly expansionist (even subversive), and was a danger to the rest of Greece. The difference between "Athens" and "Atticism" (as one's enemy) is precisely ideological. Athens is a city one may fight. Atticism is rather different from that. To Athens' opponents Atticism was an ideology that *other* cities might believe or with which they might be "infected." To allege Atticism as a crime is to shift one's interpretation of events from opposition to a material entity to opposition to a certain ideology or set of beliefs.

With the change this debate marks (for the Spartans demonstrate their acceptance of this new interpretation by the execution of the Plataeans), and the contemporary and complementary change at Athens (which we examined in the Mytilene debate), the Peloponnesian War as a whole entered a new phase. The consequences of this change for Peloponnesian policies and strategies were as serious as the consequences had been for Athens. The generalization of Athens into an alien and dangerous ideology solved some problems the old interpretation did not. It suggested the proper mood of intransigence necessary to continue the war now beyond the length of anyone's earlier expectations. It gave a new definition (however difficult of accomplishment) of how the war was to be won. Under the earlier interpretation, the defeat of Athens and the dismantling of the empire—if it were not accompanied by a change in the Athenian character—might still leave a residual danger that the Athenians would desire and accomplish a reconstruction of their power. The new interpretation suggested, however, that the real threat was a certain ideology. If Athens could be stripped of this ideology, if its Athenian manners—and especially its democratic system of government—could be changed, then both the immediate danger and the threat of future danger could be removed.[29]

The new interpretation also provided a rationale for previously unprecedented actions. The execution of the Plataeans was one, of course, but the new interpretation also lay behind such paradoxical statements (and the policies that required them) as Brasidas' (4.87.4) that he would set the Acanthians free *against their wills.* Such a conviction begins to seem reasonable and justifiable at the moment that freedom is no longer defined simply as autonomy, but requires also freedom from, or rejection of, the "wrong" political ideas—in this case freedom from Athenian influence.

The ground for this new policy, of course, had to be prepared in the first four years of war, in Peloponnesian fear and hatred of Athens. Part of the preparation can be seen in the speech of the Mytilenean ambassadors to the Peloponnesians at Olympia, but with this Plataean debate, the potential that ground provided was actualized, the policy and its principles were made public, and could thus become the conscious source of action and judgment for the Peloponnesians. This new interpretation was, I believe, to govern Peloponnesian policy for the remainder of the war, and was the source of the continuing and, now, eternally present Spartan fear and distrust not only of Athens' intentions, but even of its very existence.

The Spartan Speech at Athens (4.17–20), 425 B.C.

This speech of the Spartan envoys to Athens, in the seventh year of the war, was an extraordinary—even an extremely decent—effort. It was also an utter failure. The definitiveness of the Athenian rejection of this offer to establish a peace was indicative of a critical stage in the development of Athenian attitudes in the war. In part this speech was a failure because in serious rhetorical respects it was unrealistic. But the primary reason for its failure lay in the way Athens had come to feel about the war.

The speech was given in a brief hiatus in one of the most important events in the first ten years of the war. In the beginning of this seventh year, an Athenian army had been able to trap and besiege a fairly large Spartan force on the tiny island of Sphacteria, near Pylos, on the western coast of the Peloponnese. Although the site of the battle seemed to be chosen haphazardly,[30] this siege (and the eventual capture of the Spartan garrison) was the most significant battle of the Archidamian war until Brasidas' campaign in Thrace began in 424. From the moment of their defeat at Sphacteria, the Spartans were continually looking for a way to end the war; moreover, this defeat destroyed their morale to such an extent that the Spartans did not feel they had recovered from this until seven years later, in 418, at the battle of Mantinea. Even during the siege itself, before the issue had been decided, it was clear to all parties that the engagement would have a decisive effect on the war. The speech at Athens occurred during a brief cease-fire in the battle, called for the sake of negotiations. Though the battle was not yet over, the Athenian position at Sphacteria was manifestly superior to the Spartan.

The Spartan envoys suggest that the Athenians and themselves conclude a peace at this moment before the battle is decided. It is an extraordinary offer, for while they freely admit their possible defeat at Sphacteria, they try to make clear that they are not offering peace simply to cheat the Athenians of victory. They offer the Athenians a share of honor they claim will be equal to that of victory: since they are in the position of asking, and the Athenians of granting, the honor of the *peace* will fall to Athens:

> Let us choose peace instead of war, and let us make an end of evils for the rest of the Greeks. Indeed, they will believe that you were most responsible for this. For as it is they make war and find it entirely unclear as to which [of us] began it; but if an end comes—which is most in your power now—they will give their gratitude to you. [4.20.2]

What the Spartans ask of the Athenians is that they not complete the actual conquest of the garrison at Sphacteria. Sparta, they say, has not yet suffered any serious losses in the war. If the war ends now, Sparta would exit from it humbled but not humiliated, and with no strongly emotional defeat to avenge. This, to their minds, is an advantage Athens has purchased rather more cheaply than could have been expected. (Such is the implication of their statement that Athens had inflicted no serious casualities on Sparta.) On the other hand, the consequences of Athens pushing to a final victory at Sphacteria would be most serious:

> If ever it were so, now is the time a reconciliation is good for us both, before anything irreparable overtake us, on account of which we would necessarily keep an everlasting, special hatred for you, and you would be deprived of what we offer now. [4.20.1]

And as the chances of war are variable, and Sparta still a major power, so the chance that Athens will long continue in this position of advantage is small. The time to conclude the peace, therefore, is now.

This is an extremely intelligent and decent speech: intelligent in its recognition that a Spartan defeat here, quite apart from any strategic value it might have, would lead to a hardening of Spartan attitudes that would make a later peace more difficult; decent in its tacit admission of a certain guilt Sparta bore (but rarely articulated) for the start of the war. It is, unfortunately, unrealistic in its very reasonableness. The cool and rational tone of this speech, although no doubt suitable for negotiations before hostilities begin, fits badly into these critical and heated moments which followed six years of actual war. In fact, we could well ask why Sparta was not this reasonable before the war began. To expect that the passions and injuries of six years of war could now be ignored in favor of this calm consideration of how, by asking little, Athens would appear greater than by asking more is to expect too much. Although the Spartans were sensitive to the emotional realities of other Spartans as they affected the possibilities of peace, they seem to ignore the operation of these same realities among the Athenians. Nevertheless, no matter how unreasonable their expectations may have been, the way in which the Athenians rejected the offer is a shock, and reveals changes in their conceptions of the purposes of the war.

To realize the magnitude of the Athenian change, we must remember that, in Thucydides' opinion, Pericles would without doubt have accepted this peace offer.[31] His entire policy was aimed at this one end: the moment at which their possible losses came to appear so great that the Peloponnesians would realize they could not defeat Athens, and so would be forced to allow Athens to live as it pleased. Moreover, Pericles would have seen that this offer contained an unexpected benefit, for the moment came before Athens had done the Peloponnesians any injury serious enough to become itself the *casus belli* of a new war. When we recognize this, we can see that the Athenian rejection marks an ominous development.

The Athenians reveal themselves to be policy-less and without any notion of the aims for which they were fighting. They ignore or forget the fact that it was for this simple end (the Spartan admission of the impossibility of defeating Athens) that they began the war. Further, they make a pointless attempt to substitute territorial acquisition for the original goal, by demanding the restitution of four cities which in fact had been ceded to Sparta in time of peace (4.21.3). Actually, even this demand was aimless, for when the Spartan envoys are willing to negotiate even this, Cleon sets new conditions which make the Spartans feel it is impossible to continue. They feel, and Thucydides agrees, that the Athenians simply do not want to make peace (4.22.3).

The truth of the situation is simple. The Athenians were unwilling to conclude a peace because they were winning and because they lacked a general and agreed conception of their aims that could tell them when they had won. According to Pericles' strategy they had won at this moment. Even if Pericles' strategy were rejected but replaced by some other strategy, they would know that they had won when certain further conditions had been met, and perhaps they could even have been met on this occasion. But the Athenians rejected both the simple peace and also any other determinate concessions. Since they were winning, and since they had no goals which, once accomplished, could mark a successful conclusion for themselves, what was there to tell them that they should stop now? But to have reached this state meant that there could be no *satisfactory* negotiated settlement to this war. If Athens could not tell when it had won, then there remained only three possibilities: a total victory by Athens, the utter defeat of Athens, or an armistice arranged at a moment of stalemate and exhaustion on both sides. It was this latter, in fact, that terminated the first ten years of war, when Athens had lost all it had gained at this high point of its position, and when the willingness to continue was lost in both Athens and Sparta. But such an armistice, although a negotiated settlement, was not a satisfactory one, for it left on both sides unresolved feelings of enmity and material injury which, once the period of prostration was overcome, returned in force as the causes and impulsions of a new war. At this moment, perhaps, there was an opportunity to negotiate a peace which would not contain the seeds of a new war. But when, abandoning their old strategy in the flush of success, the Athenians rejected this offer, they made it that much more likely that the eventual peace would be nothing more than a papering-over of the injuries sustained in this war, which in turn would lead to another war once the exhaustion of both sides was over.

Hermocrates' Speech at Gela (4.59–64), 424 B.C.

From a moment late in the fifth year of the war in 427 B.C., Athens began to consider the possibility and desirability of a campaign in Sicily. At first the plans were both concrete and tentative. When Thucydides first mentions this development, at 3.86, he indicates that the primary purpose of Athenian intervention in the internal wars of Sicily was to hinder the shipment of grain to the Peloponnese from the west, and generally to see if some injury could be done to Syracuse, the most powerful city in Sicily, and a nominal ally of the Peloponnesians (although it had not yet given direct support to them). Insofar as this was their whole strategy, it was in keeping with the policy with which the Athenians began the war, of doing whatever injury they could to the Peloponnesians without risking a direct engagement with the Peloponnesian land forces. In this respect it was consonant with all the other Athenian engagements, which tended to occur at the peripheries of the spheres of influence of the two blocs rather than in the center of Greece. On the other hand, Thucydides also mentions that in addition to this concrete aim, the Athenians had another intention of *testing,* in this first intervention, "if it were possible that Sicilian affairs be brought under their control" (3.86.4). While this represents a departure from their original strategy, at this moment they held this new aim tentatively.

From the fifth year of the war to the occasion of this speech, an assembly called at Gela in the eighth, the Athenians returned intermittently to the consideration of the campaign in Sicily and reformulated their reasons for being interested in it. For the greater part of this period, their attention was absorbed by events occurring nearer home (notably the Sphacteria episode), and Thucydides' narrative of events in Sicily reflects this.[32] Out of this narrative, fragmentary though it is, a definite picture emerges. Having made an initial test of conditions with a small force, the Athenians decided (3.115, in 426 / 25 at the end of the sixth year of the war) to attempt the conquest of Sicily, thinking that it would be easy and that it would provide safe training for their fleet. The enlarged force that they sent to Sicily for this purpose was in fact occupied, for the greater part of a year, with the siege of Sphacteria. But with the surrender of the Spartan garrison, Sicilian matters came to a kind of climax.

The Athenian victory at Sphacteria had important material and psychological consequences that created certain expectations in the minds of participants, and which, when we read Thucydides' account of the consequences, create the same expectations in our minds. On the one hand, the Athenian victory finally freed the forty ships which were originally intended for the Sicilian campaign. This meant that Athens was able to make its move against Sicily with a considerable force. On the other hand, the Athenian victory had a tremendous demoralizing effect on the Peloponnesians, and a complementary encouraging effect on Athenian ambitions. Thucydides twice mentions (4.21.2 and 4.41.3) that Athens rejected Spartan peace proposals because "they were hungry for more" (οἱ μειζόνων ὠρέγοντο). This moment finds Athens at the very peak of both military success and adventuristic optimism. With respect to this campaign, at least, our expectation is that Athens, riding the crest of the wave, will easily and quickly assume control of Sicily, especially since Sicily was weakened by those domestic wars and conditions of *stasis* within cities that the Athenians knew how to exploit so well.

In these perilous circumstances, gestures toward peace among the cities in Sicily were begun, and led eventually to a general conference of all the cities. The conference was troubled by the same conflict of interests which had created the disordered situation in Sicily, but was able to come to a decision after all, primarily (in Thucydides' account at least) because of the proposals of Hermocrates, a Syracusan. This is the speech that Thucydides records.

Hermocrates' speech is, like all his speeches (as we shall see later), extremely intelligent in its perception of the likely moves Athens will make. The Athenians have come, he says, whatever their pretexts, to gain control of Sicily (4.60). They are likely to succeed so long as the Sicilian cities are at each other's throats. However serious the reasons were for which these internal wars were begun, the Athenian threat is an even more compelling reason to end them. What the Sicilian cities do not realize is that their isolation from the rest of Greece makes the entire island into a single community. Sicily has concerns of its own which are quite different from those of the rest of Greece, and which bind the cities together in a community of interests which transcends matters of race or of previous alliance. Internal war in Sicily is like *stasis* in a city, and the Athenians know very well how to use this for their own ends (4.60–61). Therefore, let us conclude a peace which will be no dishonor to any city, but which will allow Sicily to develop according to its separate destiny (4.63–64).

Surprisingly, the other cities agree. And although they are again embroiled in wars within two years (which situation again suggests to the Athenians the possibility of subduing Sicily), at this moment they correctly recognize the danger that Athens, with all the built-up momentum of its stunning victory at Sphacteria, poses. They make a general peace, and the cities which had invited the Athenians in now ask them to leave. Yet the greatest significance of this speech lies outside the particular importance it had for Sicily itself. Though Hermocrates apparently had an extensive vision of a Sicilian federation which could have made Sicily into a substantial power (and whose accomplishment would have made his policies intrinsically interesting), in fact the vision was a failure. All that was concluded at this assembly was an armistice of limited duration (no attempt, for instance, was ever made to establish the means for the formulation of a common Sicilian policy), and indeed within two years even this had collapsed, destroyed by the domestic rivalries to which Hermocrates alluded in his speech. Nevertheless, the minimal agreement concluded at Gela played an important part in the military history of the first ten years of the Peloponnesian War because the political decision reached here presented Athens with the first serious tactical check to its recent successes.[33]

With this single political decision, the Sicilians put a stop to an uninterrupted string of Athenian successes and suddenly frustrated the expectations that had been created by the Athenian success at Pylos. In fact, the Sicilian campaign, far from ending in another Athenian triumph, became the first step of the Athenian recession from this high-water mark of success. The progression of events that Thucydides shows us in the first ten years of the war is a complex one: of Athenian perseverance until their sudden success at Sphacteria, and of the gradual erosion of their strategic position and morale until the Athenians felt compelled to settle for the Peace of Nicias (of 421), which left them in a position no better than that with which they began the war. The unexpected withdrawal from Sicily (which infuriated the Athenians, who themselves expected only further victories—see Thucydides at 4.65.3-4) marks the moment at which the progression of events turns from a story of success to the story of Athenian failures. The withdrawal from Sicily had no connection with Brasidas' successes in the north, which were in fact what convinced the Athenians to conclude a peace. Yet it was at Sicily that Athenian hopes and ambitions received their first check, and it is from that moment that we date the growing disappointment of their hopes. It is the growth of their disappointment that forms the second part of the account of the Archidamian War.

The check in Sicily is as important as it is, not because of its intrinsic character, but because of what follows. If Athens had continued successful in the war in Greece, no doubt the Athenians would later have returned to try to take Sicily. The next two years, however, were years of failure for Athens, and the combination of those disappointments with this sudden check of their ambitions created a mood of pessimism and exhaustion which led the Athenians to peace negotiations. We may gauge how important the *mood* of failure is by considering that even after two years of failure the Athenians still manage to accomplish all of Pericles' war goals. Yet at the moment of the Peace of Nicias the Athenians cannot take any such optimistic view of their situation. It is to explain to us that Athens concluded the peace because the Athenians *believed* all their possibilities were frustrated that Thucydides has composed the narrative in the form we have it: a great Athenian progress followed by an equally great regress.[34] By our perception of these two movements, we can recreate, in his composition, the cumulative feeling of disappointment and frustration which brought the first ten years of war to an end. The decision at Gela, which this speech marks, was the first of the events which changed Athenian optimism to the exhaustion in which they concluded the Peace of Nicias.

Brasidas' Speech at Acanthus (4.85–87), 424 B.C.

In 424, the eighth year of the war, Brasidas, one of the very few Spartan generals to display any daring, marched north through Greece toward the Athenian allies in Thrace. His primary purpose was to encourage their defection from the Athenian empire, or to capture them, and so weaken Athens and bring the war to a close. This campaign was the first occasion on which the Peloponnesians themselves initiated revolts among the Athenian subject states. The first of the cities to be approached was Acanthus, on the Chalcidic peninsula, which may have been chosen either for its strategic location or, since it was in the midst of factional conflict, for its vulnerability.[35]

Brasidas' speech to the Acanthians, to convince them to

revolt from the empire, figures in two ways in the history. On the one hand, it is a critical moment in the chain of events leading to the Peace of Nicias, for the revolt of Acanthus was the first of a series of allied defections which convinced the Athenians to make an end of the war. On the other hand, the arguments he uses to convince the Acanthians clarify and extend the changes in political and military thought that had been occurring among the Peloponnesians. Brasidas uses only two arguments in this speech. The first shows the completion of the change in Peloponnesian strategic thinking which was begun with the decision to support the revolt of Mytilene. The second shows the consequences for political and strategic policies implicit in the ideologizing of the war begun at Plataea.

Brasidas' first argument, contained in chapters 4.85 and 4.86, is that he has come to the north of Greece simply to encourage the defection of the Athenian allies, and so to deny Athens their material support. Despite the fact that he has entered Acanthus because a fight was being waged there between its political factions, he says he does not intend to side with one group or the other. And although Sparta would normally arrange that its allies were oligarchs, Brasidas denies that he has come to alter the form of government in Acanthus in any way. Recognizing the power of ideological commitments, he says pointedly that this would be worse than the indirect domination from Athens that they now undergo. As far as he is concerned, the Acanthians need not even give any significant aid to the Spartan forces:

> [I have come not so that] we may hold you as an ally whom we have brought over by force or fraud, but on the contrary, so that we may be the active allies of you who have been enslaved by the Athenians. [4.86.1]

He claims he is fulfilling the original promise made by the Peloponnesians to free the imperial cities; [36] and all he requires of the Acanthians is the example of their alliance with Sparta to hold up to the other northern allies to encourage their defection.

While it is true that the example of their revolt was all

Brasidas required immediately of the Acanthians—for it was all that was needed to accomplish the general design of the Peloponnesian strategy (to bring Athens to negotiations through fear of the evaporation of its imperial support)—the rest of Brasidas' promises were probably lies. In fact, Sparta wished to acquire these northern cities as allies in order to have something to barter to the Athenians once peace negotiations began for the return of the Peloponnesian cities that Athens had captured (4.81.2). That his argument was a sort of callous deception, however, is really irrelevant, for no doubt it does represent the *hopes* the allies of Athens felt in respect of Peloponnesian aid.

His second argument (4.87) is much stranger. What he follows his promises with is nothing less than the threat that if the Acanthians should choose not to revolt, he will take the city by force. By itself, there is nothing unusual in this. The way in which he expresses the threat, however, is very unusual:

And I will call the gods and native heroes to witness that coming for a good purpose, I am not believed; and then wasting your territory I will try to compel you. Nor will I think I act unjustly, but good reason is on my side because of two necessities: the one of the Spartans, that (if you will not come over to our side) by your good will they be not injured by the money you provide the Athenians; the other of the Greeks, that they be not hindered from being freed by your slavery. We could not properly do these things, nor ought the Spartans to liberate any people against their wills, except for some common good. [4.87.2–4]

Brasidas claims that no one should free someone against his will unless there is a compelling reason of common good. Thus he justifies his threat of force. But suspect as the justification may be, it is the action to be justified itself that is incredible. The statement that one can "liberate people against their wills"—that is, that one can *compel* people to be free—should seem to us under any condition a most cynical paradox. Brasidas mentions it as if it were merely a morally unpleasant act, though one sometimes justified by circumstance. He seems to have no sensitivity to, or interest in, the patent self-contradiction of such a notion. Further, the Acanthians recognize that this is a threat and respond to it as one. It is the threat, rather than its paradoxical justification, which motivates their decision (4.84.2 and 88.1). But since they do respond to the threat, it is clear that Brasidas could have been successful with even the simplest formulation of it. This in turn makes his actual statement even more gratuitously paradoxical and cynical, yet neither the Acanthians nor Thucydides call attention to it.[37]

Under what circumstances could such a statement pass as reasonable or justifiable? Brasidas' unself-consciousness about the implicit contradiction and the Acanthians' indifference suggest that this phrase, too, had received something like the status of a slogan—something which one hears without paying it too much attention, whose meaning is understood from other sources, and whose logical structure is largely irrelevant. The statement has received its public acceptance because of the new ideological interpretation of the war, otherwise it would be nonsense or brutishness. When states (and their conflicts) are considered materialistically, then freedom is simply autonomy. According to such an interpretation, compulsion of any sort is a form of enslavement, and compelling a nation to be free, therefore, is self-contradictory. But if states are characterized ideologically, then autonomy itself is not sufficient for freedom. The acceptance of an incorrect ideology constitutes a form of slavery, too, and the promulgation of this ideology a form of enslaving others. The wrong ideology, further, may be held quite willingly, and so compulsion—in the form of reeducation—may be necessary as an act of liberation. Moreover, an unwillingness to accept reeducation provides a bad example for other states, discourages them from reeducation, is therefore an encouragement of the wrong ideology, and constitutes an act of enslavement. This is the argument that Brasidas uses, warning the Acanthians that if they will not actively revolt from Athens (for revolution is the external sign of the changing of ideologies), they will be hindering the liberation of other cities.[38]

It is in this way, by characterizing the world as divided between those who oppose and those who support the aggressive Atticist ideology, that the Spartans eliminated the notion of neutrality from their policies. Brasidas specifically warns the Acanthians that there is no way for them to remain neutral, not even if they claimed they were sympathetic to the Peloponnesian cause. They must actively oppose Athens and Atticism, or else they will be compelled to do so. Ideological oppositions are always absolute: they are oppositions of right and wrong. Where material powers, only, are opposed, there exists the status of neutrality for those who provide support to neither side. But where philosophies contend, nonparticipation is taken for acquiescence, and passivity for passive support.

Brasidas' arguments (repeated throughout Thrace—see 4.114.3-5 and 4.120.3) and his campaign in the north were widely successful, and did erode Athenian support to the extent that the Athenians feared (correctly or not) that the empire was breaking away from them. By the end of his campaign, the Athenians were ready to negotiate a peace, and the first ten years' war came to an end. Presumably, his success depended at least in part on the acceptance that the arguments of this speech (and others like it) found. That his arguments would be accepted is not entirely surprising either (paradoxical as they appear), for Athens at the height of its successes could very easily drive cities to believe that unless all stood together to stop it, its growth would continue until it enveloped all of Greece. But while we can understand the attractiveness of the arguments, we must also recognize that the ideologizing of the war that we see in this speech, and its destruction of the possibility of neutrality, had serious consequences. It made the grounds of hostility at once more absolute, more intractable, and more permanent. And in the dissipation of opportunities for neutrality it helped to create conditions which would drive the Athenians to a state of fear in which they, too, would decide that neutrality was impossible and that the compulsions to war were total, unalterable, and irreconcilable. Further, the coincidence in this belief (that the differences between the blocs were irreconcilable) of Athens and Sparta ensured that the peace concluded in the tenth year (out of mutual exhaustion) would be a peace in name only, and that Thucydides would rightly see the resumption of hostilities in the seventeenth and eighteenth years as a continuation of the original war.

3 The Speeches, 416–411 B.C.

The first ten years of the Peloponnesian War (conventionally named the Archidamian War) were brought to an end by the conclusion, in 422 / 21, of a peace between Athens and Sparta, called, after one of its prime Athenian supporters, the Peace of Nicias. In Thucydides' opinion the peace was shaky, and perhaps doomed, from the start, and he explicitly denies (5.26.2) that it ended or settled anything. Many influential members of the Peloponnesian League kept themselves outside the Peace, and without their participation any chance of success the Peace had was severely crippled. Moreover, as Thucydides presents the Peace to us, it was never completely convincing even to Athens and Sparta, and, from the very moment of the conclusion of the peace, important segments of public opinion in both cities crystallized into war parties directed toward undermining it, and toward creating opportunities to bring the two leading cities once more into open conflict. The supporters of the Peace were at first influential enough to move Athens and Sparta to approve an alliance (in 421) as a means of shoring up the original treaty, but this was far from sufficient. The alliance was the high water mark of peace sentiment, and the narrative of events in Thucydides' account of this period presents us with the spectacle of the unchecked growth in influence and activity of the war parties. No concrete good ever came of the Athenian-Spartan alliance, and, indeed, within a year and a half of its approval it is (as far as Thucydides is concerned) entirely ignored in favor of alli-

ances which were virtual copies of the original sides to the
Peloponnesian War, and which reflected the ideological interpretation of the war by then current (5.44 and 5.48). Within
two years of the alliance (5.53) the two sides are in all but direct
conflict, and, as Thucydides says (5.25.3; 5.26.2), they went
on skirmishing through intermediaries and at the peripheries
of the Greek world straight through the Peace. We will
consider the nature of the Peace, and its relation to Thucydides' belief that it constituted not a break in hostilities, but a
stage in a single, continuous Peloponnesian War in more
detail in chapter 4 (pp. 154–60). At this point we need only
take account of Thucydides' conviction that the peace gave no
respite from what we might call the war psychology, and therefore its events would have their own influence on strategic and
political thinking in the war. The next event for which Thucydides records political speeches in fact occurs in the sixth year
of the Peace.

The Melian Dialogue (5.85–111), 416 B.C.

In 416 the Athenians attacked Melos, an island off the east
coast of the Peloponnese, settled by colonists from Sparta.
Melos had managed to preserve its independence and was a
member of neither bloc. The motive of the Athenians for this
attack, according to Thucydides (5.84.2), was the desire to
make this independent island subject to the empire, as all the
other islands were. This attack was, in fact, the second campaign against Melos. In 426, during the Archidamian War, the
island had been attacked for exactly the same reasons (3.91.2).
But when the Melians resisted the Athenians, that campaign
was abandoned. This time there was to be no abandonment.
   When the Athenian forces arrived at Melos, the Athenians
attempted first to arrange the surrender of the island without a
battle. The attempt and the arguments used on both sides are
recorded in this dialogue. When the Melians refused to surrender, the Athenians besieged the town. Melian resistance was
again stronger than the Athenians expected, and when, after
some difficulty, the Athenians finally took the town, they slew
all Melian men of military age, and enslaved the women and
children. This part of the Melian episode is so well known and

so striking that the dialogue itself receives very strange treatment.

Almost all writers on the dialogue refuse to treat it as an event. For most of them, the dialogue is seen epideictically: rather than being an action, it is an exhibition or a demonstration of some sort, a kind of living treatise. For Finley,[1] it is a demonstration and indictment of Athenian depravity. This interpretation, although now either heavily qualified or rejected, had at least the virtue of implying that the dialogue exhibited some kind of historical progression—of Athenian moral decay. Most other commentators[2] insist that the Athenians here are the same as Athenians have always been. To these writers, the dialogue is a general statement—this time without euphemism—of the principles of Athenian imperial policy. For most of these writers, too, these principles have remained essentially unchanged throughout the course of the war. Méautis and Wassermann (followed in part by Liebeschuetz[3]) attempt to make the dialogue some part of a history—rather than a moral or political treatise—by linking it to the Sicilian campaign soon to come. But even here their history is epideictic: the Melian dialogue demonstrates the *irony* of the Sicilian expedition.

The Melian dialogue seems to lend itself to the epideictic interpretation because it is difficult to see any other explanation for its inclusion. The actual capture of Melos is of no strategic value, and so the event has no evident material significance. The Athenians do not ever employ the harsh measures they inflict on the Melians again, and so the event is not descriptive of any Athenian punitive policy. With the importance of the campaign unclear, so, too, is the purpose of reporting speeches from it. But as attractive as an epideictic or exemplary interpretation of this dialogue might be, before we concede and accept it, we must examine the dialogue to see whether it may serve some properly historical function.[4] That is, before we decide that the dialogue is a merely stylistically different restatement of principles we already know, or a symbolic foreshadowing of a cataclysmic disaster, we should ask whether it informs us of some new event which is an integral part of the history of this war, and which we would not know without this dialogue. This, I believe, is emphatically the case. What the Athenian speakers in this dialogue say is indeed very much like what other Athenian spokesmen (such as Pericles, Diodotus, and the envoys at Sparta) have said before, but it is not exactly the same.[5] In what they say that is the same we can see the ties these Athenians would naturally have to their past, but in what these Athenian speakers say that is different we can see the innovation and change that justify Thucydides' inclusion of this dialogue as a source of information necessary for our understanding of the events to come. In fact, it is only because some of what is said is identical to past Athenian policies that we are able to perceive any deviation from them. But we must not be seduced by a partial identity of policy into believing this statement at Melos is identical in all respects.

We should recognize one further point before proceeding to the arguments. This debate is not about Athenian cruelty. The terrible judgment which was ultimately meted out to the Melians had already been employed by the Athenians earlier in this period of peace, against the Scioneans in 420, in the first year of peace (5.32.1). Then also, with as little necessity, and despite the fact that the city had been delivered to them by the democratic faction of Scione, the Athenians slew all men of military age and sold the women and children into slavery. But Thucydides passes over that event without comment.[6] It is unlikely that with an earlier occasion available he would choose this later one if his purpose were merely to demonstrate how brutal Athens had become. Moreover, as cruel as the Athenians do appear in their principles, in terms of the concrete negotiation of this debate they began more moderately than we usually consider. The conditions they offered Melos (5.111.4) were quite reasonable: alliance and the payment of tribute. Only one other island, Chios, at this time had better of Athens. And though it is the ultimate destruction of Melos that monopolizes our attention, it is necessary to remember that this eventuality was not a concern of this debate. The Athenians offered the Melians the choice between easy conditions now and heavier ones if they had to be defeated in battle. But the Athenians did not insist at any time in the debate that the choice was between submission and annihilation. The harshness of the eventual penalty Melos paid was not foreseen by the Athenians, but was a result of the anger generated in Athens by the length of the Melian resistance. That the Melians were executed was a dreadful event of the war and of the narrative, but not a dreadful issue in this debate.[7]

Our general strategy with the debates of this history has been to regard them in relation to the future events they influence. We have searched the debates for evidence of the past to provide a sense of continuity and of the issues that arose as past patterns of thought and action came to be modified; but we have been primarily interested in discovering what new patterns the debates revealed and what consequences these new patterns would have. So, too, with this dialogue. We should not only read it in relation to the Sicilian expedition (its nearest neighbor), but also in relation to as much of the history to come as it may fruitfully illuminate. This dialogue is a prelude to the resumption of open war, and, with the Athenian speeches at the beginning of book 6, plays a role analogous to that of the speeches of book 1. Several formal tokens of this introductory role can be pointed out. First, its position, in a finished state, at the very end of the otherwise unfinished book 5. Second, its proximity to the Athenian debate about the Sicilian expedition, which forms an introduction to the next great action and next stage of the war. Third, the chapter which Thucydides includes between the end of the Melian episode and the Sicilian expedition debate, and which bears a striking resemblance to 1.146, the last chapter of book 1:

> The Athenians from Pylos took much booty from the Spartans. The Spartans did not on this account (which would have been tantamount to giving up the peace) make war on them, but decreed that whoever among them wanted to could take booty from the Athenians. And the Corinthians made war on the Athenians because of some private differences. But the rest of the Peloponnesians remained quiet. [5.115.2–3][8]

What we can see in the arguments of this dialogue are the attitudes of the Athenians toward their empire and other states as they turned their minds again to action (whereas the debate between Alcibiades and Nicias in book 6 will show their attitudes toward themselves and their future at virtually this same moment). Among these attitudes there is one which is significantly new. The Athenians at this negotiation deny the possibility of neutrality. We tend to take it for granted that this would be the natural state of affairs during a large war, but for the Athenians to deny that there is any longer any space for free movement between the blocs is in fact a new development. It is the novelty of this denial that makes the Melians incredulous, and makes them appear rather naïve or stupid to us. Once before, after all, in 426, the island had been a military objective for the Athenians, but the campaign was abandoned as not worth the time or trouble. Yet now, during a period of at least nominal peace, the Athenians were willing to carry it through to the end, for even less apparent reason. This change of mind was unexpected and inexplicable to the Melians, though the Athenian arguments demonstrate to us the changing attitudes that come to bring it about.

The discussion of neutrality runs from 5.89 to 5.99, through enough questions and specifications for us to be able to see very clearly how Athens regarded the rest of the Greek world at this time. It begins in a startling way with the Athenians warning the Melians to look only to the present situation, and as they (the Athenians) will not bring up their past, neither should the Melians: neither that they have always been neutral, not *that they have done Athens no injury* (5.89). The Melians take this paradoxical statement (that though they have done nothing to the Athenians, yet the Athenians will make war on them) to mean that Athens merely wants to subjugate new states, and, from greed, to make the empire larger still (5.90). But although the Athenians admit they are there to enlarge the empire (5.91.2, repeated at 5.97), the questions that follow make it clear that their motive is not merely greed.

At 5.94 the Melians ask directly if they can choose neutrality, and the Athenians answer:

No, for your hatred does not injure us that much: it is friendship on the part of subjects that is a clear sign of weakness; enmity is a sign of our strength. [5.95]

The Melians then ask, in turn (5.96), whether the Athenian allies will think that the case of independent Melos is the same as their own (that is, to be held only by force), and (5.98) whether Athens is not afraid of making all other neutral states their enemies by this example. The Athenian reply is extremely revelatory. They deny the Melian belief that the allies will distinguish Melos' condition from their own because, they say, there is in fact no distinction (5.97). Both are islands, and Athens has *no choice* but to subjugate all the islands. Further (5.99), they admit that the only enemies they worry about are islanders. Continental states will be a long time even preparing against Athens, but independent islands present an immediate—though indirect—threat to Athens by encouraging, by their example, Athenian allies to revolt.

From the beginning of the war, the unquestioned and even arrogant assumption of their right to the empire has been an Athenian characteristic; the principle that the strong will rule the weak was enunciated at the Spartan congress, and other Athenian arguments from that congress (that they act legally, though they need not, and that the most moral great power is the one which moderates its strength) also make their appearance in this debate at 5.111. What is new in this Athenian argument is an urgent anxiety about the solidity of their hold on their allies. For the first time, and, we should emphasize, in a moment (though waning) of peace, the Athenians represent the empire as the serious weak link in their defenses.[9] Before this moment there was no question that Athens could control the imperial cities, and only once was there any thought that the cities constituted a significant threat (which threat was presumably removed by the new ideological orientation of policy). But now, suddenly, it is the Peloponnesians that are only minor threats (since their approach will come with plenty of warning) in comparison to the imperial states which are now believed to have the potential of abruptly and seriously crippling Athens. For the first time Athens believes its control uneasy enough and its safety insecure enough that the mere existence of an independent state which it *could* control requires that it *be* controlled, or it will threaten the empire on which Athens depends.[10]

In other respects the Athenians feel secure enough. Having

ruled out neutrality as a choice, they force the Melians to bring up the possibility of involving Sparta in this action (5.103-4). The Athenians laugh at this suggestion. They cynically and correctly predict that Sparta will choose to ignore the whole affair (5.105-09). Moreover, they are not afraid even if the Spartans come in (5.111.1). They appear certain that there will, eventually, be a new war, but not now. Even if now, it will be against an accommodating enemy: no invasion of Attica has ever yet forced Athens to discontinue a campaign.

But Athenian reasoning at this debate does mark a new departure. The experience of the ten years' war, and presumably, of Brasidas' campaign in Thrace especially, has given the Athenians a new and compelling source of fear, the empire itself.[11] To deal with this fear, imperial principles have undergone a change which involves the denial of any middle, neutral ground between the two great blocs. This modification itself had extensive consequences, both for thought and action, in creating the conviction of a truly total war, and in compelling states to act according to that conviction. The phase of the Peloponnesian War which commences with book 6 is informed by this conviction, and the debate on the Sicilian expedition (which we will consider next) and the Melian dialogue (in which this conviction made its first public and articulated appearance) provide the fitting introduction to the beliefs and expectations of the Athenians as the initiators of this next stage of the war.

The Debate on the Sicilian Expedition (6.9-23), 415 B.C

In the summer after the Melian dialogue and the capture of the island of Melos, the Athenians began what was to be the most important single event of the Peloponnesian War, the Sicilian expedition. This immense campaign extended over two full years. It was the largest and most daring military enterprise of the war; it constituted the grounds for the breaking of the Peace of Nicias and the formal resumption of the war between Athens and the Peloponnesians; and in its disastrous result, dealt the Athenians their heaviest material blow and single most stunning defeat.

The Sicilian expedition is given, commensurate with its

importance, almost two complete books of the history. Book 7 contains no political speeches, merely the narration of the battles which took place around the city of Syracuse. Book 6 contains three separate debates and a single speech. The meaning of this unbalanced distribution of speech and narrative will be looked into later, but we can say, initially, that it is clear Thucydides felt the early stages of the expedition were those which required the most explanation, at least in terms of the political processes involved.

At various moments in the Archidamian War the Athenians had toyed with the idea of a full-fledged campaign to conquer Sicily. Later, in the winter of 416/15, ambassadors arrived from the Sicilian city of Segesta, asking for aid against their neighbors, and their neighbors' ally, Syracuse. The Segestan ambassadors appealed to the Athenians on the basis of their earlier alliances in Sicily, on the basis of the (supposed) threat that a strong Syracuse would pose for Athens and its allies, and on the basis of a (fictitious) large sum of money the Segestans had available for the campaign. Athens sent representatives to determine the truth of the Segestan offer of money, and when these representatives confirmed (wrongly) the existence of the money, the Athenians decided to aid Segesta. The aid to Segesta was a pretext for the conquest of the entire island (6.6.1 and 6.8.4). At the assembly called to determine how to expedite the campaign, Nicias spoke to attempt to prevent this Athenian commitment.

The debate comprises three speeches: two full statements of positions and one reply. These three speeches, together with the Melian dialogue, complete our picture of how and why Athens again became involved in a great war. Nicias' two speeches (one openly against the campaign, the other indirectly against it by the requisitions he made for the expedition) show us the dynamics of the situation quite clearly. Faced with the possibility of this immense action, the Athenians in fact cannot resist undertaking it. Moreover, the more difficult it is made to appear, the more glorious it seems to them and the more still they are in love with the idea. In this simple respect Nicias' speeches show us the limits of the situation: for no reason whatever could the Athenians think of putting it off

(Thucydides tells us, 6.15, that the vote was overwhelmingly in favor of the expedition), nor were there any limits to how difficult it might be that would have kept them from it. For what reasons they undertook the campaign is, however, a more complicated question.

Personalities are more important in this debate than in any other in the history.[12] This is the only pair of speeches reported in the history in which clearly recognizable personal attacks are employed as arguments (Nicias' attack on Alcibiades at 6.12.2, Alcibiades' answer to it in 6.16 and his patronizing reference to Nicias' luck at 6.17.1). Further, we know more about the personalities of these speakers than of any others that oppose each other in debate. The reason we need to know so much about them is that this debate is the least straightforward in its arguments. Both speakers are in a sense lying. According to Thucydides, each had, for reasons quite external to the ones he adduced in the debate, made his decision about his position on this issue. Nicias opposed the expedition because he was naturally cautious, and routinely opposed risky ventures; Alcibiades supported it because he hated Nicias and because he saw it as an opportunity to acquire the glory and money he coveted (6.15.2–3). The reasons for and against the expedition that they gave in their speeches are rather different from these. Because we are told as much as we are about these men, we can decide that they did not always believe the arguments they presented, but merely manipulated them as counters they felt would move the Athenian audience.

There is a sense in which it is important for us to know they were lying, and a sense in which it is irrelevant. It is irrelevant, of course, in the sense that in this inquiry we need only concern ourselves with the arguments that were or were not persuasive to an audience. Whether or not the speaker believed his arguments can be ignored, as long as we can judge what the audience believed.[13] And yet there is a sense in which our feelings of the dishonesty of these arguments sharpen our perception of what was in the minds of the assembly in Athens. All three speeches in this debate are terribly exaggerated, and give us a distorted picture of the generally intelligent minds of Nicias and Alcibiades. In all three cases, however, the exaggeration and distortion go unnoticed by the Athenians. This can be very revealing to us. Nicias desperately exaggerates the Spartan threat, which we would expect to have been a matter that would evoke a serious response at Athens, but even his hyperbolic representation of this traditional danger awakened no reaction or anxiety in the Athenians.[14] Alcibiades gives what to us should appear a grotesquely distorted picture of the Athenian character; but, on the other hand, this picture was accepted without protest. Serious and real distortions have occurred in Athenian attitudes, distortions that condition the way Athens sets about this expedition, and which we must know as Athens prepares again for war.

Both speeches are concerned with threats to Athens' security, both speakers express fear directly and indirectly, but they differ (and create the issue of the debate) in where they place the most serious threat. Apart from its exaggeration, the speech of Nicias is quite simple, and it is unexpected that it does not succeed. He feels that the expedition has been decided on with too little consideration of how difficult it will prove to be. The Sicilians are far off and powerful; even if the Athenians can defeat them (which is itself uncertain), they would have a most difficult time in retaining control of Sicily at such a distance (6.11.1–2). His fundamental argument against the expedition, however, concerns the Peloponnesians. The alliance and peace with the Peloponnesians, he says, is about to collapse; there are stresses on it from both sides, and some of the Spartan allies have never concluded a formal peace with Athens. The Peloponnnesians, he claims, are simply waiting for their opportunity to begin the war again. If the Athenian forces in Sicily are defeated, the Peloponnesians will attack Athens; even if Athens is not defeated in Sicily, but is heavily committed there, the Peloponnesians will give aid to Sicily, and fight their war against Athens at a distance and with little sacrifice. As it is, Athens' control of its empire is uneasy; the Thracian Chalcideans are still in revolt, and the obedience of other colonies is doubtful. Before Athens can undertake a new campaign, it must first secure the empire (6.10.5). He reiterates (at 6.11.6) ''nor must we believe that the Spartans are looking to anything else (because of their shame) than how, if they are able, they can rectify the accounts of their own disgrace by tripping us up," and ends, after attacking Alcibiades for supporting the expedition merely to increase his personal honor at public expense, by saying that the city is now "cast into surely the greatest danger up to this time" (6.13.1).

Alcibiades at first merely denies each of Nicias' arguments. He claims that his personal ambition in no wise conflicts with the safety or glory of the state (6.16—about which we will have more to say below). He denies that the Sicilians will be difficult to defeat; rather, they are, he says, an unstable mixture of nations of indifferent bravery, and are beset by internal factions which will make them even easier to control. Moreover, the Peloponnesians pose no threat, for at this moment they are more than ever in awe of Athens (6.17). That his denial of the difficulty of the enterprise would be welcome to Athenians—who were always rather too ready to believe that nothing was beyond their capabilities—is not surprising. But Alcibiades' minimization of the dangers of Sicily and Sparta does not mean that his speech is informed by an assertion of confidence. Rather, Alcibiades has found a new source for fear. In the long chapter 6.18 that concludes his speech, he presents an argument for the necessity of the expedition which is surprising, unprecedented, extreme, and, in its acceptance by the audience, revelatory of a whole new attitude of the Athenians toward their city.

Alcibiades claims that Athens must undertake the Sicilian expedition or be forced into slavery itself. Insofar as he has dismissed the Peloponnesians as a threat, one might reasonably wonder what force could effect this enslavement. Alcibiades finds the threat in the city of Athens itself. He alleges that the character of the city, of its citizens, and of its position in the world requires continual activity and growth. If the city stops expanding, it will collapse:

> Since if they [our predecessors] had all remained quiet or had judged according to race who should be assisted, then they would have made a small addition indeed to [the empire], and we would, rather, be running risks on behalf

of its very existence. For one does not defend himself only when the stronger attacks, but forestalls him so that he may not attack. Therefore it is not possible for us to take such an inventory about how much we wish to rule, but it is necessary, since we are in this state, for us to make plots against some, and not let others go, since there is the danger that we may be ruled by others if we will not rule them. And therefore inactivity is not to be considered in the same way by you (as by others), unless you are going to exchange your practices and habits for ones like theirs. [6.18.2-3]

And again:

[Consider that] a city, if it remains quiet, will wear itself away on itself just like anything else, and [that] all men's knowledge grows obsolete. But by constant struggle it will gain experience, and will get the habit of defending itself not in word but rather in deed. And I know absolutely that a city which is not inactive will soonest (it seems to me) be destroyed by a change into inactivity. . . . [6.18.6-7][15]

We are not wholly unprepared for this new Athenian interpretation of their world (for it is nothing more than the generalization and the turning inward of their expressed attitude towards their colonies that we saw in the Melian dialogue),[16] but it is startling to see it in such a radical form. This attitude is nothing like the notion of limited defense against particular threats that the Athenians claimed at the Spartan congress; it is far beyond Cleon's statement that Athens cannot afford the luxury of behaving moderately toward its allies; it is quite different from Pericles' assertion that it is unsafe for Athens to give up the empire.[17] For the first time a sort of desperation akin to paranoia begins to inform Athenian responses to other states. Under this formulation threats are no longer particular external occurrences, the threat is general and internal to the very nature of the city. In this debate, which is in response to a new expansionist venture, we see the Athenians in a dire light. (Not a dire moral light—such a judgment would be foreign to Thucydides—but a dire political light: a city whose political reasonings and reasonability have become unrealistic and replaced by fantasy.)[18] They have now come to resemble the picture of them that was drawn by the Corinthians at Sparta: uncontrollable in their activity and limitless in their designs. But it is not ambition that has made them so, it is fear, a much more compelling and intractable motivation.[19] Having internalized the necessity for expansion by believing it innate in the city's very essence, there can be for them no rest from compulsion. The independence of any state would be seen as a threat. There would be no condition of foreign relations that was secure, no moment, even of victory, after which they could stop. When they cease growing, they believe, they become slaves. Power gives them no rest, and the only end can be defeat. It is a frantic and hopeless position.

We must consider one more thing to complete our picture of Athens at the moment when (for all intents and purposes) the Peloponnesian War recommenced. The sorts of arguments that Nicias and Alcibiades used in the first two speeches reveal something about the way the Athenians thought of themselves at that moment. Nicias' speech is full of the distinction between the city and the private person. There is a "good citizen" (6.9.2 and 6.14), and "public danger" (6.12.2), a "national benefit" (6.13.1), a "care of the commonwealth" and a "physician of the country" (6.14). All of these are set in opposition to the ambitions, vices, and irresponsibility of the private citizen. But when Alcibiades comes to defend himself against these attacks (6.16), far from denying his ambitions, he claims they are for the general good of the city. In an especially cynical way, he denies that there is any distinction between the public interest and the interests of its private persons. He does not do so in the usual homiletic fashion of saying that a prosperous city makes for prosperous citizens. Rather, he does it quite the other way around, and claims that the personal excesses and ambitions of its citizens make the city ambitious and exceedingly grand. Moreover, it is to Thucydides' credit as a writer that we can have no doubt, as we read this argument, that this is truly Alcibiades speaking, and that this argument was vastly more attractive to the Athenians than Nicias' about public spiritedness.[20]

We can see that Alcibiades' public admission of his ambition must have seemed shockingly frank, and his cynicism about the springs of the city's greatness hard-nosed and realistic. Nicias' appeals to public spirit must have appeared platitudinous and naïve by contrast. But the consequences of this new conception of the city were far-reaching and disastrous. Having come to believe both in the appetitiveness and incorrigibility of human motivation and in the necessary analogy of the person and the state, the Athenians came, at least by the moment of this speech, to believe that they could expect no more of their politicians than an active personal ambition which might, in its striving for personal glory, produce incidental material benefits for the city as a whole. From this time the history of Athens at war becomes crowded with the names of political adventurers who hold brief tenure and are deposed. In book 8 we learn the names of probably more Athenian politicians than we know in the seven preceding books.[21] Certainly there must have been demagogues before, but as the city still felt there existed some common interest that shaped its policy, Thucydides could represent its actions behind the anonymous mask of "the Athenians." From this moment, however, with the reduction of public to private interest, the policy of the city (except in times of clear national emergency) is that of a particular politician, and for the first time Thucydides names them all.

With Athens in this condition, it is no surprise that Nicias' request for time to consider what supplies the expedition needed was met by a taunt to quit stalling. Nor is it surprising that when he requested an extraordinary amount of materiel the request was accepted without demur. Whatever greed made the conquest of Sicily seem desirable was reinforced by fear. The expedition was necessary for the existence of the city, the Athenians felt, and no limits could be imposed either on materials or goals. Dispatch, they felt, was of the essence. It was in this state of hectic activity that Athens again went to war.

The Debate at Syracuse (6.33–41), 415 B.C.

This debate and the one which follows at Camarina (6.76–87) share a common peculiarity. Both appear to end without decisions, and therefore both appear to result in no action.[22] At the end of the debate at Syracuse, the Syracusan generals simply decided to ready the army *in case* war should come. At the end of the Camarinean debate, the Camarineans decided to remain neutral. Both decisions owed nothing to the speeches in the debates, and both decisions appeared to have been taken rather despite than because of the speeches.

Yet we can see in these debates two critical moments of the Sicilian expedition—and of the Peloponnesian War, too, given the importance of this expedition within the general war. The outcome of the expedition was finally decided in one great trial of arms. At the beginning of the expedition, however, no such dramatic moment was expected or inevitable. Examining the arguments of Alcibiades' winning speech in the debate which authorized the expedition, we can see that the Athenians expected that whatever battles occurred would be one-sided in Athens' favor, and that this would be the result primarily of the existing political conditions both within Syracuse and throughout Sicily.[23] That political conditions did not aid the Athenians is not in itself proof that Alcibiades was wrong in his evaluation of the situation, and the Athenians in their expectations. Rather, certain events occurred which robbed the Athenians of these political opportunities, and made the expedition merely a trial of arms. The two Sicilian debates of book 6 present us with the *political* decisions which necessitated that the result of the Sicilian expedition would be decided wholly militarily. In this respect the two debates play a critical role in the organization of Thucydides' narrative of books 6 and 7.

The outline of the debate at Syracuse is strange in the apparent disjunction of the speeches and the decision. The Athenian expedition to Sicily was about to sail, but accurate information about it was unavailable in Sicily, and at Syracuse (on whom the greatest burden for the defense of Sicily would be placed) there was still doubt whether the Athenians would indeed come or not. That they will come, and what to do when they do, was argued correctly and with great strategic ingenuity by Hermocrates, recognized as an important politician through the whole of Sicily, but also, apparently, an oligarchic sympathizer in Syracuse.[24] That the Athenians will not come was argued by the leader of the democratic party in Syracuse, Athenagoras. His argument also included an attack on the political ambitions of Hermocrates. The debate was curtailed by the Syracusan military staff before a vote was taken; and the generals ended the assembly saying little more than that they would ready the army and try to get more detailed information of Athens' plans. This minimal military preparation surely had to be in the minds of the generals even before the debate, and their decision was in no way brought about by either speech. Moreover, in a matter of weeks, events themselves were to overtake this debate and make it meaningless. The Athenian expedition will be actually seen on its way to Sicily, Athenagoras' arguments will be utterly discredited (including his attack on Hermocrates, who acted in an exemplary fashion during the defense of Syracuse), and Hermocrates' alarms and strategies vindicated. That the military acted for reasons of their own external to the debate, and that the speculations of the debate were so quickly superseded by hard facts, makes it difficult to see the historical appropriateness of the inclusion of these speeches.

Hermocrates' speech is straightforward and very intelligent. Convinced that the Athenians are virtually on their way, he directs his argument toward the countermeasures to be taken. Syracuse is actually in a strong position, he says. With very little effort it can deal the Athenians a serious blow and win great honor. Even a partial success against the Athenians will seem significant, given the general opinion of Athens' chances (6.33). Further, Syracuse can count on a considerable amount of assistance which normally (because of the fear of itself that the smaller cities in Sicily have) would be denied it, but which will arrive now on account of the manifestly more serious Athenian threat (6.34.1-2). Syracuse could do even better, however, if its fleet would sail to engage the Athenian expedition before it crosses the Ionian Gulf and reaches Sicily. If the Syracusans do this, they will attack the Athenian fleet in its weakest position, lacking both maneuverability and provisions (6.34.4-5). The unexpectedness of this challenge, coupled with Nicias' reluctance about the campaign as a whole, will cause the Athenians to call off the entire expedition (6.34.6-

7). In its perception of the fundamental instability of Athenian morale, and its exploitation of the weakness of the Athenian leadership, this was a clever and striking plan. It offered the possibility of a decisive victory with no more risk than that of the defense of Sicily once the Athenian force had arrived there.[25]

Athenagoras opposes this plan first by simply denying that the Athenians can have any intention of attacking Sicily (6.36–37), and then by claiming that Hermocrates has invented the notion of an attack as part of a plot to acquire command of the armies, and by this to assume revolutionary control of Syracuse itself (6.38.1). From this point to the end of his speech, Athenagoras descends into a political attack on the oligarchs of a brutally factional nature. He accuses the oligarchs of regularly manufacturing crises to keep the city in disorder (6.38.3); he taunts them for wanting special privileges (6.38.5), and for being wealthy but stupid and malicious (6.39.1).

In reading Athenagoras' speech in the context of this debate, three aspects of its character must be noted. It is unintelligent, irrelevant, and bloodthirsty. Athenagoras' denial of even the possibility of Athens being interested in attacking Sicily is simply stupid, since the Athenians have been interested before, and therefore might be now. Further, it will be shown to be stupid in this specific instance almost immediately by events. But it is hardly sufficient to say that this debate is recorded to reveal Hermocrates' intelligence and Athenagoras' stupidity. Indeed, we never even hear of Athenagoras again in the history. What, then, may we say the debate reveals that would be important to our understanding of the events Thucydides was recording?

Paradoxically, it is the irrelevance and the bloodthirstiness of Athenagoras' speech that makes the event clear. Athenagoras' attack on Hermocrates and his arguments about oligarchs and democracy are, strictly speaking, irrelevant to the military and deliberative situation.[26] Further, its tone is shocking both in relation to the measured tone of Hermocrates' speech, and to the necessities of political order. (The generals who ended the debate were clearly concerned lest the rhetorical attacks arouse factional passions and hinder the common defense [6.41.2].) Yet in a different sense the speech is not irrelevant, nor its tone surprising, if we see it as occurring in a context of latent *stasis,* in which all political proposals seem to be and are taken to be partisan political opportunities.

That such a condition of near-*stasis* characterized the political situation in Syracuse at this moment is what Thucydides reconstructs and exhibits to us in Athenagoras' unexpected attack on Hermocrates in this debate. In this light we can see that Athenagoras' comparision of democracy and oligarchy in chapter 39 is not a philosophical statement, it is a bitterly partisan one. His trope, "democracy is named for the whole people, oligarchy for a part" (6.39.1), is a way of suggesting the isolation of Hermocrates; his references to unequal wealth and danger is a way of evoking ill-will towards the "oligarchs" so isolated. The purpose of the whole chapter is to suggest to Hermocrates that he (Athenagoras) can indeed carry out the threats he has made in chapter 38. In attitude and often in the language it uses, the speech corresponds to the picture of political fears and reactions that we have seen before in other cities in the middle of a full-blown *stasis.*[27] In these attitudes we can see that beneath the surface of Syracusan politics lay serious ideological fears, jealousies, and intrigues. Further, to make sure that we not overlook the phenomenon of *stasis* in Syracuse, Thucydides calls our attention to it in his own voice just before Athenagoras' speech: "So Hermocrates spoke, but the populace of Syracuse was in great strife [ἐν πολλῇ ἔριδι] amongst themselves" (6.35.1).

Political strife in Syracuse represented Athens' best hope for success in Sicily, and this debate, therefore, exhibits the real possibility of that success by displaying the existence of the necessary political passions. At the same time, however, it shows the disappointment of this Athenian hope. In a way, both speeches in this debate lose. Hermocrates' strategy, which might have prevented the Athenian fleet from even reaching Sicily, was tabled in the face of Athenagoras' opposition. But the generals' decision to begin defensive preparations was in itself a defeat for Athenagoras' attempt to discredit Hermocrates' position. In the political strife which robbed

Hermocrates of his effectiveness lay Athens' best hope; in the decision of the generals to stop that contention and to begin a common defense lay the end of that hope.

Alcibiades had claimed (6.17.2–5) that *stasis* in Sicily would make it an easily defeated opponent, for from this condition of *stasis* two potential results could reasonably be expected to benefit the Athenians. On the one hand it was possible that internal jealousies would so paralyze the operation of the state that Athens would be able to come against a city that was wholly unprepared for war. On the other hand there was the even more welcome possibility (with sufficient precedent) that the democratic faction in the city, faced with the external threat of Athens and the internal threat of its own oligarchs, would judge Athens the lesser of the evils, and deliver the city to it without a fight. Athens was prepared for a strictly military campaign against Sicily, but was also aware that, if internal Sicilian politics followed the usual patterns (and the fact, embodied in this debate, that factional hatred paralyzed the only far-sighted plan for a general defense of Sicily shows us how real the chances of *stasis* were),[28] the war might be even easier than expected.[29]

While this debate shows us the potential for an early Athenian success, the decision of the generals indicates that this hope was to be disappointed. Syracuse, acting on the advice of the generals, put together a common, though conservative, defense policy. The chance for an easy Athenian conquest of Sicily vanished at that moment. That this was not the only chance that Athens had to win in Sicily is, of course, true. But we must take note of the way in which Thucydides has constructed his account of the Sicilian expedition. Books 6 and 7 display a special relation to each other. In book 6 the initiative of the campaign rests in the hands of the Athenians. In book 7 the initiative has swung over to the Syracusans. Not only is this the case, but in the account of book 6 we can see another structure: of the initiative slipping more and more out of Athenian control, from the acceptance of Nicias' most timid general strategy for the campaign (and also the one least likely to succeed), to the recall of Alcibiades, to the Athenian failure to acquire any new allies, to the failure to exploit the first decisive victory over the Syracusans, to the dispatch of Gylippus to Syracuse, and, finally, to the inability of the Athenians to complete the encirclement of Syracuse. The letter Nicias sends to the Athenian assembly (7.11–15) is the summary of this whole process, and comes in the history at what Thucydides clearly felt to be the turning point of the campaign.[30] In book 7, the strategic dominance is in the possession of Syracuse, and following a desperate attempt (in the night attack on Epipolae) to regain the initiative, the Athenian position steadily deteriorated.

It is in the light of this progression that this debate acquires significance. While not the only, nor the last, Athenian hope for success, the exploitation of the possibility of *stasis* was an important part of Athenian chances. The decision, despite the appropriate soil for *stasis,* to remain united against the Athenian expedition was the first of the sequence of events by which Athenian possibilities were drastically narrowed.

The Debate at Camarina (6.76–87), 415/14 B.C.

This debate, to the assembly at Camarina, is the last debate in the history as we have it. No doubt Thucydides would have recorded further debates had he been able to complete his history, but this last debate is in fact sufficient to introduce the remainder of the account that he was able to complete. The political decision taken at this debate had grave consequences for the entire Athenian campaign in Sicily, and therefore cast its influence over the rest of the Peloponnesian War. Further, the political attitudes behind this decision, embodied in the speeches of the Syracusan and Athenian envoys to this debate, have an extension beyond the single instance of this deliberation, and provide us with the grounds for understanding the actions of the Athenians (and their enemies) at this stage of the war and onwards.

The Athenians came to this debate to ask the Camarineans for direct assistance in the war with Syracuse. They were encouraged to believe they would receive this aid because Camarina was already nominally allied to Athens,[31] and, more importantly, because Athens had emerged victorious from its first major battle at Syracuse. The Syracusans who came to Camarina were seriously concerned by the prospect of this alliance, both because Camarina was a neighbor to Syracuse (and so would make an uncomfortably convenient base for Athenian forces) and much more because they feared that a Camarinean defection to Athens here would become the first of a wave of defections among Sicilian states, a trend made likely by the recent Syracusan defeat.

If internal disorder (especially at Syracuse) was the best Athenian hope for an easy Sicilian victory, the isolation of Syracuse by alliances with other cities that were convinced of Athens' ultimate success was their second best hope. An alliance here would have had consequences for the future of the entire campaign, and Camarina was in fact essential to this strategy, since it was at Camarina that Athens had the best chance of succeeding (both because Camarina, as a neighboring city, should have had the strongest fear of Syracuse, and because the psychological effect of the recent Athenian victory would have been greatest at this moment).[32] The Athenian failure in this attempt to isolate Syracuse did not, again, mean that the Sicilian expedition as a whole was doomed to failure, but it did mean that the outcome of the expedition could now be decided only in battle.

Hermocrates' speech to persuade the Camarineans to support Syracuse rather than Athens is almost entirely straightforward. There is an unexpected (and self-contradictory) evocation of racial animus (6.76.2, 6.77.1, and 6.80.3),[33] but in the main his argument is very simple. He admits frankly that traditionally the other Sicilian states have seen their greatest threat in Syracuse. He does not deny that Syracuse has had designs on the hegemony of Sicily. But, he argues, those states which want the Athenians to humble Syracuse but not destroy it (so that, while Syracuse could no longer have offensive capacities, it might still form a strong defense for Sicily) are wishing for what is impossible. If Syracuse is defeated, then the rest of Sicily will fall in turn, for none of the other states is capable of resisting Athens (6.78). That Athens will subjugate the rest of Sicily if Syracuse is defeated can be inferred from the way the Athenians act in Greece. Further, it would be unjust for a Sicilian city to ally itself with a foreign nation to destroy another Sicilian city (6.79). Athens, he concludes, rather than Syracuse, is Sicily's greatest threat, and if the Athenians are successful, both the blame and the greatest danger will belong to Camarina: it could have stopped the Athenians, and it is (being the nearest neighbor to Syracuse) their second target if they are not stopped (6.80).

At this point let us sketch in the argument of the Athenian speaker, Euphemus', speech (which we will consider in greater detail below) in order to complete the picture of the action of this debate. Euphemus counters Hermocrates' argument by trying to prove that Athens is not a threat to Sicily generally (but only to Syracuse), and that therefore Syracuse remains the only real threat to the smaller Sicilian cities (making Athens, then, an ally to be welcomed). The Athenians, he says, got and hold their empire only because of fear (6.82); and fear will also explain their actions in Greece (6.83). Athens does not subjugate cities in order to exploit them, but only to increase its own security. The only city in Sicily that Athens fears is Syracuse; the rest of the cities pose it no threat. Consequently, this expedition has come against Syracuse alone, and, in fact, far from wanting to subjugate the rest of Sicily, Athens wants these cities as strong as possible, so they can keep Syracuse from regaining its power (6.84–86). Therefore, since Camarina has nothing to fear from Athens, it should remind itself of its traditional fear of Syracuse, and exploit the opportune presence of the Athenian forces to destroy the Syracusan threat once and for all (6.87).

At the end of this debate the Camarineans decided to remain neutral between these two powers. Thucydides tells us (6.88.1) that they were still afraid of Syracuse (and so did not want to help the Syracusans too much lest they win), but also thought that in fact Athens did intend to subjugate all of Sicily. While this appears to be no decision at all, it is actually an important action. First, Athens was unable to convince this most likely new ally to help it defeat Syracuse. With this failure, any potential rush of Sicilian defections to Athens was checked, and the Athenians' last hope of an easy and inexpensive victory in Sicily was lost. Second, when the Camarineans decided to remain neutral, the Athenians took no action to

compel them to the alliance. Far from there being a rush to
Athens, this example of Athenian unwillingness or inability to
compel allegiance encouraged other Sicilian states to remain
neutral or even to adopt attitudes of semihostility to Athens.
Instead of the Athenians beginning to isolate Syracuse, this
debate in fact began the process by which the Athenian force
itself became isolated in Sicily. The results of this debate and
of the debate at Syracuse were those two *political* actions which
conditioned the steady deterioration of the Athenian position
in Sicily, and which therefore conditioned the deterioration of
the Athenian military position as well.

Although it was probably not apparent to either speaker,
Hermocrates was the victor in this debate. He insisted that
Syracuse needed unequivocal Camarinean support, but in fact
the simple denial to the Athenians of this same support, and
the denial of the *example* of Camarinean support, was sufficient to turn the tide in the political aspect of the campaign
against the Athenians.[34] The argument which made this possible (and which must have been constantly present in Hermocrates' mind, for we find it also in his speech at Gela
[4.64.4] in the eighth year of the war) was that the arrival of a
foreign enemy (of course, given the context of this war, the
Athenians) must always constitute the most serious and immediate threat to any region in Greece, and must put an end to
any existing "domestic" hostilities. This, in fact, became the
pattern of the later years of the war, as more and more states
entered the war for the first time against Athens, especially
after the Athenian defeat at Syracuse. Book 8 of the history
sees the extension of the war to Asia Minor, and the alliance of
Persia with Ionian Greeks and with the Spartans. At the extremities of its influence, Athens came to find uniform and
determined opposition to its presence.

On the Athenian side, a new attitude developed in response
to this, and is strikingly embodied in Euphemus' speech. In
justification of Athens' imperial status, Euphemus gives an
account of the origin of the empire which is simply not true:

Now the greatest testimony [to the propriety of possessing
the empire] [Hermocrates] gave himself: that the Ionians
have at every moment been enemies to the Dorians. And

this is so. And we, being Ionians, looked to see in what way we could be least subject to the Peloponnesians, who are Dorians, and are numerous, and live near us. And after the war with the Medes, acquiring a navy, we were delivered from Spartan rule and leadership. . . . And we live having made ourselves the leaders of those who earlier were subject to the King, having thought that in this way we would be least subject to the Peloponnesians, by possessing the power with which to defend ourselves. [6.82.2–3]

When this account of the empire is compared to that given by the Athenian speakers at the Spartan congress, two points stand out. Although fear is said to be the source of the empire in both cases, the kinds and objects of fear are different. On the one hand, the fears of Sparta the Athenians originally claimed to have, which at the congress were described as political and whose commencement was located (in time) after the Persian War, are here alleged to be located long before that war and are described as fundamentally racial. On the other hand, the indefinite consequences of the fears suggested at the congress are here reduced to the simple and unequivocal fear of slavery. In the Athenian speech to the Spartan congress there was a sort of balance between statements of general principles ("fear, honor, profit") and statements of particular results or events or advice (the empire, the war or peace to come). In Euphemus' speech, however, the force of particular events or circumstances on men's actions or emotions has disappeared, to be replaced solely by abstract principles and abstract terrors.

In Euphemus' account of the empire, the already simplified account given at Sparta has been further reduced to a story of constant racial animosity. This is, of course, a lie, and was as much a lie at the moment Euphemus gave his speech as it was during the foundation of the empire and during the early years of the Peloponnesian War. Euphemus himself sees he must admit in his speech that the Athenians sometimes form alliances with Dorians and sometimes subjugate Ionians. Why, then, does he assert that the underlying force of the war is racial hatred, when history and even current events contradict him? The answer, I believe, lies in the sudden appropriateness of a racial explanation to the novel sort of fear the Athenians were experiencing as they regarded their situation in these moments long into the war.[35] Racial divisions are utter and immutable. Racial fears are general and irremediable. As a metaphor for a total and irreconcilable conflict, a racial explanation is perfect, and so the Athenians "invented" it—that is, exploited it for the first time in this war—to describe the opposition they encountered, and express the fear this implacability created in them.[36]

It is not hard to discover the origins of this undeniably (but, I believe, unconsciously) false account of the empire, nor the origins of the attitude which lay behind it. We must consider, on the one hand, the developing situation of universal opposition to Athenian influence; on the other, Alcibiades' characterization of the nature of the city (in the debate on the Sicilian expedition). Euphemus has accepted Alcibiades' characterization of Athens as a city which must continually expand or else will decay.[37] He invites the Camarineans to make use of Athens' "restless activity and character [πολυπραγμοσύνη καὶ τρόπος]" (6.87.3).[38] *Polypragmosynē* had originally been a term of reproach directed at Athens, but now the Athenians have adopted it as their own. And when this Alcibiadean interpretation of the city's nature was coupled to the developing military situation, the result was a belief in the city's position entirely new to this history:

> But to a tyrant or to a city which possesses an empire nothing is illogical that is profitable nor can anything be one's own that is not trustworthy. In each particular case, enemy or friend it must be as the occasion demands. [6.85.1]

> For we say we rule [cities] over there so that we be not subject to another; . . . and we are compelled to do many things because we are on our guard against many things. [6.87.2]

The attitude of the Athenians toward themselves and their future has undergone a radical change which brings them to a position virtually opposite to that with which they began the war (if we take Pericles' three speeches as exemplary of the earlier position). When the war began, the empire was seen as a luxury which enabled the Athenians to create a manner and style of life impossible anywhere else in the world. The maintenance of the empire required a level of civic activity which was unusually high, but which the Athenians willingly accepted for the freedoms it gave them: personal freedom realizable with the riches and opportunities the empire presented, that removed the constraint of subsistence farming and provided the economic foundation of the democracy; national freedom realized in Athenian overseas possessions, which removed the physical compulsion which would otherwise have been theirs had they been landlocked. At this point in the war, however, the position of the Athenians is utterly different. Far from being a source of freedom, the empire is Athens' constant and irremovable source of compulsion. The maintenance of the empire is no longer seen as a voluntary chore, it is, they believe, a necessity. Constant fear and compulsion have now indeed made compulsive activity a part of the Athenian character (a characteristic which, if previously alleged by its enemies, was denied by its own spokesmen, Pericles in the Funeral Oration and the Athenian envoys at Sparta).

The destruction of the Athenian army at Syracuse of course reinforced this mood and this attitude toward the range of action. With the news of the loss Athens' enemies multiplied, the possibility of total defeat became imminent, and Athenian fears naturally were strengthened. Their attitudes became more and more paranoiacal, and universal fear and distrust became extended even to parts of Athens itself (as we see in book 8) as suspicion traveled inward. As fear and feelings of compulsion became generalized, Athenian policies became at once more frantic and less deliberate. If Thucydides' history had been completed, we would surely have further debates in it, but not, I think, for a while. The dual characterization we have by now received—of Athens (from this debate) and its enemies (from the debate at Plataea) both committed to notions of total war—is quite sufficient to enable us to understand the origin of the policies which shaped the events of that most bitter and active final stage that Thucydides calls the Ionian War.

Alcibiades' Speech at Sparta (6.89–92), 415/14 B.C.

During the summer of 415, a series of bizarre events occurred which leads us to the dramatic occasion of the last political speech that Thucydides records in his history. Some time
between the decision to undertake the Sicilian expedition and
the actual sailing of the Athenian force, the religious statues
called herms in the city of Athens were defaced in an act of
sacrilege or vandalism. In the anxious climate of Athens on the
eve of the expedition, the act was variously interpreted as an ill
omen for the expedition or as the first act of a political con-
spiracy to overthrow the democracy. Under either interpretation, the incident came to be treated with a seriousness bor-
dering on hysteria, and many persons were suspected or
denounced, among them Alcibiades.

With the expedition about to sail, Alcibiades called for an
immediate trial to resolve the situation so that he would not
have to assume his command under a cloud of suspicion. Thucydides says (6.29.3) that Alcibiades' political enemies postponed the decision in order to bring charges against him in his
absence. Alcibiades sailed with the fleet. The next few months
of the summer saw Athens increasingly unsettled over this
matter. Denunciations became common (though Thucydides
says [6.60.2] that they made the facts of the matter no clearer),
and punishment followed denunciation. Finally, Alcibiades
was directly implicated in an act of profanation (although not
in the defacing of the herms). The religious crimes had, by this
point, become thoroughly associated with the notion of the
overthrow of the democracy.[39] The assembly, urged on by
Alcibiades' opponents, voted his recall from Sicily, not so
much, Thucydides says (6.61.4), to stand trial as to be put to
death. Alcibiades and a number of other persons who were also
accused sailed from Sicily in company with the Athenian state
galley as far as Thurii, but there—either because they then
learned that they were to be killed, or because they had never
intended to go farther—escaped. In time Alcibiades made his
way to the Peloponnese, and then to Sparta. He was condemned to death in absentia, and it was in this circumstance,
as a fugitive and defector, that he addressed the Spartan
assembly.

Although Alcibiades' speech is a striking one, I believe we can treat it quite briefly. It completes our understanding of the major participants on the eve of a new stage of the war (the resumption of hostilities in year eighteen, 414 B.C.) by informing us both of a concrete event which took place at Sparta and of a more abstract condition subsisting at Athens. Let us consider the latter first.

Alcibiades' defection to Sparta itself gives us new information about Athens, and his apologia to the Spartan assembly exhibits the attitudes on which it depends. While it would be tempting to claim that Alcibiades' unprecedented defection depended only on his own erratic character, we cannot really do so. While we find no other example in Thucydides of an actual defection (which would have to include geographical movement to another city), the preference of personal success to the success of the city—even to the point of aiding the city's enemies when that will advance one's own interests—becomes an alarmingly common pattern of behavior in Athens. We can also see evidence of this same personalization of politics and action among the Peloponnesians,[40] but inasmuch as this pattern had developed further among the Athenians, and insofar as its effects were manifestly of greater consequence for the Athenians, it is among Athenian speakers that Thucydides has selected a speech for its exhibition. The coincidence of Alcibiades' defense of his behavior with his influence on the resumption of the war made this speech the most attractive one for Thucydides' purposes. Although any human—and therefore any politician—is always in part motivated by simple personal interest, the extremity of personalization is a new event to Thucydides, and depended upon belief in a new set of attitudes explained by Alcibiades.

The apologia has two parts. At first, at 6.89, Alcibiades explains why he had been an enemy to Sparta, but the explanation implies attitudes toward Athens as well. He had been Sparta's best friend, he says, but because of their insulting treatment of him he resolved to injure them as badly as he could. There is nothing strange in this, he asserts, nor in his being willing to be a politician in a democracy, as long as there were prospects for personal glory in it. The implication, of course (which he certainly intended to have recognized by the Spartans), is that for the same reason of personal injury he can now as easily change from being the leader of the democratic faction of Athens to its most resentful enemy. Since the reasons for being a politician are purely personal, when one's honors are taken from one, one takes revenge on the city as on a personal rival.

The position is elaborated in an arresting passage in the second part of his apology:

> I feel no patriotism insofar as I am done injustice, but insofar as I could safely act as a citizen. Nor do I believe that I am attacking a city which is still my fatherland; rather that I am recovering that city which is not my fatherland. And the true patriot is not he who would not attack his own unjustly lost city, but he who, through desire for it, will try in every possible way to get it back. [6.92.4]

What we see here is the furthest extreme of the personalization of Athenian politics, whose first symptom we saw in Alcibiades' speech in the debate on the Sicilian expedition. Even if the new Athenian interpretation of their relations to other cities had not already been driving the Athenians into a state of policy-less reaction to external stimuli, their lack of a coherent common policy would still come as no surprise to us given this sort of thinking by their politicians. There is no such thing, for Alcibiades, as a national interest. The only interests whose existence he admits are those of the leaders at any given moment. To change leaders is to change policy and to create enemies to that policy. In this total reduction of the public to the private, considerations of public good and determinations of genuinely public policy disappear. We had first seen such a reduction in Alcibiades' speech at 6.16, but at that time we had nowhere as extreme a statement as here, nor did we know that such attitudes were widespread. By this moment of the war,[41] these attitudes have caught on, and have begun to take their effect. Thucydides directly attributes the political disorder which so crippled Athenian deliberations after the Sicilian expedition to these new attitudes (8.89.3). Phrynichus' direct echo of these Alcibiadean statements, at 8.50.5, indicates the currency of these attitudes among Athenian politicians. That Alcibiades expected these arguments to be acceptable to the Spartans—and that they were in fact accepted—suggests that the attitudes were now common among all Greek states.

In addition to the exhibition of this development in attitudes, Alcibiades' speech is also the occasion of a concrete military event, Sparta's reentry into the war. Not only is the speech instrumental in procuring this reentry, the arguments on which it depends also give us evidence of Sparta's considerations at this moment. That this speech is meant to show us how the Spartans recommenced the war (to complement our understanding of how Athens went to war which we received from the debate on the Sicilian expedition) may be seen by a stylistic peculiarity. The context in which this speech is given is described by Thucydides (6.88.7-10) in such a way that it appears almost a parody (appropriate to this late date in the war) of the first Spartan congress which began the Peloponnesian War eighteen years before. At 1.67.1, Thucydides described how the Corinthians, themselves and their allies suffering defeats they could no longer bear, and the Spartans procrastinating, marshaled all the aggrieved allies at Sparta to force the Spartans to take action. At 6.88.8-10, the scene is repeated. The Syracusans, believing their defeat was imminent, requested Corinthian aid, and again the Corinthians trooped off to Sparta, this time dragging in train the Syracusan ambassadors and Alcibiades. Again, the Spartans, though sympathetic, were slow to act. This time, however, it was not the Corinthians who drove the Spartans into the field, but Alcibiades. This is the parody. The final key to the symmetry which Thucydides sees and means to express between these two occasions is the identity of the language that he uses. At 1.67.5 he says: "But the Corinthians came forward also and counselled these things, having allowed the others first to whet the Spartans' anger [παροξῦναι]." And at 6.88.10 the same words are there: "but as [the Spartans] were not anxious to send aid, Alcibiades came forward and, saying these things, urged them on, and whetted their anger [παρώξυνε]."[42]

There is room for serious doubt whether there is any truth in the arguments Alcibiades gave the Spartans. I believe they were not true, but in the long run this is irrelevant, since the Spartans acted on them true or not, and since it is this fact that they *did* act on them that is historically revealing. As the Corinthians at the first Spartan congress constructed a picture of the Athenian character which was frightening to Sparta, so at this mock congress Alcibiades gave a picture of Athenian ambitions whose acceptance by the Spartans—seen in their undertaking all of the strategies he proposed—reveals the nature and extent of their fear of the Athenians.

In chapters 6.90 and 6.91, Alcibiades constructs an argument to frighten the Spartans into action and to propose positive lines of strategy. He was successful in both. He claims that Athens is on campaign in Sicily merely to prepare for the subjugation of all of Greece. First Sicily, then Carthage, then, with the accession of men, materiel, and money from the west, an unstoppable campaign against the Peloponnese. Although this bald statement of a plan for world conquest sounds almost comically exaggerated, its effectiveness suggests its consonance with prevailing Spartan fears of Athens.[43] Such a design would not seem far-fetched to a Sparta which believed, as we have seen in the discussion of the debate at Plataea, that Athens was more like Persia in its ambitions and the dangers it created than like any of the Greeks. Moreover, this plan might even appear likely, in the light of contemporary Athenian successes.

Sparta too, then, reentered the war in a state of fear akin to that in which Athens undertook the Sicilian expedition. In place of Athenian paranoia, Sparta went to war convinced that unless Athens was stopped at this point, its designs for world conquest were assured. It is important for us to notice that both sides recommenced hostilities in states of mind near terror, for after eighteen years of continuous war, it was only the mortal dread of defeat which gave them the will to continue. The tactics that Alcibiades suggested, and that the Spartans, after their habitual delay in execution, followed, were those which eventually won the war for them: immediate aid to Syracuse in the form of a Spartan commander (and it was with this commander's arrival in Sicily that Athenian military fortunes there began their serious decline); declaration of war on

Athens; fortification of Deceleia and the bleeding off of Athenian monetary resources from the silver mines nearby; and the encouragement of imperial defections. While it is true that Athens held out for nine more years, what brought it down were the deprivations caused by this strategy.

With this speech Thucydides completes his portrayal of the combatants as they entered this final phase of the Peloponnesian War, but with an important difference between this introduction to the Ionian War and the earlier introduction to the Archidamian. In Thucydides' account of the Archidamian War, the war proceeds both by battle and by speech. From this point in book 6, however, there are no further political speeches. It would be rash to say there would have been *no* other speeches in Thucydides' history until the final great change of the war, the change from war to peace, Athens' surrender. Yet it is not impossible that Thucydides meant to construct his narrative without speeches for a time. If he believed—as indeed was the case at this moment—that every opportunity for political action had been played out, there would be no need for speeches to explain action. The construction of his account of the Sicilian expedition (undoubtedly in its finished form) follows this pattern. With the end of book 6, all occasions for political movement have occurred. What remains is only the trial by arms, and book 7 appropriately contains no political speeches, only those of the generals to their troops before a battle. Book 8 is surely incomplete and unrevised, and yet its absence of speeches may have more to do with the character of the war than with its unfinished state. With both sides now believing in a notion of total, irreconcilable conflict whose stakes were survival itself, there is no room for political maneuver, and so, no need—and perhaps no propriety—for political speeches in the history. From this point in the war it is the battlefield that will decide the outcome.

Having completed our examination of the political speeches in Thucydides' history, we should recapitulate what we have so far accomplished, and what remains to be done. In these first three chapters we have discriminated seventeen occasions at which political decisions were taken that gave shape or direction to the military events which comprise the other great part of the history.[44] There remains another job to be done to reveal Thucydides' interpretation of the Peloponnesian War.

Our seventeen occasions represent, as it were, instantaneous appearances of policies or attitudes. Yet these instantaneous appearances were merely the momentary expressions of policies and attitudes in a constant process of development and change, which took place as the cities acted and reacted to events as they occurred. In the next chapter we must reconstruct the lines of process and of consequence and connection between these occasions. We will also examine the crucial military events of the history, either as they were executions of policies decided upon, or as their fortuitous occurrence enforced reconsideration and reformulation of policies. Throughout, the speeches will remain our focus as we try to discover that process of thought and action (and that complex notion of cause) that Thucydides felt was the story and the meaning of this war.

4 | Thucydides' Interpretation of the War

In the first three chapters of this book we isolated seventeen occasions at which political events occurred which influenced the policies (military and political) of the war. In each case we were able to characterize the immediate application or significance of these political events, and we were able to locate them in a context of prior events and policies and to suggest their more important consequences. The task of this fourth chapter is to consider these seventeen occasions, not in isolation, but as forming moments of a continuous process of thought and action, and, by taking these occasions together with the events recorded in the narrative passages of the history, to discover the account that the sum of occasions and events is meant to convey to us.

Throughout the first three chapters of this essay it was assumed that since the speeches gave emphasis to certain events, they provided a natural starting point for the discovery of what Thucydides considered the significant events of his history. But as we shall see in this fourth chapter, the speeches also provide a framework for discovering the structure of Thucydides' written account of the war and the interpretation of the war that Thucydides presents through his account. The speeches alone, of course, do not comprise the history as a whole. The story of this war, for Thucydides, lies somewhere between the political events and the military events, and is found in the relation of thought and action. In this relation the
speeches are the primary means of conveying to us the sub-

stance of the public thought and considerations of the participants. They enable us to observe the more "material" events of the history (movements of armies, diplomatic maneuvers) either as attempts to actualize the intentions of the participants or as circumstances which require or suggest new thoughts and purposes. Insofar as debates contain in their structure traces of the past, present, and future (as we have noted in chapter one), and insofar as the single speeches embody elaborations and evolutions of the policies presented by debates, the speeches of the history themselves embody internal lines of connection and continuity which we can utilize as a framework for reconstructing the continuous process of thought and action which is, indeed, the story of the war.

Further reflection would also indicate the primacy of the speeches in reconstructing Thucydides' interpretation of the events of the war. Considered before the fact, men's thoughts inform action. Men have intentions and desires, and act to try to achieve them. Action is seen as purposive and reasonable by knowing what it was intended to accomplish. Insofar as the actions of a war are public actions, so too the intentions must be publicly held and expressed, and these public expressions provide us with the evidence we need to understand the actions as intentional and deliberate. By far the simplest cases of this are the generals' speeches which precede the accounts of certain battles in this history. Opposing generals explain their tactical plans and the grounds of their expectations of success. *We* can then make sense of the description of the battle itself because we know its strategic design. In fact, the speeches give meaning even to the unforeseen accidents of battle (or make discovery of that meaning possible) because we can see in the accidents the unexpected achievement or disappointment of hopes and designs.[1] Although the generals' speeches are the simplest example of this relation of thought and action, the same relation exists between political speeches and the actions that follow them. The consequences of course appear in a wider variety of kinds of action and over a longer period of time, but the relation is still there. We understand, for example, the diverse actions of the Athenians in the first years of the war in terms of the policies outlined in Pericles' first speech;

we recognize the dangerous weaknesses of the Sicilian expedition by watching the frustration, step by step, of the intentions and predictions of Alcibiades' speech in the debate on the expedition.

Looked at after the fact, speeches attribute significance to events, as agents deal with changing circumstances and find in them new intentions and necessities. One of the more unexpected events of this war is also one of the most significant: the Athenian victory at Sphacteria. The significance of this event, however, does not exist in the event per se, but rather emerges from the particular responses to it. The size of the Spartan loss was relatively large, but did not materially cripple Sparta. The morale of the Spartans was, however, disproportionately disturbed by this defeat. (This psychological effect was probably the result of the unexpectedness of *any* large Spartan defeat.) Consideration of the merely material consequences of Sphacteria would leave us unaware of its significance. That significance is given it in the speeches and subsequent actions of the Spartans. On the Athenian side the same potential ambiguity exists. Their victory could be considered simply a fortunate accident, and therefore without any real significance. This, certainly, is what the Spartan envoys try to persuade the Athenians (4.17-21). But the rejection of the Spartan peace proposal shows that the Athenians gave the victory a different meaning. The Athenians took their victory over the Spartans in this case as a sign of their virtual inconquerability, and this interpretation of the event led them into other and riskier military engagements.

There is another reason for considering the speeches as crucial to the meaning of the war. In his introduction (1.22.4) Thucydides implies that in some sense the history can teach us something. Even if he means this only in the sense of giving us the picture of experience outside our own lives, the speeches play a critical part. Except in a genuinely materialistic history (and few now believe that Thucydides' is such a history), the lines of cause and effect do not run directly from event to event. Rather, they run from events, through men and their deliberations, to subsequent events. The removal of the human link in this chain ($\tau\grave{o}$ $\grave{\alpha}\nu\theta\rho\acute{\omega}\pi\iota\nu\nu\nu$) deprives the events

($\tau\grave{\alpha}$ $\gamma\epsilon\nu\acute{o}\mu\epsilon\nu\alpha$, $\tau\grave{\alpha}$ $\mu\acute{\epsilon}\lambda\lambda o\nu\tau\alpha$), of their initiation and their meaning, renders their causes ambiguous and a clear perception of them ($\tau\grave{o}$ $\sigma\alpha\phi\grave{\epsilon}s$ $\sigma\kappa o\pi\epsilon\hat{\iota}\nu$) impossible. Without the speeches the events would become mere matter, mere accident. But experience, even additional experience, of accident per se teaches us nothing. Accident is incomprehensible. But what there is in the history that can be reflected upon and internalized (that is, learned) are the examples of men trying to deal with matter and accidents and trying to impose their designs on this recalcitrant material. Information concerning this can only be found in the speeches, with their presentations of men's thoughts and designs, and in our comparison of the designs with their attempted executions and their success or failure.

Much information about the relation of thought to action has already been gathered in the examination of individual events that we have made in the first three chapters. Further information, of a more general nature, can be gathered by examining, from speech to speech, the changes of thought on subjects that remain reasonably constant. The process of re-interpretation of fundamental policy, the process of changing emotional attitudes toward events and peoples, and even the process of deliberation itself are parts of the wider relation of thought to action during this war. We can discover these processes by exploiting information we have developed in the first three chapters. In order to do this properly, however, and to construct a continuous account of the war, we must first recognize a very peculiar datum of the arrangement and composition of Thucydides' history. Let us consider, for the moment, simply the debates recorded in this history. These comprise eight occasions at which, as we have assumed, political decisions were taken of the greatest significance to the conduct and direction of the war as a whole. Eight critical political occasions during a war is not an unlikely number, especially when these are supplemented by other occasions at which decisions were taken to modify or elaborate them. Yet we are rarely conscious of a strange fact. Insofar as Thucydides' history covers no less than twenty-two years of action (twenty-one years of war and one year of prewar preparation), we might reasonably expect that the eight crucial decisions of this war would be, if not absolutely regularly, at least widely spread throughout this extended canvas of events. But, contrary to these expectations, all eight political events which Thucydides selected as most significant in their influence on the actions of the parties to the war (and therefore most worthy of extended treatment) in fact occur in only *three calendar years*. This is an unexpected and provocative datum.

Equally strange as the datum itself is how little it obtrudes on our consciousness. We hardly notice that between the debates of the first book and those of the third five years pass, and that between those of the third and those of the sixth (and let us include the Melian dialogue) more than ten. Do we usually notice at all that each of these clusters of debates is compactly contained within the account of a single year? Although the three sets of debates were widely separated in time, they are much more closely arranged in the text of Thucydides' history. We are unaware of their chronological separation because their influence is continually felt in the text as we read it. Throughout, chronological time has been telescoped, and in our reading the passage of time seems to be marked by the passage of speeches more than by the passage of seasons, though Thucydides notes these, too.

As we recognize the peculiarity of the arrangement of the speeches, so do we recognize the radical liberties Thucydides has taken with the material and chronological aspects of the war.[2] The progress of the war is marked for us more by the changing concerns of the participants than by Thucydides' calendar. That this is the result of Thucydides' deliberate arrangement is, I think, unquestionable. And that this deliberate arrangement embodies and emphasizes a definite judgment by Thucydides as to what were the actual processes of the war, seems to me equally indubitable.

When these three considerations are put together (first, the irregularity of the presentation of debates; second, that when debates do occur, all are clustered within the space of a single year; third, that this involves a judgment by Thucydides on the processes of action in the war), it seems to me that an inescapable conclusion follows. The three occasions marked by these clusters are thereby given special emphasis by Thucydides. And when, exploiting our analyses of chapters 1–3, we examine the content of the debates in these clusters, the judgment that Thucydides is making about the progress of the war appears to be that on these three occasions radical turning points were passed in the direction and attributed significance of the war. In chapter 1 of this essay it was suggested that the decisions of debates should be seen as authoritative over the policies of the states concerned, until superseded by another debate. Now, examining the debates not individually, but in their clusters, and further, examining where these clusters are placed in relation to the narrative as a whole, I believe we can make a different sort of statement about the role and influence of the debates.

A single debate represents only a single state's policies. The clusters, however, contain expressions of policy from both sides. I believe that the clusters of speeches are Thucydides' way of marking, embodying, and explaining to us wholesale changes in the orientation of all parties to the war. Where clusters exist, we are informed of more than changes in the strategy with which an individual state prosecuted the war. These clusters (as distinct from individual debates) mark the moments at which the entire situation of the war changed and was redefined. Because these clusters involve all the combatants, it is as if the war itself changed on these occasions. States change their relations with other states, their alliances, and their images of themselves. New meanings are attributed to the occurrences of the war and to the characters and destinies of the participants. New hopes, fears, and expectations are created. New needs are recognized and new goals decided upon. On each of these occasions the war as a whole is seen in a new light, and its meaning is redefined. At each of these three moments the shape of the past, present, and future is changed, and with it the reasons for fighting, the stakes involved, and the conditions for concluding the war.

One of the consequences of such changes is, of course, alteration of strategic design, of which we have already spoken in the three preceding chapters. But there are other, more extended, consequences. At these three turning points the general attitudes of all the participants undergo sweeping and serious transformations. The whole atmosphere of the war seems to change; the war itself seems to be renewed in a new guise. What is common to all of these changes is that they are characterized by a deepening of the hostility felt, and by explanations of this hostility in terms of principles which become progressively more abstract and more irreconcilable. The new shapes of the war tend also to involve more and more of the peoples originally outside the war and to involve them in more intense, brutal, and cruel ways.

The occasions marked by the clusters of debates give structure and significance to the war as a whole in two senses. Particular changes of policy and action (by individual states) originate in, take their meaning, and become comprehensible to us in their relations to these general changes of interpretation. Further, the periodic reinterpretations of the war which occur on these occasions, and which involve increasing abstraction and growing implacability and hostility, are themselves events in an underlying political process that constitutes the essential structure of this war and that, according to Thucydides, informs the actions of men generally.

Of the three occasions at which the war reached a turning point, the first is embodied in the three debates that occur in book 1: one concerning Corcyra at Athens, and two at the first Spartan congress. This turning point is the moment of the first great movement of this history, the change from peace to war. Naturally, the shape of events, and the relations between states change thereby. As we consider this first movement, we must examine the meaning the participants gave to the war as they began it in order to characterize the nature of the actions during this first stage of the war. We must also explain why, for Thucydides, the Corcyrean episode properly begins the history of the war.

The second turning point occurs in the fifth year, and is embodied in the debates of book 3: at Athens (about Mytilene) and at Plataea. At this moment, too, the shape of the war changed, for the actions and motives of the combatants were given new meanings. The change was characterized generally by an ideologizing of the reasons for war and of the relations that subsist between states. From an initial perception of the war as a material conflict between national entities, the nations on both sides turned toward an interpretation of the war as merely a material manifestation of underlying conflicts of political systems and ways of life. Again, the overall shape of action changes as new motivations suggest new avenues of expression. Once the major powers conceived of their hostility ideologically, their support could be obtained by interested parties by persuasion along ideological lines. This turning point stands at the beginning of a period of epidemic political *stasis* in the smaller cities of the Greek world (because of the outside support available to such actions) and of the encouragement of this internecine political warfare by Athens and Sparta. Further, as the interpretation of the war changed, so did perceptions of who were one's enemies and friends, and this shift found expression in new kinds of political and military activities. Dependent upon this new interpretation, new principles of association were invoked, and new bonds of association created whose effect was to make alliances more homogeneous. In peacetime, this would perhaps have reduced the chances of unintended or unwanted war, but in the context of the ongoing war, the evil consequences of this change far outweighed any good. The scope of the war was extended at the same time that its grounds were made to appear more serious and more intractable. The nature of this second stage of the war not only renders the actions of the period significant by exhibiting the appropriateness of such actions to the new attitudes and interpretations, it also provides an explanation of Thucydides' conviction that the entire twenty-seven years of conflict constituted but a single war.

The third turning point of the war, which occurred during its sixteenth and seventeenth years, is embodied in the debates of book 6 and the Melian dialogue of book 5. Once again, the general attitudes of the participants changed, as they began to resume open hostilities. On this occasion the consequences of the ideologizing of the war took a final turn, and the combatants came to consider the war as one upon which their very survival depended. In addition to the ideological interpretation of the origin of the war, both sides came to believe that the grounds of the conflict were finally irreconcilable, and that therefore their actual existence was at stake. The mere presence of the other side was seen as a threat, and from this point the conflict was believed to admit of no solution other than the total defeat of the enemy. This, too, led to its appropriate forms of action, as existing fears and hatreds were intensified and magnified at the same time that the range of hostilities was further extended. The nature of this change also explains the prolongation and vehemence of the last stage of the war.

Finally, there are three general observations to be made about these turning points. First, we can notice that, although in the second turning point both sides are equally represented by debates, the first turning point is concerned rather more with the Peloponnesians, and the third with the Athenians. This, too, must embody a specific judgment by Thucydides as to the nature of these events, and in the course of our examination we will attempt to understand its significance. Second, although I have everywhere written as though the occasions of these debates were also the actual moments of change, clearly this could not have been so. Rather, in a continuous process, the ground must have been prepared for each of these changes in the months or years which preceded the speeches. Nonetheless, the occasions of the debates are the significant moments to emphasize, for the actions and consequences we are considering are *public* actions, and it was on these occasions that the new interpretations were publicly articulated and thereby made available for use either as sources for policy invention or as justifications and explanations of actions. Third, on the basis of these turning points we can now correctly name the true phases of the Peloponnesian War. In the first three chapters I often spoke of three parts of the war by a nomenclature now conventional, and occasionally even employed by Thucydides: years one to ten, the Archidamian War, followed by the Peace of Nicias (book 5); the Sicilian expedition; and years seventeen to the end, the Ionian War. These names, clearly, are arbitrary to Thucydides, since he felt the full twenty-seven years were a single war. For him, the Peace of Nicias was an event of no greater significance than many others, nor was it in any sense a true end of the fighting. Rather, I believe that the war can be differently divided into three phases (which division I shall use henceforward in this essay) suggested by this chapter, and corresponding to actual differences in the nature of the war: the beginning of the war, conceived along traditional lines (years one to five); the advent of ideology (years five to seventeen); and the final life-and-death struggle (years seventeen to twenty-seven).

The First Phase of the War

If we are to understand the structure of Thucydides' history, the initial question we must ask about Thucydides' account of the first phase of the war is: Why does he begin it where he does, with the Corcyrean episode? The question is not a simple one, of course, primarily because of Thucydides' own ambiguous distinction (at 1.23.5–6) between the true and the apparent causes of the war (respectively, $\pi\rho\acute{o}\phi\alpha\sigma\iota\varsigma$ and $\alpha\emph{i}\tau\acute{\iota}\alpha\iota$). The incidents of Corcyra and Potidaea were only $\alpha\emph{i}\tau\acute{\iota}\alpha\iota$, he says; the truest cause of the war was Sparta's fear of Athens' growing greatness. It was this fear that Thucydides says "necessitated the war." But if this was the truest cause of the war (although what "truest cause" might mean requires explanation), why then does the account of the war begin with Corcyra? Why does the account not begin with the Pentecontaetia, the synopsis of the growth of the Athenian empire? This synopsis is, in fact, postponed until the conclusion of Thucydides' account of the first Spartan congress, even though the Pentecontaetia clearly relates to the "truest cause," while the incidents of Corcyra, Potidaea, and the Spartan congress relate directly only to the "allegations."[3]

The answers to these questions are intricately bound up with Thucydides' notions of the relation between political thought and action and of the way in which thoughts and actions are the causes of events. Without an explicit statement of cause by the historian, or, as in our case, with an ambiguous statement, we must use as evidence of the historian's understanding of cause the order in which he presents information at the beginning of his history, since order in a narrative necessarily implies and embodies judgments of priority, both in the sense of time and in the sense of importance. Given that Sparta's fear made the war necessary, Thucydides' construction of the story of the beginning of the war embodies an extremely compact and sophisticated picture of the ways in which actions, opinions, and deliberation interact in the creation of events.

There are simple notions of the relation of thought and action in politics, but these Thucydides deliberately eschews. Nothing would have been simpler than to begin the account of this war with the Pentecontaetia. Every possible simple historical reason would have been on the side of such an arrangement. First of all, the Pentecontaetia follows chronologically on chapter 1.21 of the Archaeology, and if Thucydides had had any doubt about where the Peloponnesian War, as a discrete event, began, he would have had to take the cautious route and proceed merely in sequence of time. Second, if his purpose had been to demonstrate a simple notion of the necessity of the war, then to have placed the account of the growth of the Athenian empire before the deliberations at Athens and Sparta would have driven us ineluctably to this interpretation.[4] But of this one conclusion we must be certain: by placing the Pentecontaetia *after* the Spartan congress, Thucydides has deliberately subordinated that account of the empire to the records of the debates as an explanation both of the outbreak of the war and of its necessity. Whatever the role of the Pentecontaetia in either the creation of events or in a subsequent explanation of them, Thucydides has declared by his arrangement that it is a role which can be properly understood only *after* a consideration of the debates. The necessity which Thucydides is conveying to us is no simple, material necessity.

For Thucydides' purpose, for the understanding of his interpretation of these events, all that we need to know about the Athenian empire when the first decisions which lead to war are taken is that it exists. To know more than this would obscure the processes which Thucydides is trying to display. If we knew the empire's history, and if that history were followed by the account of the war, we would have to conclude that the historical process Thucydides has exhibited is that once an imperial power has become established, it inevitably involves all other nations in war. But while there may be a sense in which this is true, this sense manifestly would not satisfy Thucydides' perception of the political processes which govern action.

From their reaction to Sthenelaidas' speech at the first congress, we can see that at the moment the Spartans made their decision they indeed felt this simple process was true. They felt that the existence of the empire was a compelling reason for war, in exactly the same way that we would have, had Thucydides told his story in chronological order and begun his history with the Pentecontaetia. Naturally, for the Spartans had undergone the real experience of those fifty years in just that order. And yet Thucydides chose to delay the presentation of this "compelling reason" for war until after he had presented no fewer than six speeches—which are concerned primarily with the "allegations" and which include the decision that the peace was broken—occupying no less space than one half of book 1. By arranging the beginning of his history in this way, Thucydides has exhibited quite another sort of historical process, one which we will trace throughout this fourth chapter.

As far as Thucydides conceives of the origin of events, whatever "necessities" the material circumstances of nations may imply, certain processes of thought and action must intervene before nations can act on these "necessities." The existence of an imperial power undoubtedly creates a radically unstable international situation and creates the sorts of anxieties which drive nations to war. Yet, before a war actually breaks out, the nations concerned must make conscious judgments about the belligerency of the empire, and must be able to justify the fears they feel and the war they look to for relief of these fears. These judgments and justifications are more than mere diplomatic forms to make war appear honorable. Having lived in peace with the imperial power for years (even if anxiously), nations must reorient their policies and principles to account for why now, but not before, war has become the only course. Certainly, material circumstances create "necessities" which states must obey. The existence of an aggressive imperial power demands countermeasures to contain it if autonomy is to be preserved. But so, too, does the political process create political "necessities" to which men must submit, even in

their obedience to the necessities of circumstance. The change
from peace to war demands a variety of political acts: a determination that the opposing power is in fact aggressive, a cata-
lyzing event, its promotion to the status of a grievance, representations to the offending power, refusals, hardening of
positions, preparation of public opinion, ultimatums. These
are not mere political displays and diplomatic forms. They are
necessary acts in the political process that results in a judgment
that peace is no longer possible and that war is desirable. They
are necessary because men, not states, make war, and yet make
war in nations rather than as individuals. It is because of the
complex relation of men, states, and action that Thucydides
has placed the political processes in the foreground of his
history.

It is the complexity of the lines of efficiency between the
men who are the agents in the direction of the state (on the one
hand) and the nations which are the agents of the events of the
war (on the other) that has dictated to Thucydides the isolation
of two kinds of cause. Nations are, ultimately, directed by the
men who compose them. The directions given to nations depend not only on those events which occur in the world, but
also on the attitudes of men toward the events that have occurred, and on the desires of men for the results of events that
are to occur. The occurrence of an identical event may result in
quite different responses depending on the differing emotions
and desires of the respondents. In this respect the ultimate
explanation of an event resides in the motivations of the men
who are the agents or the directors of the action. Such an
explanation is Thucydides' $\pi\rho\acute{o}\phi\alpha\sigma\iota\varsigma$—it was Spartan fear
which necessitated the war. But these motivations are, in
essence, the possessions of individuals, and it is not individuals
who make war. Needed, also, for the explanation of national
events is some explanation of the translation of essentially
individual motives into public, national activity. It is this explanation that Thucydides provides with his $\alpha\acute{\iota}\tau\iota\alpha\iota$—those
public and political acts and interpretations which, in combi-
nation with the individual motivations of the populace of the
nations, result in public decisions and national policies.

What Thucydides is exhibiting to us in the first cluster of

speeches are the changes of conception and attitude (and the events through which these changes were realized) that made the Peloponnesian War occur. He is showing us the making-active of that Spartan fear which necessitated the war, in the sense of showing the political transformation of a state of mind into a concrete policy. (And as it was developments in Peloponnesian attitudes which opened the war, it is appropriate that two-thirds of the speeches in this cluster are given by Peloponnesians.) As far as Thucydides is concerned, the actualization of this fear began unequivocally with the episode over Corcyra. Before this incident the conditions for the fear may have existed (and in this respect the mere existence of the empire may have rendered the international balance unstable), but there was neither cause for the fear to be acted upon, nor even for it to appear as a justifiable or articulable political motive. The fear itself may even have existed in the minds of individuals in the Peloponnesian cities, but there was as yet no way (no evidence, no cause) to turn this individual fear into a specific course of national (or allied) action. The balance of power that was in existence at the start of the Peloponnesian War had been in existence exactly as it was for fourteen years. Perhaps it was an unstable political situation, and perhaps the highly visible Athenian empire preyed on the minds of the Spartans and made them uneasy. Nevertheless, nothing had occurred which could be pointed to to demonstrate that the situation had changed in any important way, that Athens would not merely remain quiet, that in fact it was an immediate threat to the Peloponnese. Not only were there no pretexts for war, neither was there anything to indicate that war was a necessary or justifiable course.

Corcyra changed all of that. It was a pretext for war, but it was not merely an excuse. It was the event which, when added to the scales with the mere existence of the empire, demonstrated to the Peloponnesians (correctly or not) that the empire was something to be feared. It provided a concrete object for the previously inchoate Spartan anxiety (and made this anxiety a definite and immediate fear of Athens and its empire) at the same time that it demonstrated that Athens was a state justly and reasonably to be feared. For the first time there was evidence to which one could point to explain the existence of one's fears. And the preexistence of the fear made this event a danger, something which demanded counteraction. It is only later, once the war had begun, that one could cynically say: "Corcyra was just an excuse; it was really Sparta's fear which made the war happen." In the dynamics of events and of deliberation, Corcyra was also the event which enabled the fear to become an object of deliberation and to take its place as a motivation and a cause. Even amid the undeniable pressures of the merely material aspects of the powers in collision here— the unprecedented size of the Athenian empire, the almost inevitable commercial conflicts between Athens and Corinth, the instability and suspicion of a world split between two great power blocs—political events must occur, on a completely human level, before the imperatives of power politics can find their expression.

It is these events that are Thucydides' concern in this first cluster of speeches, and the political processes displayed there are minutely and subtly portrayed. At the moment of its beginning there was nothing to distinguish the Corcyrean affair as especially significant or consequential. It was, at first, nothing more than a factional war on the peripheries of Greece. The Epidamnians were able to secure Corinthian assistance thanks to longer standing, fairly restrained, hostilities existing between Corinth and Corcyra. The Corcyreans, in turn, faced with the prospect of defeat, appealed to Athens for support, with expectations of success based on the possibility of exploiting whatever jealousies existed between Athens and the Peloponnese. Even the Corinthians come to Athens for quite minimal reasons. They worry about the Athenians as an obstacle to their plans for Corcyra, not yet as enemies in a general war (1.31.3). It is at this moment that Thucydides records the first debate of his history, for it was at this moment that events first occurred to which meanings were given and responses made that definitely tended to war—all of this through the deliberate choice of the agents in a political context which made this choice univocal.

Until the debate at Athens there was nothing in this situation which necessitated a general war. With that debate, however, an important political gesture was made, a threshold was crossed, and a radical change in political attitudes was begun. As we have seen in the section on this debate in chapter 1, the Corinthians did not deny the existence of the jealousies the Corcyreans hoped to exploit. In fact, they admitted that these had given them grounds for suspicion of Athenian intentions, and they made the matter of Corcyra a test of the true nature of Athenian-Corinthian relations. When the Athenians decided to assist the Corcyreans, they took a course of action whose significance had been unequivocally defined in this debate: they accepted the Corcyrean interpretation of the near-belligerency of the Peloponnesians, and they declared that it was indeed a state of hostility that existed between Athens and Corinth.

Even at this moment the *Peloponnesian* War was not yet necessary, for it could have been possible to consider the hostility a private matter between Athens and Corinth.[5] But in the context of existing material relations and political attitudes, the Athenian declaration of belligerency had a political consequence that far outweighed the material consequences of the addition of the Corcyrean navy. The Corcyrean affair led to conflict over Potidaea, not because of any directly hostile intention, but through a certain necessity of making defensive arrangements. When this second confrontation had occurred between Athens and Corinth, the actions were taken which made possible and necessary the completion of this first great change of orientation in the history of the war.

It was at this moment that in Thucydides' terms the war can be said to have become necessary, for it was at this moment that the necessitating cause of the war—the *prophasis,* Spartan fear—could be given form and expression. Athens had made only one choice, and had acted upon it but twice, but these two actions provided the material grounds for a reinterpretation of the international situation by all of the Peloponnesians. The previous hypothetical interpretation of conditions subsisting before this war—of an Athenian empire of great material strength but no patently hostile intention—could no longer be credibly proposed to the Peloponnesians. Something like this hypothetical statement was given as the Athenian argument at

Sparta, but is seen to have been impossible for the Spartans to accept. The Athenian decision concerning Corcyra, and their merely automatic response at Potidaea, gave the Corinthians the rhetorical material to demonstrate that the Athenian empire was not only large, but dangerous.

If Athens had come into conflict with Corinth, but had had no empire, than the conflict would have been private, with no necessity of a general war. If Athens, possessing its empire, had avoided a direct confrontation with the Peloponnesians, the case for a general war would have been weak, if not politically unjustifiable. But on the one hand, there was the existing empire, and on the other, the deliberate declaration of Athenian hostility to Corinth. When these two data were brought together, the rhetorical grounds were complete both for the demonstration that Athens' empire was clearly belligerent and therefore a general threat (since it was an empire and not simply another city), and for the actualization of the Spartan fear which "necessitated the war."

In these first three debates of his history Thucydides has done much more than merely to portray the diplomatic stages by which the two powers came to war. He has actually embodied the processes of political action which brought the war about, as individual motivations became public ones, as events were interpreted in the light of these attitudes, and as responses appropriate to both event and attitude were formulated. Embodied as well are the relations of actions and thoughts in their interdependence which underlie all events. In a context of mutual suspicion, one party draws a line and makes a particular decision the test of the truth or falsity of those suspicions. The other party makes a decision which itself is still particular. That decision, however, creates both further actions (dictated by the policy of the first decision) and the necessity of the reinterpretation of political attitudes and programs in the light of, and taking account of, the original decision and its material consequences. The reinterpretation itself, then, becomes the source of new decisions, attitudes, and actions of a kind different from those which existed under the old interpretation. It is these processes that Thucydides exhibits in the first three debates. They are more than diplomatic forms followed on such occasions, they are, in fact, generically the political activities states perform under these circumstances and specifically the ones which brought this war into being. These are processes of thought and choice which show us the combatants as conscious agents, and also give us a sense in which a war can be necessary without forcing us to say that states are moved only by hidden material factors. These processes exhibit to us the way in which there may be both "truest causes" (πρόφασεις) and "allegations" (αἰτίαι) without our being misled into believing that only one of these embodies the reality of the historical situation.

Without the *prophasis* of Athenian growth and Spartan fear there could be no general war. It is for this reason that the *prophasis* can be spoken of as the "truest" cause of the *Peloponnesian* War. Without the *prophasis* the events at Corcyra and Potidaea would not have been *aitiai* of any larger war. They would merely have been particular occasions of hostility between Athens and Corinth. Yet the *prophasis* as cause of the war is in itself merely potential, not actual. Without the *aitiai*, the fear Sparta had of Athens' growth would not have been the *prophasis* of any war, for without some initiating event there would be no means by which this fear could itself become active as the cause of further events. It requires something to bring it into actuality, and this is the role of the *aitiai*. For a *prophasis* to become the *prophasis* of something there must be *aitiai*. The moment of the *aitiai* is therefore also the moment of the actualization of the *prophasis*, and therefore of the event of which it is the *prophasis*, in this case the war. It is for this reason that Thucydides can say with assurance, "I have recorded the *aitiai* first. . . so that no one need ever inquire as to *when* this great war among the Hellenes began" (1.23.5), and can begin his account of the war with Corcyra and Potidaea rather than with the Pentecontaetia. We must notice that in this recognition of two different notions of cause a premium is placed on the understanding of the political acts that lie behind events.

We must now characterize what this turning point is a turning *toward*, and how it stamps its character on the first phase of the war (the first five years). The nature of the threats felt by both sides, and their responses and aims, were at this moment extremely concrete. For both sides this was a war of nations, rather than of anything deeper or more abstract, like political philosophies or ways of life. To the Peloponnesians, Athens was a threat because of its size and wealth. Its aggressiveness (or alleged aggressiveness) was not seen as unnatural or idiosyncratic, even by the Corinthians. The aggressiveness was natural to nations of a certain size, and that Athens acted upon this universal impulse was no cause for surprise. As the impulse was felt to be natural, and therefore not alterable, all that made Athens a special danger was its size and its empire. The war against Athens, to remove the danger, was therefore one whose goal was to reduce Athens' power to the scale of the other Greek nations. At the beginning of this war the Corinthians say that Athens alone is a match for all the cities of the Peloponnesian alliance. This imbalance must be ended. At which point, so the Peloponnesians believed at this moment, although the innate aggressiveness of nations would remain, Athens would no longer have the material capability to threaten the independence of the Greek states generally. What is most important to notice is that at its beginning the grounds of the war and the manner in which it was to be carried out and concluded were all thought of materially.

On the Athenian side, the war of defense was conceived no less materially. Athens had been attacked because it was a power of a certain sort. It had not been attacked on political or moral grounds. Its enemies, the Peloponnesians, were thought of as being no different in their basic drives than the Athenians. Even when Pericles came to characterize the Athenians as different from other Greeks, it was in a limited way. The Athenians have different institutions which lead to a style of life freer and more complete than that in other states. Yet there was no idea of a radical otherness between Athens and the rest of the world, nor was there any distinction of motives or desires. Given the same opportunities, the Athenian speakers at Sparta suggested, any Greek city would act as Athens has acted. The other Greek cities were considered inferior to Athens, but not conceived of as natural enemies. The differences of institution are merely said to make Athenian life better than that of the other cities, but are not seen as having any relation to the causes of the war. Athens had been attacked by other *nations,* and its strategy would be to outlast them, drawing upon its vast material resources. The conclusion of the war would be one between nations: a readjustment of the relations of the states, which would allow Athens to pursue its individual course.

As the strategies dependent on this general interpretation were spelled out (in the second Spartan congress and in Pericles' first speech), we can trace on both sides the elaborations of attitudes toward, and expectations of, this first part of the war. For both sides, although with some differences dictated by their material circumstances, the war was thought of in an extremely limited way. It was limited in scope, in strategy, in length, and in the depth of feeling involved. On the Peloponnesian side, the belief was that the war would be brief.[6] Their strategy was essentially traditional: invasion, and the hope of a decisive victory between armies. When the Athenian forces had been beaten in battle, the empire, they believed, would evaporate, order would be restored in international relations, and the war and hostility would be over. On the Athenian side, though the duration of the war was expected to be greater, the aims and designs were no larger. To endure, to avoid risky combat, and to retain control of the imperial cities was the sum total of the strategy. The length of the war was solely dependent on how long it would take the Peloponnesians to spend all their money or to decide they could not win. At the beginning of the war, Athens expected no widespread Peloponnesian threat, nor did it expect any danger to the empire. Nor did it have any larger design of its own. It was believed on both sides that the war would be decided in the weighing of the material resources and strength of the nations at war. Injuries were material, the danger on both sides had a material basis, and the conclusion would be decided by material. The war began without the hint of ideology or philosophy, and, like all nonideological conflicts, was believed to have definite, concrete aims and limits.

The limited and material conception of what had brought the war about and of what its purposes were put a characteristic stamp on the conduct of the first five years of the war. Military actions were traditional in design, cautious, rather static and inconclusive. It was five years of war virtually without any significant military event, though in the five years we can see both the testing and the failure of the conventional military strategies. On the Peloponnesian side tactics were limited to the invasion of Attica (four times in the five years) and the siege of Plataea. Both of these maneuvers had almost no effect. The invasion of Attica, traditional as it was with Spartan commanders, had no material effect on the Athenian capacity for war. The siege of Plataea, though eventually successful, seems primarily to show us a general Peloponnesian military ineptitude and bankruptcy of imagination.[7]

On the Athenian side the list is no longer nor more interesting. Athens contented itself with campaigns against the nearby cities it traditionally harrassed during a war, Aegina and Megara. In addition, almost yearly, it sent a fleet around the Peloponnese to harrass the coastal cities. Beyond this, the Athenians undertook alliances and minor campaigns at the remoter parts of the Greek world, Thrace and Acharnania. In no sense were any of these actions conclusive. The far-flung alliances shifted from one year to the next. Their raison d'être was never clear in any case. Megara was not captured. The coastal raids apparently bothered the Peloponnesians no more than the invasion of Attica did the Athenians.

Both sides avoided direct confrontations whenever they felt the circumstances at all disadvantageous. The war was fought through intermediaries (as, for instance, most of the fighting in Thrace) or on the peripheries of the spheres of influence. On the peripheries, both sides felt secure: no threat directly impended on the principals, the Peloponnesians felt Athenian control was weakest at the extremities, but the Athenians believed the superior mobility of their fleet made up for this. In the third year of the war a direct confrontation of the fleets took place in the Gulf of Corinth. The results of this battle, too, were inconclusive, but a marginal Peloponnesian defeat and habitual Spartan naval timidity served later to keep the Spartans from utilizing their fleet at all if an Athenian force was present. This was of some consequence in the fifth year.

There were, in these first five years, only three events of any importance, and characteristically with this static beginning, none of them was of any *military* significance. The first was the initial invasion of Attica, which, although foreseen, delivered a psychological shock to the Athenians. The second, of much greater importance, was the outbreak of the plague at Athens, in the second year of the war. These two events were the only ones which offered any hope to the Peloponnesians' initial expectations of the progress of the war. Yet, in the face of the initial shock and the much greater blow of the plague, the Athenians nevertheless continued the war, for reasons we have brought out in chapter one. The third event of importance, in the fourth year of the war, was the revolt of Mytilene, which, though unsuccessful, delivered a third serious shock to the Athenians.

That Thucydides, too, felt the first five years of war were of lessened importance seems clear from his treatment of them. All five years are telescoped into only slightly more than one book of the history, a book which, moreover, includes three important speeches and several generals' speeches. Virtually all that we need to know of this first phase of the war is that five full years passed, in which the war was in progress yet nothing was decided or even near decision. It was the length of time, more than what happened in that time, which brought about the changes of the next phase of the war. With the passage of time, two complementary processes took place which undermined the original conceptions of the war.

On the one hand we can see the utter disappointment of the hopes and expectations with which the Peloponnesians began the war. They could point to no clear victory, to no moment at which their numbers or their strategy had played a decisive part. Their demoralization was so deep that when, in the fifth year of the war, the Peloponnesian fleet might have done Athens some serious damage among the allied cities in Ionia, the Spartan commander preferred to withdraw rather than risk defeat by the small Athenian force in the area. Faced with such a complete reversal of their designs, their original attitudes toward the war clearly had to be revised. An explanation had to be found for the lack of success of the materially based policy.

The explanation had to show why, despite Athenian material losses (especially due to the plague), the war had not ended. An interpretation had to be found which took account of the obvious devaluation of the simply material aspects of the war, and which provided a new goal for which the Peloponnesians could continue the war, even now, long past its anticipated length.

On the Athenian side there were pressures for reorientation every bit as great. Although Pericles had foreseen a long war, the five years weighed even more heavily on the Athenians than on the Peloponnesians. Pericles had designed a passive strategy, but five years without clear success were just as hard for the Athenians to bear as for the Peloponnesians. Moreover, the plague had produced hardships far in excess of any expectation. Beyond these general pressures, the Athenians had a special anxiety. The entire Periclean strategy and all their hopes were based on the continued availability of the vast resources of the empire. With the debilitation of internal Athenian resources by the plague and by the expense of the campaigns at the edges of the world, the empire assumed a larger and larger importance in Athenian designs. In the fourth year of the war the first serious revolt from the Athenian empire occurred (Mytilene), and for the first time the possibility of the loss of the empire was presented to their deliberations. The empire had always been taken for granted, but its loss would have (at this stage of thinking) necessarily implied an Athenian defeat. As this special fear was added to the general restlessness and discomfort of the Athenians, the conditions were created for a reinterpretation of the war which would deal directly with the empire and how control of it was to be preserved.

These two processes bring us to the next turning point of the war. To understand the changes in attitude (as well as of interpretation) which occurred at this point, however, we must recollect one other aspect of the situation at this time. Inconclusive as these first five years had been, they were five years of open war. And the enmities with which the war began had had the opportunity to deepen and to become increasingly entrenched in the attitudes of the participants. The new formulations which were to be conceived had also to take account, and to allow the expression, of the feelings which had been generated and intensified by the first part of the war.

The Second Phase of the War

In the debates of book 3 at Athens and Plataea, we find the change in orientation which shapes the second phase of the war. The material and nonideological orientation with which both sides began succumbed to the frustration of five years of inconclusive war. In particular it succumbed to its failure to explain the continued resistance of the enemy and its failure to provide political explanations and programs which justified further pursuit of the war. In these debates we discover the new formulations made in response to these pressures. On both sides the new rationalizations of the situation were ideological, though in slightly different molds which reflect the different circumstances and traditions of the two blocs. These ideological formulations were at once abstract and compelling. Their abstraction was rhetorically advantageous since it could be used to explain the prolongation of the war to this moment and to demonstrate the necessity of continuing the war even though no definite ending date could be set. Wars fought for material purposes, after all, have material goals and benefits against which costs must be weighed. Once the costs outweigh the potential benefits, one ought rationally to give the war up. Obviously, the combatants in this war were hardly going to abandon the war despite its unexpected length and cost. Yet to justify this open-ended war, new goals and explanations were needed which could not be attacked as more costly than they were worth. Insofar as they were abstract and spoke of abstract forces, dangers, and goals, the ideological formulations were immune to materialistic criticism based on cost. Further, in their abstraction and simplicity, they displayed a compelling quality important in enlisting support for this open-ended future of conflict. Finally, the new formulations had tremendous endurance. Although the use of these formulations later shifted once more, the ideological distinctions made in this fifth year continued in force as one of the sources of emotion and action to the very end of the war.

When Athens began the war, one *casus belli* was its alliance with Corcyra. At the time that this alliance was made (1.24–26), the democracy in Athens sided with the Corcyreans and the oligarchs of Epidamnus against the democrats of Epidamnus. If we needed a clear example of the nonideological character of political thought at the beginning of the war, this is it. The decisions on both sides were made solely in terms of material power, and of the possibilities that changes in power alignments gave for the exercise of influence over various nations and parts of the world. Such nonideological thinking can be seen in the speeches of the Corinthians, Athenians, and Spartans at the first Spartan congress, and in Pericles' speeches. This same sort of thought characterized Cleon's arguments in the Mytilenean debate. In response to the revolt of Mytilene and the threat that that implied to Athenian control of the empire, Cleon suggested the use of simple force.

Diodotus' argument in the Mytilene debate heralded a new stage of Athenian policy-making by articulating a new model for the relations between states. Diodotus asserted that a response which considered only material bases of power would not lessen the danger that Athens felt from the empire, nor would it take account of the actual political forces in operation. What the Athenians must recognize as their greatest political resource, he said, is the automatic sympathy of the democratic factions in cities for the Athenian democracy, and the hatred these factions feel for their own indigenous oligarchic parties. Diodotus suggested that the new relations between Athens and its allies be constructed along these ideological lines. Athens should cultivate the good-will of the democrats in its subject cities. This would assure Athens' control over these cities.[8]

In some ways Diodotus' speech was not very ideological at all. He himself does not show any particularly strong sympathy for the other democrats.[9] Further, in *intent* his speech was limited in its application to relations with Athens' allies. All that Diodotus suggested was the manipulation of this ideological factor to Athens' material benefit. And yet, as we see in the events that follow, in *action* the principle came to have a much greater effect. The principle was initially invented to solve a particular imperial problem. But its simplicity and attractiveness led to its generalization over the whole spectrum of Athenian international relations. It was true, to Athenian eyes, that all Athens' enemies were oligarchies. It was true, further, that the existence of the democracy at Athens was part of its peculiar heritage and character. By a natural sort of rhetorical impulsion, and under the pressure of finding a rationalization of the war which explained its length and the necessity of continuing it still longer, the Athenians came to consider the war as one between democracies and oligarchies.

The consequences of this new orientation were many and weighty. Directly, in terms of the actions Athens took, it caused a wholesale reorientation of Athenian alliances. From this moment all of Athens' associations were with other democracies. Alliances were only considered with democrats, and where important cities existed under the control of oligarchs, support was given to democratic factions to overthrow the oligarchies in order to bring the cities into the Athenian orbit. The enlisting or capture of cities was accomplished, from this point, more often by subversion than by siege.

In addition to specific military and political consequences, the new orientation had profound effects on Athenian attitudes and emotions. The change of interpretation deepened the Athenians' commitment to the war and made them less inclined to compromise or negotiation. It was no longer the case that the stakes of the war were merely Athens' surplus possessions (that is, the empire). At stake now was the democratic basis of the life they led. The war became a necessity to the Athenian *demos,* and, as they felt oligarchs were never to be trusted, the chances for a negotiated settlement of the war receded.[10] The war now became associated, in Athenian minds, with one of the crucial springs of Athenian emotion and commitment, its democracy, and its situation, alone against all the oligarchs. Naturally, with the connection of the war to this traditional source of emotion, Athenian feelings of hostility toward the Peloponnesians were intensified.

On the Peloponnesian side, at this turning point of the war, a reorientation of thought was made which, though characteristically different, similarly generalized the attributed meaning of the war and associated it with traditional sources of bitterness and hatred. The Peloponnesians were not as given to political explanations as the Athenians,[11] and so their reformulation of the meaning of the war was not as directly political as was the Athenians'. It was, nonetheless, ideological.

The appeal the Plataeans made to the Spartan judges was based on the older assumption that *states* were the significant entities, and that therefore the relations between states were particular and adapted to the particular situation. Under this assumption the Plataeans claimed a special relation to Sparta —which existed—and which they felt warranted merciful treatment. Their argument was countered and defeated by the Thebans, who made the Plataean arguments apparently irrelevant by moving consideration of the case under a new and general, rather than particular, rubric. In doing so they articulated the new orientation of the Peloponnesians. When the Thebans argued that the Plataeans should be condemned for the new crime of Atticism, they announced the appearance of a principle as abstract and compelling as the complementary Athenian ideologization of the war.

The reorientation of the war from being against the power of the Athenian empire to being against Atticism fulfilled important rhetorical needs. The frustration of Peloponnesian designs and hopes in the first phase of the war can be mainly attributed to the impossibility of defeating Athens if the contest was merely material. Athens simply had greater resources. As long as Athens, although sustaining serious material losses, still continued the war, the Peloponnesians were faced with a choice. They must either give the war up, or find an explanation for the failure of their expectations that would also demonstrate the necessity of perseverance. The new formulation which was found was successful not only because it satisfied these needs, but also because it came as an easy development of existing Peloponnesian attitudes.

Already at the first Spartan congress the character of the Athenians (and its difference from that of the Spartans, if not of all the Peloponnesians) was a matter of concern. At that early stage, however, the material consequences of that character were seen as a greater threat than the character itself. The recognition of the difference remained, however, and in the fourth year of the war the Mytileneans used this difference as an argument for Peloponnesian support of their revolt. They claimed that alliances could exist only between states with the same traditions and beliefs. The next step was that which the Thebans took, claiming that the Athenian character was alien to all Greeks, and *a fortiori* to the Peloponnesians.

This formulation was immensely satisfying. The Theban generalization of Athenian imperialism into an abstract force called Atticism (in effect, an ideology) provided tremendous rhetorical resources. It put Athens in the same rhetorical category as Persia, from which two dividends accrued: on the one hand, the Peloponnesians could flatter themselves that their war with Athens was being conducted for principles as holy as those for which the Persian War was fought (this would provide, of course, both encouragement for the Peloponnesians and an attractive slogan to recruit new allies); on the other hand, Athenian imperialism could take on a special meaning. Instead of remaining a word descriptive of a certain (and indeed, according to the Corinthians, natural) form of political activity, "imperialism" could become an especially pejorative term. The war would no longer be merely to reduce Athenian power, it could be seen as a desperate and necessary struggle against slavery. "Imperialism," as a conceivably natural manner of national aggrandizement, could not evoke the same sort of response that "Atticism" could. "Atticism," in this respect, was something of a wholly different character— rhetorically—from imperialism. Atticism could be seen as something as potentially expansive and subversive of Greek principles as the other great alien threat, Medism, had been.[12]

By seeing Athenian actions under the guise of Atticism, the Peloponnesians were able to establish a motive for the necessary continuation of the war even though no prediction could be given of how long the continuation might have to be. If Atticism aimed at nothing less than the complete enslavement of Greece, then the Peloponnesian allies could consider nothing less than an unceasing struggle for their freedom. Further, the linkage of Athens with an alien enslaver, and the implication that Atticism was "un-Greek," suggested that the grounds of conflict were innate and natural, and this provided additional emotional fuel to continue resistance by supplying an appropriate expression for the feelings of hatred created in the first five years of war.

The reorientation of the Peloponnesians to their ideologization of the war caused changes, material and psychological, as deep and widespread as did the Athenian. Peloponnesian policies made much the same change of direction as did the Athenian. In all cities the oligarchs were seen as those who preserved the proper Greek values, and the democrats were seen as those most seriously tainted with Atticism. The Peloponnesians, therefore, also came to exploit the civil wars of Greek states in an attempt to detach cities from Athens' ideological influence. The new interpretation also suggested the only tactic likely to succeed in encouraging defections from the Athenian empire: support of oligarchic revolutions within the imperial cities.

In addition to these material changes, the new orientation brought about an intensification of feelings complementary to that on the Athenian side. As the Persians were hated and feared, so must be the Athenians. And as there was no possible compromise with Medism, so there could be no compromise with Atticism. With this reorientation the Peloponnesians, both in the completeness of the opposition they perceived and in the depth of feeling evoked by associating this opposition with that against Persia, entered a state of total war.[13] An individual state might, under special circumstances, be willing to come to an accommodation with Athens, as Sparta was, in its anxiety for the men trapped at Sphacteria. Yet the intransigence would reemerge, under more favorable circumstances, and among the other Peloponnesian states we can find evidence that it never wavered. The Corinthians, Boeotians, and Megarians not only never concluded an actual peace with Athens at the end of the first ten years of war, they separated themselves from Sparta because it had. That this was not simply the action of states more immediately threatened by Athens, but that it, too, had an ideological basis, can be seen from Megarian and Boeotian unwillingness to conclude an alliance (though they needed one to replace their alliance with Sparta) with the democratic cities of the Peloponnese (5.31.6).

The new ideological orientations were in fact to remain influential on both sides until the end of the war, and Thucydides wastes no time in exhibiting the effect they had on the
shape of the war. In this same fifth year which saw the change
of interpretation, there occurred an event which Thucydides
describes in great detail within a few pages of the completion
of the debate at Plataea. This was the virulent *stasis* at Corcyra.
It was, for Thucydides, the most horrible and most complete
stasis that occurred in the war. It was also the first of many of
this kind, and he uses it as representative of all the others.
Factional conflicts were not a new phenomenon in Greece, but
Thucydides' introduction to his account of it makes clear his
reasons for considering the one at Corcyra an extraordinary
development.

> So this cruel *stasis* proceeded. And it seemed even worse
> because it was the first; since after this the whole Greek
> world, as it were, was in commotion, differences existing
> everywhere between the leaders of the *demos,* trying to
> bring in the Athenians, and the oligarchs, trying to bring in
> the Spartans. And though in times of peace they would not
> have had any pretext, nor would they have been ready, to
> ask aid of them, yet, when they were at war, and there was
> an alliance for either side (for harming their enemies and
> adding to their own strength at the same time), induce-
> ments were easily provided for those who had any wish to
> make a revolution. [3.82.1]

What made this *stasis* the first of its kind, and what made it
so terrible in its consequences, was that it was the first *stasis*
which, rather than remaining purely an internal matter, en-
listed the support of the two great powers, and which used
their support to feed existing hatreds and to make novel kinds
of cruelty possible. That the occurrence of this new kind of
stasis at this precise moment was not mere happenstance, but
was a direct consequence of the ideologizing of the war is
indicated not only by Thucydides' placement and emphatic
treatment of the episode immediately after the debates which
exhibit the new ideological interpretation, but also by Thucydides' second comment on the *stasis*. While Thucydides at

first seems to say that it was the war which created the opportunity for this new form of *stasis*, we must notice that five years of war had passed before any state took advantage of it. If it were war alone that made this kind of *stasis* possible, we might expect to have encountered it before this. In fact, Thucydides insists on a double condition for the occurrence of this new model of factional warfare, and that it is only now that this new phenomenon arises gives us further evidence of a new stage in the war. Thucydides says that it is not only war, but the availability of appropriate alliances which makes this new *stasis* possible. Yet the required pattern of alliance is itself of a new sort: not of government with government, but of great powers with particular political factions within a state, often a faction precisely not in power as the government of the state. For this new kind of alliance to become available takes not war in an unqualified sense, but a war of a certain sort—an ideologically perceived war, in which the political orientation of groups, rather than their political authority, provides sufficient grounds for association. For smaller states to act in this way requires that they know the great powers are willing to offer this new pattern of alliance, and this, in turn, requires the *public* enunciation by the major powers that they perceive the war as ideological, and are willing to shape their actions to it. This enunciation is given in the debates on Mytilene and Plataea, and it is only after them, then, that we find the new model of *stasis* occurring in Greece responding directly to the new interpretation of the war.

At 3.82.1 Thucydides is explicit that this new form of *stasis* and this pattern of great power intervention became the rule in the war from this point onward. It is the accident, however, that the first instance of it occurred in Corcyra that makes it easy for us to see what a revolution in attitudes and interpretation is implied by it. If after this moment it was to seem natural that Athens would support the democrats in other cities (both its allies and independent states) and Sparta the oligarchs, before this moment there was nothing natural about it. Were it so, we would expect that Athens' original alliance with Corcyra would have exhibited some trace of this pattern, but in fact the opposite was the case. As has been mentioned before, the initial event in the episode of Epidamnus is the expulsion of the Epidamnian oligarchs (1.24.5). When the democratic government of Epidamnus approaches Corcyra for aid (1.24 .6-7), it is refused. It receives help, however, from the oligarchic government of Corinth (1.25.3). When, on the other hand, the now outnumbered Epidamnian oligarchs ask for Corcyrean aid (1.26.3), they receive it. It is with, in fact, this oligarchically inclined (or perhaps merely politically indifferent) Corcyrean government that the Athenians make their alliance against the democracy of Epidamnus.

It is worth putting this baldly: in one of the events which led to the outbreak of the Peloponnesian War, oligarchic Corinth supported the democrats of Epidamnus, and democratic Athens supported the oligarchs of Epidamnus and the oligarchically inclined government of Corcyra. At the least we must say that in their relations with independent nations at this crucial moment in the war the Athenians acted according to motives that had nothing whatever to do with the internal politics of these nations or with ideology. Indeed, the Corinthians acted this way too. Yet by the fifth year of the war we find Athens supporting the democrats in Corcyra and the Spartans (or the Peloponnesians, replacing the Corinthians) supporting the oligarchs. And it is at this point that we have Thucydides' direct statement that this was to occur not in Corcyra alone, but all over the Greek world.

However natural this alignment seemed to be by the fifth year of the war, it was not natural in 433. In Thucydides' interpretation of the war there is represented a dramatic and radical political shift in the opinions of the nations of Greece. In their dealings with cities outside their immediate blocs, the major powers have apparently switched the sides that they support. Or, perhaps more accurately, they have now decided that there is an appropriate side for each of them to support, where previously sides in internal political conflicts were irrelevant. Impelling this change in policy, and the basis of the attitudinal shift which makes it possible, is the fundamental transformation of the interpretation of the nature of the war and of its underlying sources of conflict that we see represented in Thucydides' narrative of the fifth year of the war.

Through the willing involvement of the great powers, the *stasis* at Corcyra was the first fruit of this new orientation of the war, and the events and excesses of this *stasis* were also representative of the attitudes and emotions of this new orientation and predictive of the conduct of the general war. The bitterness and cruelty of events in Corcyra were due in great part to the smallness of the city, to there being no place into which to retire from the conflict. ("And the citizens in the middle were destroyed by both sides, either because they would not side with them, or through envy that they might survive" [3.82 .8].) But, indeed, one of the general consequences of the ideologizing of the war was the virtual disappearance of this neutral ground even in the larger context of the Greek world as a whole. Corcyra was ahead of its time in the intensity of these emotions and the cruelty of their expression. Thucydides notes this, too (3.82.3, 3.84.1, 3.85.1). These emotions and attitudes were the ones appropriate to the ideological orientation, and in the progress of the history we can watch these attitudes gain increasingly general acceptance, and can perceive the feelings of the combatants deepen along these same lines.

The three major characteristics of the *stasis* that Thucydides describes are: the utterness of the opposition of parties, the destruction of any middle, neutral ground, and the distortion of thought and speech by the spirit of partisanship. All of these were the necessary, though most radical, extensions of the ideological conception of the war. That Thucydides spends so much time on his account of this event, and that he does so in such close proximity to the two debates which precede it, indicates to me both that he saw the connection between this event and the new orientation of the war and that he meant the description of Corcyra to represent to us the most starkly drawn picture of the new shape that the war took under this new orientation. At Corcyra, he says, words changed their meanings, and entire habitual patterns of thought and action were overthrown or reversed. Everything came to be seen as representative of party passions; ordinary words had special political meanings given them. The possibility of speaking or deliberating about events in other than a party mold disappeared because the words for framing these thoughts no longer existed.[14] Though this is the most extreme case, the process at work in this rhetorical and perceptual reduction is common to all changes of interpretation. When the general schema of political thought changes, so do the sorts of policies that may be considered. If one's vocabulary takes on special meanings, the range of subjects that can be articulated in debate becomes limited and shaped in that same mold. What occurred at Corcyra was programmatic of changes in rhetoric and deliberation to occur among all the states involved in the war.

That such radical changes in conceptualization occurred at Corcyra is attributable primarily to the abstractness of the ideological orientation of their civil war (and, by extension, of the second phase of the war). To this abstractness are also attributable the two other characteristics of the *stasis*. As long as a war is conceived materially, interpretations of events may periodically change without one of them necessarily gaining complete ascendency. But abstractions like ideologies carry with them a single, authoritative interpretation and its proper vocabulary, and these necessarily drive out all other alternatives. A further consequence of abstractness is that it enables men to draw oppositions which are both unequivocal and complete. In a material dispute, compromise is always possible. Where differences are drawn on philosophical or ideological bases, compromise is almost by definition impossible. The emotions, too, are more intensely engaged with symbols than with matter. It is possible to hate a man more thoroughly for his philosophy than for his possession of a certain piece of land. At least if you remove him from that land, the grounds for hatred cease. There is, however, no necessary cessation of a philosophical opposition. Finally, when the opposition is drawn as starkly and implacably as this, it is possible to require everyone to take sides and to condemn all who do not. In these ways, as the possibility of a middle position evaporates between two radically expressed oppositions, neutrality disappears, and with it any chance of softening the effects of the conflict. Because the grounds of conflict were abstract, or at least were seen as abstract insofar as even concrete material differences were described by or cloaked in ideological terms, the *stasis* at Corcyra came to involve everyone, and did so with an intensity of emotion never before seen in Greek political life. This same engulfing in an ever-expanding conflict of constantly deepening hostility was also characteristic of the whole Peloponnesian War from the time of this second turning.

On both sides this second phase of the war was marked by greater reliance on ideological factors, increased activity, extension of hostility to new arenas, and a deepening of this hostility. It was a long phase, extending through the six-year Peace of Nicias, to the eve of the resumption of open war. We can examine it only in the briefest way. Both sides extended the range of their activities, expanding the circle of conflict from a small part of central Greece (with a few tentative forays at its peripheries) to new parts of the world previously untouched by war: Sicily, western Greece, new parts of Thrace. Further, the war expanded in "density" by involving cities within the center which had previously remained aloof: Elis, Mantinea, Argos. In almost all of these instances, factional politics played a crucial part. They were either the means of the capture of cities (one party within the city betraying it to the appropriate advancing army), or they were the reason for the war's entrance into a new area. The list of cities and battles where ideological discriminations either initiated a campaign or decided its outcome is long, comprising, among others, many of the most significant military events of this second phase: the Athenian campaigns in Sicily (in the seventh year), at Megara and in Boeotia (in the eighth), and Athenian diplomatic interference in Sicily (in the tenth); Brasidas' campaign in Thrace, especially at Amphipolis, Torone, and Mende (in the eighth and ninth years), and Spartan campaigns through the Peloponnese and in Achaea (during the Peace of Nicias).

Ideological considerations played a crucial part, moreover, in all of the alliances which were made during the Peace of Nicias. By far the most important alliances of this period were made with Argos, and Argive alignment with one or the other side changed no fewer than four times in the six-year period, and twice involved actual oligarchic or democratic revolutions as the precondition of the change of allegiance (5.76–82). Finally, when the democrats resumed power in Argos (in the fifteenth year), an alliance was made with Athens which endured to the end of the war (5.82.5). In addition to Argos, ideological changes influenced alliances of Mantinea and Elis with either side.

The ideological nature of these shifting alignments has a special significance both to Thucydides' (and our) perception of the war as a whole and also to the dynamics of events which led to the third turning point and to the resumption of open war. That the alliances of the Peace of Nicias were grounded in ideology provides evidence of a fundamental continuity between the Archidamian and Ionian Wars, and therefore of Thucydides' claim that the full span of twenty-seven years constituted a single war.[15] In the fifth year of the Archidamian War both sides altered their original conceptions of the basis of the war, adopting, as we have seen, explanations which discovered the source of hostility and the reasons for prosecuting the war in ideological oppositions between the two blocs. This ideological interpretation remained unchanged throughout, and unmitigated by, the Peace of Nicias.[16] The wholly ideological content of the alliances in this period convinces us of that. Indeed, as we consider the events of the Peace, the ideological interpretation may well have been reinforced by them.

The Peace was concluded at a fortuitous moment of mutual exhaustion. Those who favored it constituted, according to Thucydides, a very specific and limited group of politicians in both Athens and Sparta, to whom the peace offered specific political advantages (5.16.1). At the same moment, however, there also existed "war parties" in both cities (5.21.2-3; 5.36.1; 5.43.1), and their existence both puts us on notice of the essential fragility of the Peace (it was concluded at what—in Thucydides' narrative—appears the only moment during which the peace parties were more active and influential than the war parties), and makes it necessary for us to consider what were the continuing grounds of hostility that gave support and rhetorical justification to the war parties. As far as the terms of the peace were concerned, the drafters of the treaty cast the agreement in an entirely material or territorial mold. The treaty would recognize the authority of the Athenians and Spartans in their respective spheres of influence, and the grounds of conflict were to be removed by the return of captured men or territory to their original homes or possessors.

There were material benefits both Athens and Sparta could expect from the Peace. Athens would have returned to it some important tributary cities, and more generally, would get the time it needed to regain secure control of its allies. Sparta would recover the men captured at Sphacteria, and—especially with the alliance concluded between itself and Athens in 421 under the impulsion of the identical peace parties—would acquire Athenian support in preparation for what it expected would be Argive hostility once its peace treaty with Argos expired. With both sides looking to these material benefits, it is undeniable that the failure of both sides (but especially of the Peloponnesians) to make a complete return of the territory demanded by the terms of the treaty led to suspicion and anger that undermined any efforts the forces of peace might have made. Yet, despite these material grounds for anger and conflict, the essence of the breakdown of the Peace of Nicias (and, therefore, of the underlying continuity of the Peloponnesian War) is to be found in ideological oppositions, not in any chain of material grievances.

In a critical sense the Peace of Nicias never addressed the by then actual grounds of conflict. Despite the attempt of the framers to interpret the war materially and territorially, such an interpretation, given the currency of ideological orientations to the war, could be only partially convincing or satisfactory. The existence of war parties even as the Peace (and subsequent alliance) was ratified demonstrates that there were members of both sides who believed in grounds for hostility untouched by territorial settlements (and who were eager for war even before there had been any breakdown in the territorial reparations). The nature of the political maneuvers and their diplomatic results during this period provide us with what Thucydides believed was the content of these grounds. In the moments that immediately follow the Peace of Nicias there appears to be a great deal of fluidity to the political alignments of the cities of Greece. Athens and Sparta are newly allies; older, important Spartan allies, such as Corinth, Boeotia, and Megara, have broken away from Sparta; the entrance of Argos

on the political scene has caused further movement of Peloponnesian cities away from Sparta. Yet, despite this apparent
fluidity, within a year and a half of the alliance of Athens and
Sparta the original blocs have reformed, and what few differences there are between their composition on this occasion and
their composition in 432 in fact tend toward the more complete ideological homogeneity of the blocs. Athens has acquired as allies those Peloponnesian cities (Argos, Elis, Mantinea) that are democracies. The previously disaffected Spartan
allies (Boeotia, Corinth, Megara) have returned to the Spartan
orbit precisely because Sparta and they are oligarchies.

It is in this way that the events of the Peace of Nicias both
find their own coherence and give a concrete foundation to
Thucydides' belief in the continuity of the war as a whole. The
ideological interpretation of the latter half of the Archidamian
War not only continues into the period of the Peace, in Thucydides' narrative we can see its continued influence on the
action of states.[17] It is because the Peace did not affect the
ideological grounds of conflict, because these grounds continued to provide opportunities for conflict during the Peace
(diplomatic and military), and because these grounds continued to inform the war during its third phase that Thucydides believes it is proper to speak of the Peloponnesian War as a
single, protracted conflict.

That the Peace of Nicias did not change the grounds of
hostility, but, rather, that throughout it one could see a continual unfolding of ideologically inspired or informed maneuvers also played a crucial part in the dynamics that brought
about the third turning of the war. What in effect happened,
because of the continued vitality of ideological hatreds, was
that at no point in the first seventeen years of the war did
conflict ever cease. There was no moment at which tempers
could cool, at which the emotions involved could become less
intense. The hatreds were continually fueled by relatively
minor incidents. What was worst, perhaps, was that all this
happened during a period of nominal peace. Actions that
during wartime would be routine seemed excessive and sometimes even treacherous in the context of what was supposed to
be peace. Both sides had to be constantly prepared for battle,

for warfare had never really ceased; but to the natural strain that such preparation produces would be added the unnatural strain of the legal duplicity of this preparation and of the restlessness and anxiety of waiting for the hidden war to become open. Both sides were in a constant, hyperactive state of preparedness. Old hatreds remained unchanged, and perhaps intensified through their intermittent outbreak in battle. But both sides were also in a state of terrible suspense, and of the fear that that awakens. This is the context of the third turning point of the war.

The Third Phase of the War

The third turning point (embodied in the Melian dialogue and the debates of book 6), during the sixteenth and seventeenth years of the war, had the most serious consequences of all. The third phase of the war, which it initiated, was characterized by the greatest activity and the cruellest fighting of the entire twenty-seven year period. This was the part of the war in which military actions assumed prime importance. The character of this third reorientation conditioned both the nature of the third phase of the war and the manner in which Thucydides has written his account of it. By examining what this turning point turned *toward*, we can explain why the final phase was so bitter and its military events so important.

Let us examine first the origins of this third turning point and then consider what the shape of the new orientation was. The conditions out of which this reorientation arose were the feelings of fear and anticipation generated by the Peace of Nicias and certain material circumstances which were both results and reinforcements of these feelings. Athens had come to the Peace of Nicias relatively demoralized, or at least feeling vulnerable and insecure (the result of their steady series of reversals that began with their withdrawal from Sicily in 424). They had not, however, suffered any decisive defeat. So, although the Athenians themselves may have felt insecure about their capabilities in the tenth year, their outward appearance remained as formidable as it had been at the moments of their greatest confidence and military extent in, say, years seven and eight. The image of Athens that the Peloponnesians perceived, therefore, was unchanged. Athens appeared as aggressive and as potentially expansionist as it had been at any moment during the period before the Peace. And not only did the Peloponnesians have to endure the sight of an already worrisome enemy, they had to endure the sight of an addition to it: the Athenian alliance with Argos that was concluded during the Peace of Nicias. As it turned out, Argos was a rather ineffective military power, but this was to be seen only later, and during the Peace Argos was the city Sparta feared most after Athens because of its wealth and traditional hostility. These two cities had become allied in a patently democratic alliance against the Peloponnesian oligarchies, and, moreover, had been able to persuade other Peloponnesian democracies to join them in this homogeneous military-political bloc. Athens, then, had become to Peloponnesian eyes even stronger during the Peace, and its strength had been developed along clearly ideological lines.[18] In addition to these diplomatic changes, the Peloponnesians could see, by the time of this turning point, signals of reawakening Athenian interest in war and expansion in still relatively minor, yet clearly aggressive, incidents in the Peloponnese and in Sicily.

From the Athenian side, the image of its enemies caused equal anxiety. The Peace of Nicias had apparently dissolved the Peloponnesian alliance (for roughly the first half of the Peace, Corinth and the Boeotian states were diplomatically at odds with Sparta), ending thereby any immediate threat to Athens. But the events which occurred during the Peace, although each was apparently particular and unrelated to the others, served in fact to drive the old allies back together in opposition to Athens. The length of the Peace is critical to our perception of the Athenian change in attitude. During a period of six years, a large number of events occurred, none of them a part of any apparent plan or design by either side. Out of this confused mass of genuinely discrete events (spread over a long period of time), the two original blocs were re-formed. The appearance this created—on both sides—was of a certain inevitability which drew the two sides again into conflict. To the Athenians, too, the newly reconstituted Peloponnesian alliance had a definitely ideological shape. It was composed of oligarchies which had tried throughout the Peace to overthrow democracies in all parts of Greece.

To the anxiety caused by these diplomatic perceptions must also be added a special Athenian fear bred of the belief that all other states in Greece were their enemies. We see the origin of this belief in the seventh year of the war, when, with Athens at its greatest extent, it seemed suddenly to find new dangers everywhere it turned.[19] It had been this belief in universal opposition and danger, combined with a few military defeats, that demoralized the Athenians and persuaded them to accept the Peace of Nicias. Now again, during the Peace, the Athenians saw their actions driving other states into resistance, and again they felt themselves surrounded by enemies.

To these particular fears and attitudes must be added the general anxiety impending over both sides that the war would begin again soon, and the stresses generated by the feeling that one had to be prepared for this war when it came. It was in this atmosphere that the third reorientation of the war took place. This reorientation did not change the interpretation of the grounds of hostility. These remained ideological. What changed were the interpretation of the stakes involved and the reasons for continuing. At this turning point the war became what we would call a total war, and both sides came to believe that it was a war of survival.

Increasing the stakes had a complicated effect on the ideological interpretation of the war. Through some processes it could lead to "purer" and more intense ideological perceptions and responses. The increased use of racial explanations in this phase of the war is no departure from ideology; rather, it is a search for an ideological explanation that is more abstract, simpler, and more emotionally charged. Similarly, in the actions of the Athenian navy in 411 (8.75-76), following the temporary dissolution of the democracy in Athens, we can perceive an extraordinarily pure form of political ideology. The navy in effect claims that it—not the geographical site—is the true city of Athens. The physical city is to be dealt with as if it were an ally that had revolted. Underlying these striking and powerful new judgments is the principle that a city is constituted and recognized not so much by it material existence in a specific physical location as by its ideological position and beliefs.

But although the grounds of opposition between the Athenians and the Peloponnesians remained ideological, the change of orientation to the belief in a total war sometimes had the effect of attenuating the specifically ideological content of deliberations. Particular ideological appeals would sometimes lose efficacy in the face of more generalized appeals to the concept of total war or the necessity of continuous struggle. As I have suggested in the section of chapter 3 concerned with the Camarina debate, Athenian thinking about the war became peculiarly abstract. Concrete expressions of danger or of policy lost their "attractiveness" or rhetorical success to more abstract ones. Consequently, concrete statements of ideological dangers or of policies suggested by ideological considerations were sometimes ignored in favor of much more abstract statements which took off from the ideological base but which generalized this into philosophies of continual conflict. Thus, clearly marking the change from the second to the third phase of the war, Nicias' concrete appeal to postpone the Sicilian expedition in order to deal with the immediate ideological enemy, Sparta (6.11.7), fell on deaf ears when confronted with Alcibiades' abstract formulation that without constant struggle Athens would decay (6.18.6). And, in fact, when faced with the necessity of continuing the war under what they felt were the most dangerous conditions up to that time, in 412 the Athenians were even willing to end the democracy if it would be possible to continue the war thereby (8.53.3-54.1). (Yet this dissolution is also the occasion of the navy reasserting the ideological basis of the war. Both responses could result from the new orientation of the war.)

On both sides, however the content of the conflict was viewed on specific occasions, there was an intensification of hostility and of the fears appropriate to this. Both sides came to believe that the war would now have to be fought to its final end, that the grounds of the war were wholly irreconcilable, and that, therefore, the consequence of defeat was annihilation. With this change deliberate policies began to disappear, and the only conclusions that could be conceived were total victory and unconditional surrender.

There were three general consequences of this deepening hatred and this belief that the war was one of survival. All were terrible in certain ways. First, the war came to encompass all the cities of Greece. As cities came to consider the war a war of survival, there could no longer be any question of standing aloof from the struggle. Neutrality disappeared as a choice.[20] Second, the actions on both sides became more brutal and cruel. This was the result of believing that anything might be thinkable or necessary with survival at stake. It was also the result of the new emotional intensity of the war, as revenge became an acceptable political principle. Moreover, with every middle ground between the combatants eliminated, mercy served no further purpose. Persuasion and good-will were seen as luxuries for which neither side felt it had the need or the opportunity. Third, deliberation was replaced by simple re-action.[21] This third change, though no more terrible in its consequences than the other two, is worthy of separate consideration, for it forms a part of the general development of this war, and influences the shape of Thucydides' account.

In Thucydides' portrayal of political processes and of the relation of thought to action, this turning point brings about the gravest condition of political rhetoric and deliberation during the war. When nothing less than survival is at stake, and when the differences between states are conceived of as utterly irrevocable, rhetoric and deliberation lose both their utility and their place in the political process. This happens in two ways: internationally, there is no place for deliberation, for nothing that could be said would change the implacability of one's opponents; within a nation, deliberation has no usefulness, for on the one hand there are no better or worse courses among which to choose—everything can and must be tried—and on the other hand, one's actions are believed to be forced by the enemy. If the one side acts in a certain way, the other feels it must *necessarily* act to counter the initial action. Freedom of choice and deliberation are replaced by a kind of involuntary reflex based on fear. In these moments nations become slaves to circumstance. The most arresting statement of this condition is given by the Athenian, Euphemus, in the last debate of the history, when this final reorientation reaches its completion:

> But to a tyrant or to a city which possesses an empire, nothing is illogical that is profitable, nor can anything be one's own that is not trustworthy. In each particular case, enemy or friend it must be as the occasion demands. [6.85.1]

> For we say we rule [cities] over there so that we be not subject to another; and we liberate some there so that we be not injured by them; and we are compelled to do many things because we are on our guard against many things. . . . [6.87.2]

Athens had been named a tyrant before, but never in the sense Euphemus meant to imply. When the Corinthians called Athens a tyrant city at the second Spartan congress, they meant only that its rule was arbitrary and unlawful as a tyrant's. What they meant was in keeping with their earlier characterization of Athens: that its empire was illegal and that its desires were unlimited. When Pericles and Cleon called Athens a tyrant city, all that they meant was that it had to exercise its control over its allies by force, and that it could expect no gratitude or even sympathy from those it subjugated. But Euphemus' meaning of tyrant here is quite different, and almost pathetic. Euphemus meant that Athens was like a tyrant in a sense we later find echoed by Plato. A tyrant has no friends, only enemies. And because he is surrounded by enemies, a tyrant in fact has no freedom, as paradoxical as this at first may seem.[22] All of his energy is spent in dealing with necessities: satisfying internal needs to avoid coming apart at the seams, fending off external dangers in order to stay alive. All of his actions are taken in response to others', and he has no opportunity to initiate actions of his own. As Plato's character of the tyrant was opposite to the conventional usage of the term, so, too, is Euphemus' the opposite of the Corinthians'. Both Plato and Euphemus ring the same change on the same word. The Corinthians, using the word in its customary sense, say a tyrant is arbitrary because he is unfettered by law, and therefore can do whatever he wants; Euphemus (and later Plato) knows that a tyrant is arbitrary because he has no autonomous choice, and in fact can do nothing that he really wants. Euphemus' meaning of Athens' tyranny is as appropriate to the character of this third phase of the war (in which all the cities felt that they acted only on compulsion) as the Corinthian, Periclean, and Cleonic uses were to the first.

The meaning Euphemus gives to tyranny is characteristic of more than Athens alone in this last phase of the war. Both sides believed that their responses were determined by what their enemies did, and both sides felt that they had lost the opportunity to choose their own courses. As we have noted in the section of chapter 3 on the debate at Camarina, at this moment, for the first time, racial explanations were given of the war. This war was not racial, as we have said above, but the racial explanation was emblematic both of the feeling of the irreconcilability of the opposition and of the depth of hatred which this generated. A racial explanation is a kind of ideological explanation, but one of a special kind. Race is a symbolic and abstract distinction, and is therefore a kind of ideology. But it is an ideology that no one can change merely by choice. A racial explanation is appropriate, then, when one wants to indicate the irreconcilability of the opposed positions, as indeed was the tendency during this third phase of the war.

Because his history is incomplete, any statement about the treatment Thucydides might have given to those parts of the war left unrecorded is necessarily speculative. Yet that the war reached the state it did with this third reorientation suggests some hypotheses about Thucydides' plans for his account of the remainder of the war, and also some explanations of his practices in the later books of the history. Once nations come to believe that their differences are unalterably hostile, that the only resolution can be victory or defeat, and that their only possibilities of action are direct reactions to their enemies' moves, and if such a war is carried out to its conclusion (with no events or accidents intervening to compel a reconsideration of this position), then in fact no further change in men's attitudes or orientations is possible. When positions become as rigid as this, there are two direct consequences: strategy is replaced by tactics, and deliberation disappears.

These consequences will explain the character of the concluding books of Thucydides' history and also the character of the war they describe. The absence of speeches from book 8 of the history—usually attributed to its unfinished state—might well be deliberate rather than accidental when considered in the light of the new shape of the war. When the positions of the combatants came to be drawn as radically as we have seen, nothing but the result of military encounters remained to decide what was to happen in the war. This would explain both the increased military activity of both sides and Thucydides' exclusion of speeches in the composition of his account. Surely speeches were given continually throughout the last ten years of the war. But no speech would be able to elaborate or qualify the historical process Thucydides describes. Once one comes to believe that the war is a life-or-death struggle, and that there is no middle ground of compromise or even rest, then all the historian can do is describe the outcome of that struggle. Military options naturally remain (though even they undergo limitation in one critical way), but as long as conviction of the totality of war is firm, there is no option other than commitment to the military solution. This commitment perhaps even encourages the search for novel and more numerous military avenues, yet even here a limit is imposed: all the avenues remain essentially tactical exercises. Once it is decided that all one's actions are determined by the actions of one's enemy, the historian cannot even describe strategy, for strategy presupposes the possibility of choice and design, and these are excluded by the belief that one's responses are determined. Without freedom of maneuver in the realm of deliberation, speeches become useless to the actors and useless as well to the historian. All that remains for him to describe are the battles. The moment at which these conditions are met is found at the end of book 6, with the resumption of the war. Significantly, book 7 contains no *political* speeches, although no one denies that book 7 is in its finished form.[23] Although such a conclusion is necessarily speculative, I believe that the reason book 8 has no speeches is the same as the reason for book 7: the character of the war, not its lack of revision. And I believe that Thucydides would have shown this orientation of the war in operation continuously until the end of the war, when, of course, the Athenian defeat would require one final reorientation to bring the combatants from war to peace.

On the Peloponnesian side, this final turning point involved little change in interpretation or attitude. Even in the second phase of the war the Peloponnesians had described Atticism as unalterably hostile to their own way of life. Nothing in the intervening years would have changed this attitude. All that characterized their new orientation in this last phase was a hardening of their position and a deepening of their antagonism and their fear. On the Athenian side a rather greater change had to occur to make possible the development of the belief that survival itself was at stake. It is this shift that we have seen in stages, first in the increase of fear and the erosion of the middle ground in the Melian dialogue, and then in the transference of these fears to fear for the very survival of Athens in the debate on the Sicilian expedition. It is because this third phase involved a greater Athenian than a Peloponnesian change that most of the speeches recorded during this turning point are Athenian.

It is hard to characterize this period of war beyond saying that as the stakes were increased and with them the fears on both sides, so was the tempo of activity increased, and beyond saying that the actions taken were crueller and the conflict more bitter. The reason for the difficulty of making a clear and consistent characterization is that when the war came to be seen as one of survival, any action became conceivable as every action was felt necessary. Actions appear both as automatic responses and as gratuitous or unexpected. It was a period of simple revenge, against the Melians, against the Athenian hostages in Sicily. It was a period in which alliances were made which normally would make the nations involved uncomfortable: of Sparta with Persia,[24] of Athens with Persia, even of cities in Ionia with Persia. Actions were taken by both sides which were entirely at odds with their customary behavior: Sparta was willing to rely solely on the Peloponnesian navy, Athens was willing at different times to end the democracy or to move it to Samos, if either would mean victory. As the participants came to feel they had no freedom to choose their courses, so did the actions of this part of the war become random, unpredictable, and without a definite character. At the same time, the fear each side had drove it into more and more desperate or extreme measures. The war was not really directed by either side in this last phase; the course it followed was governed solely by the circumstances of the military engagements.

The most serious consequence of the third turning, and most characteristic of it, was the prolongation of the war. No one, at its beginning, foresaw a war of twenty-seven years (or, even if we except the period of peace, of two stages each ten years long). Of course, once the war was thought of as a life-or-death matter, it had to be fought to its conclusion. But this reorientation was also the source of energies and willpower which served to postpone that conclusion and to drag the war out even longer. On the Peloponnesian side the new interpretation assisted in making possible for the first time the composition of a truly vast united front (whose dependence on this interpretation can be seen in the fact that it endured only until the end of this war), comprising Sicily, Persia, and the rebellious allies of Athens in addition to the original Peloponnesian powers. Without this new, enlarged alliance the last phase of the war could not have lasted ten years, for purely Peloponnesian resources at this time were no greater than at the beginning of the war, and even with the Sicilian defeat Athens was still wealthy. From the record of their engagements in these last ten years it is very doubtful whether the Peloponnesians could have conducted such a protracted war without the access of money and materiel from Sicily and Persia.

On the Athenian side the reorientation helped to prolong their resistance, even after the crushing blow at Syracuse, in two ways. In respect of materiel, they too were aided by alliance, having been able to call at least in part on the resources of the Argives. But it was in a psychological fashion that the new interpretation most supported their resistance. With the third turning point, the war became for the Athenians a struggle both for Athens' existence and for the existence of its democracy. In the second phase, the war had been seen as a conflict of ideological forms, but it was only in this last phase that the Athenians saw as real the possibility of the abolition of the democracy. It was the depth of Athenian involvement in the democracy and the fear of its disappearance which served, in an unexpected way, to spur the Athenians into continuing the struggle.

Even before the defeat at Syracuse, Athens had been disturbed by internal political conflict. Athenian fear or paranoia with respect to the international situation began to manifest itself in internal suspicion and near-hysteria (6.53.2-3, 6.60.1-5, 6.61.2-3). With the Sicilian disaster, open class warfare erupted in Athens, and the political situation there was marked by almost complete disorder. But the *stasis* which occurred, and which usually had the effect of paralyzing foreign and military policy in a city, had the opposite effect on the Athenians. Since the war had become, for them, the final struggle of the democracy against its political enemies, the very outbreak of *stasis* itself was a confirmation of the necessity of continuing the war: every attempt by oligarchs to overthrow the democracy provided a goad which encouraged the Athenians in their resistance. In these last ten years Athens fed off its factional warfare, and found in it the confirmation of the necessity for continuing, and the will to continue, the war.

This, I believe, in its broadest outlines was the story Thucydides meant to tell of the origins of the Peloponnesian War, of the developing shape and meaning of the war, and of the sources of those developments. I have slighted the military events of his history because of limitation of space, but also from choice. As I have said earlier, in themselves the physical actions of the war would teach us little. In their relations to the thoughts and passions of the men who fought this war (their relations both as causes of thought and as the execution of policy), however, even their accidents have significance for us. This is how, I believe, Thucydides composed and constructed his history: as a history primarily of the political processes of the participants, marked by three great stages of attitude which impress their characters on the events which follow them. The history is at once a history of the particular events which depended on these three orientations, and a history of the general process of thought and action which brought the participants from one interpretation to another and from the range of actions characteristic of the beginning of the war to that of the end. It is a history both of what was done and of the processes of thought which informed what was done.

Part Two

The Nature of Thucydides' History

5 Principles and Historical Understanding

Although we have now accomplished the determination of Thucydides' interpretation of the Peloponnesian War, our general investigation of the nature of his history is only partially completed. There remains a further inquiry to be undertaken, toward which Thucydides' own words direct us. His history is intended as a possession for all time, he tells us at 1.22.4, something useful to those who wish to understand the true and constant origin of human action. As such a possession, with such a purpose, its meaning must be found not only in the specific facts of the Peloponnesian War as Thucydides saw and developed them, but especially in an inquiry through these facts to truths about action and history of a more abstract nature and more general application. Since histories are written to manifest and explain events and their causes, the natures of histories vary as different conceptions of the nature of events are held by historians, for each historian chooses that character of historical writing which seems most appropriate to the character of the events which are the material of the writing. For this reason it is possible for us to work in the reverse direction: to use an examination of the character of the written history as a means of discovering the conceptions of action and event held by the writer and embodied in the composition.

It is this inquiry into the character or nature of Thucydides' history—no longer the examination of specific facts and interpretations of this war—which lies before us now. As the

speeches of the history have been crucial to our discovery of the facts and connections of fact, so are they also crucial to our determination of the history's character. No longer concentrating on the content or arrangement of the speeches, we must now examine the general practice Thucydides employs in his use of speeches in this history. Reflection on this practice— on the locations and purposes and relations of the speeches— enables us to articulate our first statement of the character of events as Thucydides conceives them.

The interpretation of the Peloponnesian War that we have seen established in the history is of a war directed throughout by the deliberate choices of the participants. At no moment have we seen the participants—as initiators of events—driven by forces outside of their control; rather, the only source of all events (though not, of course, necessarily of their issues) has been the conscious intent of the human agents. Fundamental to this interpretation of the war as something always within the direction of the human agents have been the speeches, both as the vehicle for the exhibition of the content of deliberations and also in another way, to manifest to us not the content but the fact of deliberation. Prior to their sophisticated employment in representing the content of political action, the speeches that Thucydides records are used in one role so simple and immediate that it is often overlooked. While all the events in the history (as distinguished from the events omitted from it) were, of course, significant to Thucydides, some can be said to be of primary significance and others to receive their significance through their dependence on these primary events. Perhaps the earliest responsibility of the historian is to decide upon and represent these priorities and dependencies, and Thucydides has brought the speeches immediately into play here. Insofar as the appearance of a speech in the midst of the narrative naturally calls attention to its occasion, Thucydides has used the speeches to locate and give emphasis to the events of primary significance.

In part 1 of this inquiry this role of marking events of primary significance did not need attention called to it, since the speeches themselves were the events of significance, and those events that followed were seen to be significant in their relation to the speeches and debates. But, returning to the history with our eyes on Thucydides' general practice in employing speeches, we can now discover other less obvious occasions on which the speeches have fulfilled the function of indicating events of preeminent significance. We will notice that every critical battle, whether on sea or land, is preceded by one or a pair of speeches by the commanders of the opposing forces. There is no circularity to our reasoning, for it is not by the presence of speeches alone that we know that these battles are the critical battles, but also by the amount of space that Thucydides gives them in his narrative and by their consequences for the participants. The speeches are not needed to make the battles important, the battles are important in their own right. Yet we can correctly say both that the speeches add emphasis and attract attention to the event, and also that by utilizing *speeches* for this purpose Thucydides simultaneously exhibits the deliberateness of the event. Generals' speeches on these occasions, as de Romilly has pointed out,[1] provide us with the intentions of the commanders, and enable us to understand the battle that follows as an attempt at the execution of these intentions. Within the purposive and deliberate framework the speeches establish, the confused motion of the two armies acquires intelligibility, and even nonmaterial factors and chance itself are understood in their proper consequentiality as they reinforce or obstruct the intended operations. The generals' speeches, then, enable us to see the battle as more than the collision of two masses. We can see even battles (fortuitous as their unfolding may be) as deliberate actions whose shape is the result of planning and choice. Speeches mark the critical battles because for those battles Thucydides felt it important that we understand the deliberation and choice that preceded them.

In this respect Thucydides is consistent in his employment of speeches, whether they merely accompany other events (as with battles) or are themselves the event (in the articulation of policies). They mark important events because insofar as the event is important Thucydides wants its deliberateness understood. An example of one such event is the decision to undertake the Sicilian expedition. That this decision was the turning point of the war would be certain even without the speeches given on its occasion. The consequences themselves would prove it to us. But the inclusion of the debate on the occasion demonstrates something else. It shows us how entirely aware of the dangers they undertook the Athenians were. (Or, it might be more properly said, how much effort they put into paying no attention to the specific dangers mentioned by Nicias.) Even as the expedition turned into a disaster, it is clear it was no unwitting disaster; the Athenians passionately desired this campaign, even to the extent of reinforcing it at the very moment they should have been reducing it. The record of the debate enables us to discover the strength of this desire, and also to discover how definite and strange an idea of the political necessities of their city the Athenians had to have in order to have come to this decision. A necessary condition for our ability later to understand the unwillingness of the Athenians to cut their losses in Sicily while it was still possible to do so is that we be able to recognize both the deliberateness of the event and its unusual political and psychological grounds. Nicias' fear, the army's hesitation to press him, and the assembly's willingness to shore up the expedition are all explained, at least in part, by the earnestness with which the Athenians originally decided for the expedition, and this deliberateness is made accessible to us through the speeches Thucydides records.

So consistent is Thucydides in this practice that we can discover two occasions for which speeches have been provided although no action occurred. On these two occasions inaction turned out to be the significant, if obscure, event, for which, therefore, Thucydides felt it important to exhibit the deliberation (that is, that the inaction was deliberate). The first of these is the short speech of Teutiaplus (3.30) proposing a counterattack on the Athenian forces at Mytilene. No counterattack was undertaken. Alcidas, the Spartan commander of the Peloponnesian fleet in Ionia, preferred to return home without running such a risk. As nothing happened, had Thucydides omitted this short speech, we would not even be aware that there had been any event, any rejection of an untried alternative. With the record of the speech we see the Peloponnesian retirement as a deliberate action. Inasmuch as a counterattack on the Athenians might have had serious consequences, the decision not to attack is of consequence, and so Thucydides is careful to present it to us as a decision. Insofar as we can see it as deliberate, the decision also reveals certain Peloponnesian—or at least Spartan—attitudes at this time. Alcidas' decision reflects a characteristic Spartan diffidence toward unauthorized military actions and probably a specific Peloponnesian timidity about naval confrontations with the Athenians—this timidity the result of the Spartan estimation of Athenian naval prowess following Phormio's victory in the Gulf of Corinth. It is worth emphasizing that these attitudes are accessible for our consideration *only* because Thucydides included Teutiaplus' speech which enabled us to see that a decision (which reflects attitudes) was taken.[2]

The second of these occasions at which a speech is given although no new pattern of action is evident is the Spartan peace offer in the seventh year of the war (4.17–20). There had been active warfare up to the moment of this speech, and after the speech active warfare resumed. Had the speech not been included, once again it would appear that no event had occurred. Thucydides, however, recorded the speech, and by doing so exhibited that the continuation of the war from this moment was in fact a matter of conscious choice by the Athenians. In seeing this moment of choice we are again able to make assessments of the attitudes and intentions of the participants, and to perceive continuities and changes. But, again, we are able to do so only because Thucydides has been at pains to make clear that a deliberate choice had taken place.

If recording a speech on a given occasion calls attention to it as a moment of deliberate action, the content of the speeches recorded naturally provides us with information about the subject of the deliberation and the intentions of the deliberators. Bearing this in mind, we can now make an initial characterization of the nature of Thucydides' history. We can reasonably assert that Thucydides provides us, throughout the history, with that evidence necessary for our understanding of the war as an event under the continuously deliberate direction of the participants. Speeches are recorded to make clear that deliberation occurred to direct the war, and also to exhibit what the results of the deliberations were. Even where chance intervenes to frustrate the original intentions of the agents, Thucydides stresses the deliberateness of the war by presenting us (1) an original picture of human deliberation under the influence of chance and (2) a subsequent picture of humans again deliberating in an attempt to deal with the unexpected issues of their original deliberation.

Yet no sooner have we said this than something in the very nature of such a history, and something in the actual practice of Thucydides' history push us to revise and go beyond this first formulation. It is in the nature of such a "deliberate" history to have a serious shortcoming. While exhibiting the deliberateness that lies behind and informs events restores to events a certain human dimension, events do not thereby necessarily become entirely comprehensible, even on the simply human plane. Inevitably there will appear certain choices made by states that, although we are able to see well enough that they were deliberate, will remain incomprehensible by virtue of their unexpectedness, perversity, or plain stupidity. The Peloponnesian War had its fair share of these. Why did Athens continue the war at the height of the plague? After the Sicilian disaster? Why did Athens reject the Spartan peace offer of the seventh year? Why did Athens undertake the Sicilian expedition? Such questions as these might remain opaque to us even if we saw the war in terms of its direction by human deliberation, for while the answers to these questions may be found in the circumstances and activity of deliberating, they are often not to be found in the deliberate policy per se. Had Thucydides limited his history merely to the demonstration of the war's deliberateness, we would feel the history inadequate on many occasions.

That Thucydides did not so limit the history is indicated by his practice in recording speeches. We must begin by recognizing that to the extent that deliberation is an act of reason, the fact (and content) of deliberation is relatively easily represented. One exhibits it by exhibiting the goals that are desired, the means proposed for their accomplishment, and the reasons adduced in support of them. To do this does not require reporting the entire speech given on the occasion of the decision; excerpts from the speech will be easily sufficient. Indeed, we have composed a history very like this in the first four chapters, and in making known the deliberations and their contents have required nothing more than excerpted citations from the speeches Thucydides records.

To say this brings to our attention the peculiarity of Thucydides' employment of speeches. When we excerpt the rational arguments from the speeches in the history we leave behind a residuum that does not, apparently, have any direct relevance to a history of the rational element of the deliberations that caused events. In fact, Thucydides did not report merely those arguments by which ends and means were proposed and judged. In the composition of his history an attempt has been made to preserve the experience of the original speech as an integral whole, as a piece of public rhetoric with beginning, middle, and end, mixing rational with emotive appeal, yet rational as a whole insofar as constructed by art for the purpose of persuasion. Thucydides does not limit himself to excerpts of speeches, and thus indicates that the understanding of events must be found in explanations more complex than the mere deliberateness of their origin. The peculiarity of his recomposition of whole (if abbreviated) speeches is related to the natural deficiency of ''deliberate'' history as solution to problem. Embodied in Thucydides' use of whole speeches is his judgment on the character of events, and, therefore, on the character of the explanation that must be given of them.

Our inquiry is, in fact, a search for the principles of Thucydides' history, principles which—despite the particularity that distinguishes history from the abstraction and universality of science and philosophy—exercise as strict and formative an influence over the composition of the history as principles in scientific or philosophical researches. The relation of principles to inquiry in history is perhaps more complex or more concealed than it is in abstract inquiries. It could hardly be otherwise, given the fundamentally greater complexity of the phenomena of human action when compared to the phenomena of science, and given the necessary dependence of history on concrete and particular actions (which in their concrete actuality embody the effects of accident as well as principle) rather than on universal and abstracted forms of action. Nevertheless, as historians select what they believe to be their relevant material and data not haphazardly but systematically, so, necessarily, are these selections (and the equally deliberate and systematic treatments given them) informed and directed by principle. That the concrete events and descriptions of histories embody principles which are understood through the events is the ground of that more general understanding which history provides; that the concreteness of history renders the discovery of these principles more difficult is true, yet is also a guarantee of the appropriateness and (in an existential sense) the validity of these principles.

The discrimination of the principles of a history (and the determination of its character as a history) is difficult primarily because of the difficulty and complexity of the subject matter. While historians and philosophers or critics of history sometimes take the lack of consensus among historians as to the nature of action and history as evidence that history is no science, a more proper and sympathetic evaluation of this evidence would conclude that the lack of consensus merely indicates that the jury is still out. The actions of human beings (leaving aside for a moment the actions of their sophisticated and recalcitrant instruments, such as cultures, nations, and other institutions) are so much more complicated than the actions of atoms that, when one considers how relatively recent it is that the physical sciences have reached anything like a consensus on principles, it is not even discouraging—and certainly not surprising—that no consensus has yet been reached.[3]

Because of the complexity of human action as a phenomenon for study, the disciplines which consider it are many, corresponding to different aspects of it. Each of these disciplines (the social sciences generally, and also many of the humanistic fields) possesses its own proper principles, each makes a special aspect of the phenomenon, action, the object of its study and the subject about which significant assertions can be made. Indeed, within each discipline there exist competing schools of thought, and each school works from principles slightly (or radically) different from the others, and therefore delimits the field of study differently, gathers different evidence, and makes different assertions. Any of these disciplines, any of the schools within these disciplines could inform and direct the composition of a history. As each did so, it would look at specific actions from standpoints different from those of the other disciplines; action, indeed, would appear a phenomenon of a quite different sort from one discipline to another. Each discipline would likewise direct the accumulation of evidence proper to its principles (and different thereby from evidence relevant to another discipline), and would direct and warrant conclusions as to relation, cause, and meaning proper to these same principles. Each history as written, then, would contain facts and interpretations proper to a given discipline, but quite different in appearance from those of a history directed by another discipline.

Were this all, determining the character of a history would be difficult enough. But that it is in fact even harder is due to the recognition by historians of the very complexity of human action and to their efforts to deal adequately with it. Historians take deserved pride in their ability to give accounts of events more rounded and complete than those possible through reliance on the principles of any single discipline, accounts which are therefore more adequate reflections of the actual complexity of action. In constructing these accounts historians make systematic borrowings of principles and methods from the individual disciplines. They constitute, thereby, new historical disciplines based on the sophisticated weighting of different abstract conceptions of forces in action, and the combination of these forces into a complex and not easily articulable network of influences on and explanations of concrete events. Given the large number of existing special disciplines concerned with action and the lack of any single science to dictate in what proportion the forces they study should be mixed to replicate the influences that do occur in action, the intelligent and systematic weaving together of principles from the disciplines ought to be susceptible of almost limitless variation.[4]

With no science to direct the constitution of such a system of principles and influences, success in doing so—indicated by a perceived adequacy of the explanation to our existential awareness of the complexity of events—becomes very much a matter of prudence. In fact, the constitution of a system of principles for the understanding of the influences on action would be the knowledge (or science) called prudence if it were directed to action rather than to inquiry. The relation of history to prudence establishes the ground of the utility of history and also explains some of the peculiarities of historical understanding. It is because of its relation to prudence that we feel that history has something to teach us. For the nonspecialist, and for the specialist, too, at the end of his researches, the past is believed to be significant for our actions in the present. But the past per se is no more significant to the present than the present is. Both are ambiguous and require interpretation. It is *histories* of the past that have significance: not because of the facts about the past that they present, but because the presentation of those facts is simultaneously a presentation of the group of factors (as distinct from individual facts—though embodied in the facts) that the historian believes influence events. And as these are the factors which influenced the past, so are they generically the factors which must be understood in order to understand, or to act prudently in, the present. That is, when a historian presents an event and whatever he feels is necessary for the proper understanding of that event, he has presented what he feels constituted the causes (specifically) of that event. The genera of these individual causes are the universal causes of any events of that sort, and a prudent act, therefore, would require (at whatever moment it was undertaken) a consideration and understanding of those generic causes or influences (in order to discover their momentary specific manifestations).

In this respect the variety (actual and potential) of histories is an advantage for our understanding. As each history differs in its choice and combination of principles, so it reveals and throws emphasis on different aspects of actions and of situations calling for action. As we find the explanations of histories persuasive, or at least reasonable, we bring ourselves to recognize the efficacy of these different factors and we learn to be attentive to them. Reading a variety of histories provides us with enlarged ''vocabularies'' of possible factors of action, and with alternative ''syntaxes'' of these factors. Insofar as the existence of such a great variety of histories and principles of history testifies to a lack of agreement about the science of history, the provision of extended vocabularies and syntaxes of principles would itself seem a prudent course of action.

There is one other aspect of the relation of history to prudence to be considered. It is not altogether necessary to be explicit about the principles which direct one's history. That is, as prudence is learned from experience and has its only application in other concrete acts of experience, so, in a sense, the best explanation of the principles of history is produced by the embodiment of these principles in a specific history, rather than in an abstract treatise on action. Indeed, it is not only possible, but even a frequent occurrence, that a historian who has no intention of writing any such abstract treatise, who even denies having any systematic set of principles can and does write a history of compelling explanatory power. We must make no mistake. It is the historian's possession of a certain set of principles that has dictated the appropriate selection and presentation of materials in the history. (Or, put another way, the historian's systematic consideration of certain kinds of evidence, and consistent provision of explanations and interpretations of a certain sort gathered from this evidence are themselves proof that the historian's practice is directed by principles, whether they are articulated or not.) Indeed, the relation of principle to history sometimes passes unnoticed by the principal; the writing of history is sometimes believed to be simply a knack, or the fruit of experience, or perhaps an art. It is believed to be thus for the same reasons that cause prudent people, when they are asked how it is that they act so successfully, to give almost identical responses. The prudent person's, and the historian's, skill in dealing with the concrete particulars of experience obscures the existence and operation of the principles and knowledge that inform it. But the principles are there, latent in the action or the history, and that they are means that the writing of history renders accessible to us the useful knowledge of many experienced and prudent persons who would not be likely to deal abstractly with their theories of action, but who do write history. Although unabstracted, their "theories" are not lost.

Finally, the relations of principles to history and of prudence to history suggest the reasons we would desire to make an articulation of the principles of a history, and also the benefits we can rationally propose as the goals of this articulation. There are three reasons, and three coordinate benefits. First, although the principles of prudence and history are said—and seen—to operate most properly in the concrete particulars of action, they are not best understood there. The very concreteness of actions renders their principles obscure and ambiguous. It is this that accounts for both the difficulty of prudent action and the necessity of histories for the interpretation of the past. We do not understand or learn concrete particulars. For this reason, our understanding of those general truths a given history may provide (in addition to specific facts of particular events in the past) can only be aided and augmented by an articulation of its principles removed from the concrete details of past experience.

Second, insofar as principles are adapted to specific subject matters and respond to specific problems connected with them, the principles of an inquiry provide trustworthy and proper answers only to those questions proper to the principles and the aspects of the subject matter to which they are directed. This is as true in historical researches as in any others. As a consequence, however, we must realize that different histories of the same event will provide different information about it (corresponding to their different principles), and that the proper use of histories demands our prior determination of which questions they answer and which not, so that we may make use of their strengths and not blame them for omissions which can be judged weaknesses only from the standpoint of principles different from their own. Again, the discrimination and articulation of the principles of a history will bring as well the determination of the subject matter, problems, and questions appropriate to these principles, and will therefore make possible and secure the proper and fruitful use of the history.

Third, although the potential for combinations of principles from various disciplines seems theoretically limitless, it is not the case—as is sometimes asserted—that as long as a historian works honestly and diligently within his chosen principles, his history will be the equal of every other in its propriety and significance. Not all persons are equally prudent. Similarly, not all choices of principle are equally prudently directed. Some historians are, with respect to understanding rather than action, more "prudent" than other historians. We recognize that their accounts of events are sensibly closer to our notions of the ways in which events come to occur than other accounts. The separation of the histories whose prudence makes them superior sources of both particular[5] and general truths from those whose results seem nowhere near as adequate (though their fidelity to their principles cannot be faulted) is obviously an important task in the critical reading of history. At the base of this distinction is the evaluation of the principles of the histories. All principles—all mixtures of principles—are not equal. They vary in value in relation to the prudence of the historian who has chosen them. Insofar as principles are obscured in their embodiment in concrete events, the abstract articulation of the principles renders their evaluation easier and surer, and the opportunity to consider and weigh the value of the principles of the history comprises the third goal of this undertaking. With these goals in mind, the remainder of this essay will be concerned with the discovery and an evaluation of the principles of Thucydides' history.

The determination of the principles would be a much more difficult job had Thucydides not made a direct and explicit statement about them. When he states, at 1.22.4, that his history will be judged useful by those who wish to understand what has happened and what will happen—of the same sort or much like it—"on account of the human thing" ($\kappa\alpha\tau\grave{\alpha}\ \tau\grave{o}\ \grave{\alpha}\nu\theta\rho\acute{\omega}\pi\iota\nu o\nu$ [v.l. $\grave{\alpha}\nu\theta\rho\acute{\omega}\pi\epsilon\iota o\nu$]), he gives us his judgment of the underlying cause of events, and, therefore, also of the proper material of history. For, whatever meaning we decide to assign to $\tau\grave{o}\ \grave{\alpha}\nu\theta\rho\acute{\omega}\pi\iota\nu o\nu$ (a question which will be the subject of this inquiry), it is certain that $\tau\grave{o}\ \grave{\alpha}\nu\theta\rho\acute{\omega}\pi\iota\nu o\nu$ performs precisely the role we recognize as the principle of the history. According to Thucydides, it is $\tau\grave{o}\ \grave{\alpha}\nu\theta\rho\acute{\omega}\pi\iota\nu o\nu$ which accounts for the predictable occurrence of events of a determinate sort ("of this kind or much like it"). Inasmuch as Thucydides is not here speaking of specific causes of particular events, but of the operating causes considered in their most general description, he is naming what we mean by the principle of a history.

Further, as the cause of events of a certain sort, τὸ ἀνθρώ-πινον also necessarily serves as the principle of the composition of the history. Events must find their explanation in the exhibition of their causes, and the material of this history is to be found in the facts and events which display the cause (τὸ ἀνθρώπινον) and render it comprehensible.

Unfortunately, if Thucydides has been explicit in naming the principle of his history, he has not been explicit in indicating the meaning of the term τὸ ἀνθρώπινον. Although most frequently translated as "human nature," the term literally means "the human thing," and there are in fact good reasons for exercising caution in assigning a content to it. The term is peculiarly abstract, and though Thucydides does indeed exhibit a stylistic tendency to prefer abstractions to more concrete or familiar nouns, this instance is most likely not an example of it. The most straightforward way to refer to human nature, in Greek, would be to construct the phrase literally: ἀνθρωπεία φύσις. In fact, Thucydides uses this phrase, too, elsewhere in the history, so that his avoidance of it at 1.22.4 is not a quirk of his personal style. By considering the cases in which Thucydides does speak of human nature (using the phrase ἀνθρωπεία φύσις), we can discover grounds for a systematic discrimination of τὸ ἀνθρώπινον from it, and reasons for Thucydides' choice of one or the other term under specific circumstances. The two terms, we find, are applied to quite different orders of phenomena.

Thucydides uses the words ἀνθρωπεία φύσις (or φύσις ἀνθρώπων) twice (and possibly three times) in propria persona. (The words—and also substantives made from the adjective, ἀνθρώπινον—are also used occasionally by speakers in the debates of the history. It is, however, not only prudent but essential that we initiate our examination of the words by considering only those uses which we can unequivocally attribute to Thucydides.) In both uses the Thucydidean meaning of "human nature" would seem to involve a direct reference to nature in its most concrete sense.

The first use, at 2.50.1 in his discussion of the plague in Athens, is ambiguous, but only within a range close to the literally natural or biological. Thucydides says that the plague was worse even than appeared by the accounts of it, and that it struck people "harder than human nature" (χαλεπωτέρως ἢ κατὰ τὴν ἀνθρωπείαν φύσιν). Whether this phrase means "beyond the capacity of human nature to endure" (Warner) or "being crueller even than human nature" (Hobbes' unorthodox but appealing translation), the meaning of ἀνθρωπεία φύσις can be referred to the specific biological content of our natures. If the former meaning is preferred, φύσις is directly and explicitly biological; if the latter, φύσις refers to the cruel and rapacious behavior that appetite and desire occasion, and that has its origin—with our appetites—in our biological nature.

Thucydides' second use of ἀνθρωπεία φύσις occurs during his discussion of the *stasis* at Corcyra. At 3.82.2 he says:

> And many and terrible were the things that happened in cities because of *stasis,* and are happening and will continue to happen, as long as human nature [φύσις ἀνθρώπων] is the same.[6]

In this instance (and in both instances connected with the *stasis,* should we accept 3.84) the meaning of "human nature" remains straightforward, as do the kinds of events of which it is the cause. Human nature is again conceived of as a particularly amoral (if not immoral), selfish, often cruel manner of acting attributable to appetite, and, therefore, ultimately to our animal or biological nature. In this discussion of the *staseis* at Corcyra and elsewhere, ἀνθρωπεία φύσις is identical in content to the second of the alternative interpretations of φύσις in the passage from the description of the plague. That Thomas Hobbes should have found Thucydides congenial enough to warrant translation is hardly surprising. The two share an almost identical view of the nature of mankind, of its motives, of the origin of those motives, and of the usual result when this nature is allowed a free rein to operate.[7]

This selfish, appetitive nature is, for Thucydides, the cause of crimes of all descriptions. When men act according to their real nature, they will commit any injustices or acts of violence against others to further their own ends—which ends are usually either their own safety or the appropriation of the possessions of others. But as one reflects on the actions which Thucydides attributes to this ἀνθρωπεία φύσις (especially in 3.81–82 and 3.84), the problem with considering this human nature the principle of the history becomes apparent, and so therefore does the desirability of a distinction between this ἀνθρωπεία φύσις and τὸ ἀνθρώπινον.

The actions which Thucydides says are the result of "human nature" (ἀνθρωπεία φύσις) are simply not the same, nor even generically the same, as the actions he says are the result of the "human thing" (τὸ ἀνθρώπινον). The actions which φύσις occasions are intensely *personal* actions, even if they are sometimes widespread. In the instance of the Corcyrean *stasis,* the actions Thucydides explains by "human nature" are crimes of person against person for gain or safety. But although the commission of these crimes occurred on an unprecedented scale, as crimes they retain their personal character. They are the actions of individuals motivated by personal fears and desires, and they are actions directed at another individual or individuals. But the events which constitute the material of Thucydides' history, the events of which it is the history, the events, therefore, of which τὸ ἀνθρώπινον is the cause and principle, are not individual actions at all. They are social actions, the actions of states vis-à-vis other states.

At this point we can draw what would appear to be the significant distinction between ἀνθρωπεία φύσις and τὸ ἀνθρώπινον. Thucydides, it seems, reserves the former phrase (human nature in the literal sense) for dealing with the actions and motives of individuals. The actions of individuals are seen as the result of a human nature closely derived from— as it only could be—our biological nature. This nature is ultimately physical. It can be controlled, occasionally at least, by other forces—such as the law—but only insofar as they too are physical forces or represent the threat of physical force. On the other hand, Thucydides attributes the actions of *nations* to τὸ ἀνθρώπινον. As a nation is not a biological entity, it cannot properly be said to have a physical nature; and as it exists in a secondary relation to the people who compose it, the human agency which moves it can be called human nature only metaphorically. That nations are moved by people is indubitable for Thucydides, but even while this human force is a regular force, it operates at one remove from the physical, or biological, nature of people. This, perhaps, explains Thucydides' use of the abstraction, τὸ ἀνθρώπινον, to indicate that this cause, although certainly human, is not directly "natural" in the concrete and proper sense.

To make this systematic discrimination of two different orders of phenomena caused and explained by two different human forces, as I believe Thucydides did, itself constitutes the taking of a specific philosophical position with respect to the nature and cause of action. To say that individual human actions are to be explained by causes proper to the individual, while social actions are to be explained by properly social causes may appear uncontroversial. It is, however, only one position among other alternatives, and in his representation of political reasoning during the war, Thucydides makes clear that quite a different position was taken by his contemporaries. It is, after all, possible to explain the actions of nations simply by the operation of a single human nature if the nation is considered to be merely a person on a large scale. Such an analogy of person and state has always had tremendous philosophical vitality. It is the primary instrument of inquiry in the *Republic;* it endures to Hobbes' *Leviathan;* no doubt it antedates the Peloponnesian War, and will remain vital long into the future. The analogy is always grounded in the proposition that states are composed of individuals, and therefore can exhibit only those same motives and causes that individuals possess. In this way, it becomes possible to extend the operation of our underlying biological nature to the explanation of social phenomena. It is this philosophical position that Thucydides represents as the common view of his time, and that he represents it as current throughout the war justifies our initial restriction to purely Thucydidean citations of the examination we made of the use of the term, ἀνθρωπεία φύσις. That is, as Thucydides' use of the term is not identical to the uses made of it by speakers in the debates, had we included those uses in our examination, we would have obscured the special meaning Thucydides has given to it.

There can be no doubt that his contemporaries (at least

those represented as speakers in the history) identified what we consider the human nature of individual humans as the cause also of social actions. The speech of the Athenians before the first Spartan congress provides the first instance of such an identification. When the speakers explain the actions of the Athenian state in acquiring its empire as motivated by fear, honor, and profit (1.75.3), they attribute to a nation a set of passions and desires whose only literal and direct reference is to individuals. Even more dramatic examples of this reduction of national action to the model of individual human nature can be found in the speeches of both Cleon and Diodotus during the debate on Mytilene. Although opposed in so many other respects, these two speakers accept—as though a well-known common assumption—that the passionate and appetitive nature of persons is also an appropriate characterization of the motives and ends of cities. In these cases the identification of individual with social causes is even more elaborate, as both speakers assign considerably more complex individual motivations and patterns of action to states than had been assigned in the speech at Sparta. Cleon speaks of arrogance and admiration as qualities of cities (3.39.4-5); Diodotus finds no incongruity in speaking of hope and desire as feelings held by a city (3.45.5), and in fact makes an explicit statement of the identity of person and city: "All things are made by nature to do wrong—both in the private and the public sphere—and there is no law which can restrain this" (3.45.3).

That this identification of public and private was constantly made (and we can find it also in the Athenian responses at Melos and in Alcibiades' speech on the Sicilian expedition) allows us to assume further that the identification was accepted as reasonable by the majority of Athenians. Speakers would not be so free with their use of it unless they expected it would be welcome to the hearers.[8] Nevertheless, although Thucydides presents this view of a single genus of cause for both individuals and nations as the predominant view of the period, and although the speakers presented hold a view of individual human nature quite close to his own as far as the dominance of passion over reason and the inevitable criminality of nature, there are strong reasons to conclude that Thucydides did not

share the common belief that the nature of individuals explained as well the actions of nations. We can find evidence for
Thucydides' distinction between the realms (and causes) of
individual and social actions in the historical practices he
follows and the decisions he makes.

The actions of individuals hold no mysteries for Thucydides.
When called upon to account for the reason a particular person
did what he did, Thucydides does not hesitate, nor does he
spend much time in explanation or justification. Cleon took
the position he did on Mytilene because of the violence of his
character (3.36.6). Alcibiades supported the Sicilian expedition for personal aggrandizement and to recoup financial
losses (6.15.2). Nicias supported the peace treaty ending the
Archidamian War so as to avoid threatening his reputation for
good fortune (5.16.1). The nonchalance—even apparent care-
lessness—with which Thucydides makes these judgments has
disturbed many readers.[9] The explanation for Thucydides'
unconcern with these matters will be dealt with later in chapter
7. What is significant to us now is the simple fact of his unconcern. For whatever reasons, Thucydides evidently feels that
personal motivations are easily discovered and need but little
treatment in the history.

On the other hand, the actions of nations—if not mysterious
(and they cannot be as long as he believes he knows their
cause)—are complex and obscure enough to require lengthy,
careful, and sophisticated treatment. Were the same causes at
work in social actions as in personal ones, the actions of nations
would be as easily understood and explained as the actions of
individuals are. Such, however, is patently not the case in
Thucydides. Every effort of the historian is spent in the construction of social explanations for social actions, and the
resulting explanations are far from the kinds of explanation he
provides for the actions of specific individuals.[10]

Two examples, based on events of crucial importance in
Thucydides, will make this clear. If we consider the character
of Thucydides' explanations—as revealed in the signs of his
deliberate construction—of the beginning of the Peloponnesian War and of the origin of the *stasis* at Corcyra, the
historian's separation of individual from social causes, and his

concentration on explanations proper to the level of social phenomena will become apparent.

At 1.23.6 Thucydides insists that the truest cause of the war was the fear among the Spartans occasioned by the growth of the Athenian empire. The meaning of this assertion, and the relation of πρόφασις and αἰτία in this passage have been dealt with in chapter 4 and need not concern us here. At this point, however, we will want to recognize the kinds and levels of phenomena and explanation that Thucydides chooses to consider. As pointed out in chapter 4, having stated that two kinds of cause exist, Thucydides sets the πρόφασις aside at this moment and concerns himself with the αἰτίαι of the war. In the interest of our present inquiry, we can emphasize a different aspect of this decision: Thucydides sets aside consideration of the *emotion* that constitutes the πρόφασις— that is, he sets aside consideration of what is in its proper sense an *individual* cause—to consider instead the somewhat removed representations of states toward each other. Again, his most immediate concern in constructing his account of the beginning of this war is not with explanations that derive from the personal level, emotions, but with explanations composed of social decisions and movements.

When Thucydides makes the decision he does here (to postpone consideration of the πρόφασις in favor of the αἰτίαι) he gives evidence of his principled separation of individual and social actions. Although wars are made by men, they are not made by men acting as individuals but by men acting through states. This, of course, is a truism, but brings to our attention a specific problem in the understanding of historical events which becomes a problem if one makes the separation Thucydides has made, and which Thucydides has meant to solve by the way he wrote his history. In this concrete instance it is possible to state the problem in a very direct way. To say, as Thucydides does, that the truest cause of the war was a certain fear felt by the Spartans ('Aθηναίους φόβον παρέχοντας τοῖς Λακεδαιμονίοις) involves an elliptical construction of thought which the simplicity of the words conceals. We could ask, if we wished, "Fear among *which* Spartans? All of them, most, some?" The point of asking such a tendentious question would be to draw attention to the distinction blurred by the simple phrase Thucydides has used. Fear, or any emotion, is something felt, properly speaking, only by individuals. Sparta as a nation, as an artificial entity, is not afraid, and cannot be afraid. Yet individuals do not make wars. We can, if we wanted to, distinguish ideas from ideologies by precisely this distinction of individual and social, private and public. Ideas are held by individuals. No matter how many individuals hold them, as long as they act as individuals, they hold only ideas. Ideologies, on the other hand, are the possessions of collectivities acting as collectivities. Emotions, ideas, prejudices, opinions, are all things felt and thought by, and properly belonging to, individuals. That a great many people feel a particular emotion—that even a majority or a unanimity of people feel it—does not in itself imply or explain any *social* action. Social actions require a specific mobilization of the social body. When the social body is mobilized (however that is done), and when it acts, its actions will no doubt in some way reflect the emotions and thoughts its members had. But knowing these emotions or thoughts will not itself explain how the social action came about as the action of a society. To explain that requires a different order of fact.

Unless one believes that a nation is nothing other than an immense or extended person, then how Sparta, as a collectivity—as a nation—came to war with Athens cannot be explained by the human nature of the Spartans as individuals, nor by any of their particular emotions. It can only be explained by those actions, conditions, and events which, at the collective level, have the capacity to move a nation as a collectivity. From the very beginning of Thucydides' history it is apparent that the historian's inquiry pursues explanations based on the agency of these collective actions. The decision to explain the beginning of the war by examining the αἰτίαι and the actions surrounding them first is the proof of this, and we can see the organization of the account of the start of the war as an attempt to compose an explanation at the proper social level. The embodiment of the fear the Spartans had in a social act (that is, the war) required, according to Thucydides, a complex set of prior *social* acts. The debate at Athens about Corcyra, the alliance with Corcyra, the battles at Sybota and Potidaea, the speeches given at the first Spartan congress are all necessary to account for this. The fear the Spartans had (as individuals) may have made the war inevitable (as Thucydides states), but did not make it happen. The chain of public events which led up to the Spartan decision to declare war on Athens was the instrument by which the war *happened*. These *public* events finally created a set of circumstances that made possible a public decision and a public action by the Spartans which enabled them to express and to respond to the fears each of them had *as an individual*. This public action can be said to embody their fear, but the instrumentality by which the fear was actualized as a public action (rather than a merely private response) was the decision of a public as an authoritative body, not merely as a sum of individuals. And for that public body to have acted required public business, and prior actions of the public or other publics to present that business, all of which were provided in this instance by the public causes of the war, the αἰτίαι.

In this way we can see how the Peloponnesian War, as an event among nations, requires—for Thucydides—explanations dependent on the discovery of a kind of cause which, since it is human, may be called a kind of "human nature," but which must be a new kind, a social—not individual—human nature. The war, we have said, *happens* not because of fear, but because of a chain of public actions. The course of these actions cannot be reduced to the principles of the primary human nature of individuals, to, for example, fear, honor, and profit. The chain of public actions operates by rules far more complex than the simple principles (to Thucydides) of individual human nature. (Again, consider how easily Thucydides feels individual action can be explained, but at what length and with what detail he labors to explain the actions of nations.) And yet these public actions are actions directed and undertaken by people, and as such do not happen apart from human nature. So, for Thucydides, the appeal to a second human nature, τὸ ἀνθρώπινον, a public, not a private principle of action.

Let us consider one more example for confirmation. We can

see that Thucydides concentrates on the action of collectivities and that he distinguishes the causes and explanations of collective actions from simple human nature also in the instance of the *stasis* at Corcyra. As an event in the history, it depends on an essential change in the conduct of the war: on the introduction of ideology into the policies of the major combatants. Thucydides' explanation of the general cause of the *stasis* is to be found, then, in his representation of this crucial public event, and this change cannot be ascribed to the operation of primary human nature. Thucydides is even more explicit in this instance. What primary human nature will cause and account for are the vast array of criminal acts that occurred inside Corcyra among the people of that city. But these criminal acts present no new phenomenon. Thucydides is clear on this: these acts will always occur, human nature ($\phi\acute{v}\sigma\iota\varsigma$ $\dot{\alpha}\nu\theta\rho\acute{\omega}$-$\pi\omega\nu$) being what it is (3.82.2).[11] But neither these acts nor human nature in this primary sense caused the *stasis* which is a new phenomenon. Rather, the occurrence of the *stasis* provided an opportunity for human nature to operate freely and to produce these crimes. In this chain of priority and causation we cannot claim human nature as the cause of the *stasis*. Its cause must be found in other public actions and causes, for the *stasis* itself, unlike the crimes committed during it, is not a personal event but a public one.

No one has ever doubted, as far as I am aware, that Thucydides' interest was in, and his history was of, the social actions of the war. It might well seem odd, then, that the explanation of the action of states has been so often attributed to essentially individual causes—that is, that readers have so often assigned what we have called "primary human nature" as the content of $\tau\grave{o}$ $\dot{\alpha}\nu\theta\rho\acute{\omega}\pi\iota\nu o\nu$. Yet they have done so, I am convinced, because the distinction of levels of phenomena and cause into individual and social creates a problem of its own which demands solution. The problem can be stated in two ways. We might ask, first, "If social phenomena require social explanations, and cannot be explained by the motives and actions of individuals, how are we to explain the actions of states?" One way of solving the problem is to discover that parallel to human nature social entities have a separate nature of their own according to which they act. An example of such an explanation would be one that considered the institutional structure of nations the equivalent of a "nature," and which therefore accounted for the initiation and character of events by universal institutional necessities or by the different demands of the differing structures in different nations. Yet Thucydides' history is almost entirely devoid of institutional analysis (for reasons we will consider in chapter 7) or of explanations derived from other notions of the "nature" of social entities.

Or the problem may be stated in a second way. We could ask, "If we separate the social and individual levels of phenomena, in what sense can the social actions of the war be said to be the result of a human cause (as $\tau\grave{o}$ $\grave{\alpha}\nu\theta\rho\acute{\omega}\pi\iota\nu o\nu$ implies they must be), since humans exist only at the individual level?" Inasmuch as Thucydides ignores the institutional approach and also insists that the cause of events is ultimately human, it is apparent at this point that we stand in need of some principle to serve as a bridge between the nations which act and the individuals of whom they are composed and from whom they take their being and direction.

6 Deliberation and Rhetoric

Thucydides finds the required mediation between individual and social actions in the process of deliberation. Public deliberation is, indeed, a bridging activity: it is a public action, occurring under the auspices of, and for the sake of, a public; its issue, a public decision, is precisely the force by which a social entity (the society of which this is the public) is put into motion; but, simultaneously, it is individuals who are convened as a public; and it is individuals who, while constituted as a public, engage in deliberation.

To say even this little is to alter significantly our initial characterization of the history. We had said, originally, that Thucydides' history was of the deliberateness of the events of the war, and that his presentation of speeches and debates was for the purpose of exhibiting that deliberateness. But we can now extend this description. Thucydides is not interested only in demonstrating *that* the actions of the war were deliberate. He is interested as well in examining the very process of deliberation which is the modality by which artificial social entities are put into motion by the individual humans to whom, ultimately but not directly, the explanation of all action must be referred. To know merely that an action was deliberate we need only know that a deliberation took place; but to understand how nations are moved by people requires knowledge of a different sort—of the contents and processes of deliberation —and we will now want to discover what role Thucydides' presentation of speeches serves in the provision of this knowledge.

It is far from earth-shaking to assert that Thucydides' history concerns itself with the process of deliberation. The actions of the war were deliberate. There were, necessarily, deliberations before them. There is nothing unusual in a historian's interest in the content of these deliberations. Were we to stop at this point nothing would be added to our understanding of Thucydides. But what is unusual, and is, indeed, idiosyncratic to Thucydides' history, is the manner in which deliberation is understood, analyzed, and explained. And it is his specific interpretation of the nature of deliberation that determines the special role the speeches perform and that gives its distinctive character to the history as a whole.

There exists a serious philosophical—and historical—problem in making the process of deliberation the mediating activity between the individual natures and desires of people and the concerted actions of states. The models by which deliberation is usually analyzed provide only a partial explanation of human action, and the activity of deliberation (as represented by these models) forms, therefore, only a partial and untrustworthy bridge. The most frequent model of deliberation is one which analyzes the process as an activity of rational calculation by which, as one analyzes the circumstances in which the deliberating body must act, one recognizes and explains the decision that was made as a rational response to the circumstances and possibilities. Unfortunately, this model is inadequate to the human experience of deliberation. It is not that the model exactly falsifies the explanation of deliberation, for indeed deliberators do make rational calculations of circumstance and evaluations of alternatives. Insofar as they do, the model of deliberation as calculation correctly structures analysis and explanation of events. But reason is not the only human faculty in operation and calculation is not the only action occurring during the process of deliberation, and for this reason the merely calculating model of the activity must always be inadequate. There will be, as we have pointed out in chapter 5, events which remain opaque and incomprehensible to us when considered from their merely rational standpoint, yet which clearly occur as the result of deliberation. The occasional opacity of the results of deliberation is a consequence of the particularity of deliberative situations, a particularity which includes not only a component of rational calculation, but also the influences and effects of an array of no less human, yet not rational, forces and actions. The reconstitution of this particularility is the central problem that must be solved in the composition of any history of deliberation which is to be adequate to the actual phenomenon of deliberation; and it is to solve this problem that Thucydides casts his representation of deliberation in the unusual mold that he does.

Deliberations occur in a complicated nexus composed of the two functional divisions of the deliberating public—adviser (the ''speaker'') and the advised (the ''assembly'')—and the circumstances about which they deliberate. In every situation that requires deliberation, each of these three strands plays its part in the decision that is made. In every situation the part each plays is different; in every situation the part is itself complex. Not only are assemblies different from each other (so that Athenians may make their decisions differently than Spartans would), they are also different in their own behavior from one occasion to another. Moreover, they may respond differently to different subjects even on the same occasion. Advisers (that is, politicians giving advice) differ from one another in their intelligence, their characters, their personal responses to circumstances of different sorts. In addition, as speakers and public figures they differ in their relations to their audiences and in their skill in speaking and persuasion. By reason of this natural variability of assembly as audience and politician as speaker, circumstances, too, exhibit commensurate variation. For on no occasion whatever is the ''objective reality'' of the circumstances to be acted upon available to those persons conducting a deliberation. The best that is ever available is an agreed interpretation as to the truth of the circumstances. But this interpretation is constituted only in part by the ''objective reality'' of the occasion. Its other parts depend on the assembly and the speakers, on their ability to recognize the truth of the situation, on their habits of good or bad interpretation, on their ignorance or knowledge of relevant facts, on their weakness or skill in reasoning and communicating. In addition, the interpretation of the circumstances may deviate from the circumstances themselves under the influence of prejudice, emotion, or malice. And, of course, the deliberating body's interpretation of what constitutes a desirable or adequate response to these circumstances (that is to say, its aims) will vary in all the same ways for all the same reasons. Moreover, we must remember that our explanation of the event does not necessarily require or benefit from an understanding of the objective reality. We require to know what the "subjective" reality was, and this, of course, can be much harder to recover.

We should not be surprised, then, if sometimes, as we consider the circumstances and the arguments proposed in them, the decision that was made does not seem to follow quite as we expected. We may have interpreted the situation differently than the original assembly did. Were this so, the decision would seem improper. Or we may have understood the arguments differently than it did; or perhaps the decision was made on grounds real to the situation, but not apparent in the arguments. For example, good advice has often gone unheeded and worse been accepted because one adviser was not respected or was respected too much, or because one speech, regardless of the content of its arguments, was delivered more compellingly than another.

If we were to consider only the calculative aspects of deliberation, it would be on these occasions that the origin of a decision would remain incomprehensible to us because it lay not in the rational arguments for a policy, but in the varying subrational and extrarational aspects of the particular concrete situation. To compose a history from the standpoint of deliberation, and to make the history appear faithful to our sense of the depth and complexity of action, we must somehow find a way of considering all of these aspects of the actual activity of deliberation. A new, more complete model of deliberation must be found.

Our problem now becomes one of analysis and presentation. Precisely because the particularities of a deliberative situation are sub- and extrarational, while the potency these factors have must be admitted, so must be the difficulty of their discovery, evaluation, and articulation. The rational arguments for a policy, though insufficient by themselves to explain the occurrence of an action, have at least the virtue of being, necessarily, explicit and articulated. But habits of interpretation, or prejudice, or the assembly's emotional response to a speaker are precisely unarticulated, either because (as in the case of emotion) they are immediate or because (as habit or prejudice) they are constants which operate without explicit statement. If the discovery of these extrarational particularities is itself difficult, so is the matter of assigning appropriate weights to the influence different ones of them exercised on a given decision (for even if we could complete a list of these factors, we would have to recognize that they will not necessarily exert exactly the same force in all situations).

Thucydides' solution is to consider deliberation not as a simply logical activity, but as a rhetorical one, and to fashion, from the familiar schemata of rhetoric, a new structure adapted to historical inquiries. The utility of rhetoric, as the instrument of research, could hardly be surpassed, for rhetoric is precisely a branch of study aimed at the analysis of, and action within, specific deliberative moments. Rhetoric is an art which systematizes not only logical responses to situations, but also consideration of the state of mind of audiences, and the abilities and necessities of speaker and of speech. In this respect it provides us with a system for exactly those aspects of deliberation we might fear were unsystematizable. Rhetoric provides a model for deliberation which is not restricted to the merely rational and calculating. Its model compels us to consider speaker, assembly (now thought of in its functional role as audience), and occasion in their particularity, and provides us, in fact, with a systematic representation of the sources of the particularity and opacity of events.

Of course, Thucydides utilizes rhetoric as a historian, not as an orator. In its proper role, rhetoric is an art whose function is the discovery of the "available means of persuasion." It is an art by which the orator's attention is drawn to the aspects of the particular situation that can be turned to use in the defense or attack of a given position. Persuasion is not Thucydides' primary goal. Yet if rhetoric can be used to discover what should be chosen from a situation for use in speech (that is, if it can be used as an art of discovery), by turning its orientation 180 degrees rhetoric can be transformed into an art of recovery. If knowledge of the system of rhetoric enables one to know how to fulfill one's duties as an orator, knowledge of the system of rhetoric will also make one aware of how these same duties *have* been fulfilled in specific situations. From our knowledge of what aspects of a situation must be considered in persuasion (and these aspects are provided by the structure of rhetoric), and our knowledge of the problems to be solved by the orator (provided by the theory of rhetoric), it is possible for us to be alert to the specific solutions employed by orators on specific occasions. It is precisely by being able to recognize the specificity of individual solutions to general problems that the particular facts of particular situations can be discovered. That is, rhetorical problems are susceptible of general formulation, but are solved in a multiplicity of ways, each way, on the one hand, consonant with the general formulation, but, on the other, also responding to the necessities of the particular situation. The specific content of a problem and its solution on a given occasion is the result, then, of those particular facts that are proper to that occasion and no other; it is our knowledge of the general structure of rhetoric that enables us to discover (or recover) these particularities.

Of course, rhetoric is able to systematize particularity only by stripping it of its content. Rhetoric provides merely the empty formal relations of the acting elements of particular situations, it does not inform us of the specific content of these elements. It systematizes analysis of argument, emotive appeal, passion, character, and diction, but does not itself tell us what arguments were used, which emotions were appealed to, or what the character of the speaker was, on any single occasion. In fact, from the standpoint of historical research this formal emptiness is an advantage. Insofar as rhetoric provides a structure of communication without indicating content, the use of the structure does not prejudicially impose any specific content on the analysis of the situation. Instead it necessitates the provision of content from within the rhetorical situation itself, rather than from without. From the standpoint of the orator, the art of rhetoric does not tell one what to say. Neither does it insist that certain things must be said on all occasions. Rather, it directs one to discover those facts of the particular occasion that appropriately supply content to the previously empty formal directions of the art. From the point of view of the historian using this art, rhetoric does not indicate what was said, it directs one to consider what unique facts, arguments, and appeals supplied its content on each individual occasion. The art of rhetoric's formal emptiness allows, therefore, for the discovery of those factors which were indeed in operation in any specific situation, without prejudice either in favor of or against certain predetermined factors. Moreover, insofar as the rhetorical structure is designed for individual situations, it provides an instrument for discovering the representation of varying factors in different situations. That is, a rhetorical analysis will not represent the operation of identical factors in all circumstances. As factors become influential on deliberation, they receive rhetorical representation. Where they do not operate in some specific situation, they are unrepresented. The formal and contentless structure of the system of rhetoric serves a function, in this historical adaptation of its theory, almost identical to the function served by *loci,* places, within most systems of rhetoric. The structure of rhetoric itself now becomes a place for the discovery of the elements of rhetorical and deliberative situations generally, and for the discovery of the particular contents given to these empty places in specific situations.

Under the direction of this structure, Thucydides' account of the deliberations of the war takes on its unique character, and his practices in recording the deliberations receive their explanation. In analyzing deliberation from the perspective of rhetoric, even the extrarational aspects of deliberation become deliberate insofar as they are considered and utilized by the orator, and they are therefore recoverable and articulable by the historian working from the same model of the situation. Passion and character, as well as logic, become deliberate insofar as they find deliberate embodiment in speeches. Of course, they find their embodiment differently than do the rational arguments given in support of a policy. They are embodied in parts of speeches unconcerned with the rational arguments, or in aspects of speech—the nuances of words and expressions, for example—extrinsic to the rational content of these arguments. What this means is that to recover traces of these extrarational forces, we must have access to something like the entire speeches that were given on the occasions of deliberation. That is, the excerpts which are normally made of the arguments for and against policy (excerpts, for example, such as we have used in the first part of this inquiry) can embody and represent the calculative aspects of deliberation, but not the extrarational aspects. More of the speech—in some sense the whole speech—is required to represent these latter aspects.

Faced with the practical problem posed by the impossibility of including complete speeches for each deliberative situation in the history, we can see Thucydides' practice with respect to speeches as a daring solution. He has recorded whole speeches, but miniature ones. In their wholeness it is clear that he has made the attempt to record in these speeches not only the rational arguments for policy but also those rhetorical elements which address the extrarational aspects of deliberation. Insofar as we believe him capable of this rhetorical tour de force, there becomes available to us evidence touching on the most concrete particularity of the deliberate actions of the nations of this war. The possibility even arises of discovering facts of the period which, while not directly germane to Thucydides' interpretation of the war, are necessarily embodied in the speeches through their connection to directly relevant facts of the deliberative situation.

While we must accept on faith Thucydides' ability to re-embody all of the rhetorical elements of the original speeches in his shortened whole versions, there need be no doubt concerning the ability of the rhetorical model to provide the sorts of information about the extrarational aspects of deliberation that we require. The six examples which follow should be considered as merely illustrative of the kind of information accessible through the speeches. Far from exhausting the available information, these examples represent only a small portion of the material provided by the speeches concerning deliberations and the deliberative circumstances. Since it is precisely a function of Thucydides' method to discover the wide variety of possible contents and solutions to rhetorical problems, no exhaustive list of contents is likely. Yet the following examples are nonetheless exhaustive in a formal sense. There are two examples from each element of the rhetorical triad, audience-speaker-speech, to demonstrate that information concerning all extrarational aspects of deliberation can be found in the speeches in this history by attention to the places (*loci*) indicated by the structure of rhetoric.[1]

1. Audience

Momentary changes of states of feeling will distinguish the audience of one rhetorical situation from that of another. These changes, or the emotions in operation on specific occasions, usually leave quite clear traces in the speeches on the occasions. But in addition to these momentary states—whose influence on actions is never doubted and rarely ignored—there also exist more enduring characteristics of audiences which distinguish them from one another, which also have their effects in the creation of events, but which—precisely because of their constancy—are embodied in oratory in rather more concealed ways than the changing emotional responses to momentary circumstances. Nevertheless, difficult though it may be to disentangle these characteristics, they form part of the deliberative situation. Their traces are there, if concealed; moreover, their discovery may be critical in the explanation of actions otherwise opaque, at least in part. The first two examples consider two such enduring characteristics.

The Character of Audiences: An Intellectual Habit

What we will examine first is how habitual patterns of politics in a particular city (Athens) can lead to the creation of an idiosyncratic style of deliberation, and how that general style (or habit) may influence the outcome of debates that occur in the city. Such an analysis of the style of politics in a city might well be done for any city if the information were available (for certainly the idiosyncracies of political habits do influence decisions in those groups that have particular styles), but

Thucydides has really only furnished us with such information for Athens and Sparta. Athens has been chosen for this example primarily because we have more information in its case, and also becasue its style is more definite and perhaps more influential in the decisions it takes.

To the character of the Athenians when sitting in assembly (as perceived by the politicians who had to deal with them) we have considerable and remarkably consistent testimony in the speeches. The assembly, all politicians agree, was a nightmare. Whether their criticisms give an accurate picture or merely reflect their necessarily special relation to the assembly, the politicians uniformly condemn the assembly as impetuous, wholly irresponsible, and inappropriately sophisticated. The impetuosity and irresponsibility (that is, its eagerness to make decisions, yet its unwillingness to accept responsibility for the decisions once made) find critics in the widest gamut of Athenian orators: Pericles (2.60.1-4), Cleon (3.38.3-7), Diodotus (3.42-43), Nicias (6.93 and 7.14.4), and Alcibiades (6.89.4-6). In part, the irresponsibility was the result of the extraordinary political and rhetorical sophistication of the Athenians, a sophistication which on occasion could lead them to make political judgments on essentially aesthetic grounds, or so, at least, it could be said. Cleon makes the clearest statement of this:

> The city gives prizes for such contests [of eloquence] to others, but itself bears the risks. You yourselves are the marshals of these games, and very ill for you it is that you are, inasmuch as you are wont to be contemplators of speeches, but mere listeners to actions. You look at the possibility of future actions on the basis of the eloquent words of others, and what was done from the words of those who find fault; for you have no more confidence in what is accomplished by seeing it than by hearing about it. You are the best men to be deceived by some novelty of speech, and for not being willing to follow the tried and true. You are slaves to whatever is strange, and disdainers of the usual. [3.38.3-5]

The perception of the assembly as irresponsible (whether it was in fact or not) could itself influence the actions of politicians, and through them, of the state. Since the assembly would hold the orator (rather than itself) responsible for disaster, an individual's actions could be informed as much by fear of the assembly as by prudence. The results might be trivial (Nicias' sending a written communication to Athens, 7.8, because he was suspicious that his messengers—afraid of the reaction of their audience—would understate the gravity of the Athenian situation in Sicily), but could equally be of the greatest seriousness. Fear of the consequences the assembly would decree forms the basis of the argument with which Nicias convinced the other Athenian commanders to remain at Syracuse following the failure of the night battle (7.48.3). Nicias' own motivation (according to Thucydides) was quite different from this, yet he concealed his own reasons and presented this argument, presumably because he felt it would be most persuasive to the others. Fear of the assembly, therefore, must be counted one of the influential factors in the imprudent decision to remain.

Moreover, the perceived irresponsibility and the fear it occasioned may well also have led to political corruption as politicians looked for rewards of office other than the admiration of the public (something too fickle to be satisfactory). Pericles (2.60.6) warned of the danger of the eloquent, even intelligent, but corrupt politician, and charges of corruption were commonplace (as in the Mytilene debate, 3.38), even when unjustified. While it is impossible to evaluate how much of political corruption and self-promotion is to be attributed to the irresponsibility of the assembly, we can nevertheless account it a factor in unsettling the activity of politics throughout the war.

The rhetorical sophistication which lay at the heart of the assembly's irresponsible behavior (and which is touched on in the latter part of Cleon's criticism) had its own effect on Athenian politics, in addition to the fear it caused among politicians. It is this additional effect which is the "intellectual habit" of this example. The sophistication of the Athenians as an audience for words led them, as Cleon claims, to an unreflecting love of the novel and elegant in styles and in ideas. Their very sophistication made them vulnerable to a certain kind of argument. We can see that the Athenians believed (by the beginning of the war and throughout it) that they had fashioned international politics in a new mold, and that they —as distinct from all other nations—were finally able to recognize and admit the naked operation of power which was the principle of all political action. This belief had its influence on the content of political rhetoric and thought. In Thucydides' representations (granted compressed) of Athenian deliberations, no winning orator supports his policies with arguments from principles of justice, moderation, or mercy. When these kinds of arguments are used, they are failures. Apparently, the Athenians believed they had removed these considerations from their deliberations (as inappropriately metaphysical and emotional), and they were wont to lecture those who had not on their naïvete. In an extraordinary fashion, the entire nation seems devout believers in the roughest realpolitik.[2]

The maxims about the exercise of power as a natural behavior were, of course, popular among the sophists, and their modernity and paradoxicality no doubt were what made them attractive to the Athenians. But actual commitment to these ideas was less than complete. In fact, the Athenians often acted emotionally and unrealistically. The point we must grasp here is not that they had in fact stripped politics of these considerations, but that they believed they had. It is this belief that constitutes a certain habit of mind, and this belief (or self-image) which made them vulnerable to certain sorts of arguments. When we can see that a certain kind of argument is attractive independent of its appropriateness to the situation, we are in the presence of a *habit* of thought, rather than thinking itself.

The Athenian bent toward a politics based only on the "realities" of political processes is exhibited not only in the arguments of the orators before the assembly, but also in statements made by speakers before other groups, speakers who are identified only as "Athenians," and who must stand, on these occasions, as representatives of general Athenian opinion. On the only two of these occasions, the "realistic" political rhetoric is flaunted before the other "deluded" cities. At Sparta:

> So, we have done nothing to be wondered at, nor anything
> unnatural, if on the one hand we accepted this empire which
> was offered, and on the other did not let it go, overcome
> by the three greatest things: honor, fear, and profit. Nor
> were we the first to do such things; rather, it has been ever
> established that the weaker is kept down by the stronger. . . .
> But they are worthy of praise who, acting in accordance with
> human nature so that they rule others, are juster than they
> might be considering the power they have. [1.76.2, 3]

And at Melos:

> But from what we both truly think, let us accomplish what
> is possible, understanding (as intelligent men) that as far as
> justice is concerned, that is determined in human debate on
> the basis of that necessity which presses equally on both
> parties; but that as far as the practical is concerned: that is a
> matter of the superior doing, and the weak yielding. [5.89]

> We think about the divine (by conjecture) and about
> human conduct with clear certainty that wherever it can it
> rules: this has been true forever—the necessity of nature
> is absolute. We neither made this law, nor are we the first to
> use it having been made. But we make use of it, accepting
> it since it was there, and leaving it behind to remain for-
> ever, knowing that even you or anyone else with the power
> we have would do just the same. [5.105.2]

Two points should be made. First, it is not that political
principles per se remain constant between these two occasions.
That Athenian political thought had undergone serious
changes between the times of the Spartan congress and the
Melian dialogue has been sufficiently demonstrated, I hope,
in chapters 2 and 3. What remains constant is a style of presenting whatever the current principles are. Second, the
importance of this style of presentation for our purposes is that
it necessarily implies a complementary style of listening and
thinking. If Athenians speak this way consistently, they will
also respond consistently to being spoken to this way. The
self-image of the Athenian audience, that it was the only
realistic and unhypocritical political body in the world, made

it an easy mark for certain kinds of rhetorical argument, and its fondness for these arguments is a clear factor in several of its decisions. Our prior recognition of this habit, and of the resultant vulnerability to certain arguments, is important to our proper understanding of the origins of these decisions.

Two of these are the Mytilene debate and the debate on the Sicilian expedition. In the first case, it is not that the Athenians are looking for a new imperial policy that leads them to accept Diodotus' proposals. Simply, Diodotus outstrips even Cleon in realpolitik (or apparent realpolitik). Cleon himself was leaning heavily on "realism" by pointing out how sweet an emotion revenge is (3.38), and how much and how justly Athens was hated by its allies. But Diodotus went a step further, and claimed that even revenge was a superfluous emotion (3.44) and that human nature was worse even than Cleon supposed. He accomplished this latter riposte in the passage on love and hope, which, in addition to being a politically fashionable sentiment, was stylistically elegant, and so presumably had a double attraction for this audience. In proposing this picture of human motivation, Diodotus invited the Athenians to accept an understanding of human nature stripped ever further of illusions. As this played to Athenian self-images (independently of its truth or probability), it attracted support to the specific policy it was defending. In our conclusions about the causes of this Athenian decision, we must weigh the subtle force of this style of argument—with this specific audience—in addition to its content. Similarly, during the debate on the Sicilian expedition, Alcibiades was the orator who most successfully exploited this "realistic" bias on the part of the Athenians. Nicias tried to appear realistic by being concrete about the danger of the campaign, but it was Alcibiades who more successfully exploited the *style* of realism. On the one hand, in justifying his fitness to offer advice (in response to Nicias' attack on his character), he reduces all human motivation to simple greed (6.16); on the other, he plays upon latent Athenian fear with the allegation of a new principle of political life (that states which do not expand are necessarily subjugated) which is at once apparently hard-headed, cynical, and irrevocable.[3]

In both these cases the penchant of the Athenian audience for a certain sort of rhetoric was influential in the decisions they took, and our familiarity with the penchant is necessary for our complete comprehension of the decisions. The Athenians were not averse to taking revenge (they did at Melos and elsewhere), but in the case of Mytilene they overcame the attraction of this emotion. Without saying that this decision was paradoxical enough to worry us, it is clear that the success of Diodotus' speech (and so our understanding of the process of decision-making in this case) depended heavily on his knowing exactly whom he was addressing and what sort of arguments would appeal to them. In the case of the Sicilian debate we can see a perfect consonance of an orator's style with the predelictions of his audience, so that he produced arguments to manipulate and reinforce attitudes which had to be exaggerated and subtly distorted to explain the decision to undertake this otherwise gratuitous campaign.

Emotions and Audiences: Compelling Attitudes or Prejudices

There are two distinct ways in which certain definite emotions or attitudes may influence rhetorical situations and decisions. On the one hand, certain preceding actions or circumstances may create automatic responses in the deliberative body that have such immediate strength that they produce a disproportionate effect on any subsequent deliberation. Panic is an example, and if we had records of any of the Athenian deliberations following the defeat at Syracuse we would no doubt see its effects in them. Similarly, the release of a pent-up emotion, for example anger, may compel specific decisions, as was probably the case in the first day's debate on Mytilene, in which the Athenians originally decided to kill all the Mytileneans. On the other hand, certain attitudes or emotions may influence specific decisions not because of their momentary intensity, but because they form part of the emotional make-up of a specific audience in respect of specific objects or problems. This is a different matter from the political habits of an audience. Rather, what we are interested in here are automatic emotional responses to certain situations or certain persons, and we are interested especially in those responses which have become ingrained and which, although they might well be concealed, would form a part of any deliberative occasion on the appropriate subject.

As a particular case, let us take Spartan attitudes toward Athens. From one point of view it would be possible to ignore this altogether, for Spartan decisions always follow particular actions by Athens or its allies, and could be seen simply as responses to these. Yet to do so would be to ignore an important dimension of the decision-making processes at Sparta, for in large measure it was a preexistent general attitude toward Athens that determined what Sparta's direct responses would be whenever it felt it had to react to an Athenian action. Sparta lived in an indefinite but constant terror of Athens, and this supplied a tremendous advantage to anyone attempting to move the Spartans to take some action that was hostile to the Athenians. Moreover, the action would usually be in some way excessive in its response, no doubt the result of acting always from fear. Strangely, the Athenians seem never to understand just how strong this attitude is, though Sparta's allies always knew it was there to manipulate.

This Spartan fear was less a product of specific Athenian actions that it was of the peculiar character of the Spartan nation and of its image of itself. We are speaking of a fear different from the particular one that propelled the Spartans to war with Athens. Rather, we are concerned here with that general, chronic mistrust and incomprehension of Athens which was the result of the marked difference in constitution and character between the two cities, and which resulted in Spartan beliefs that Athens was always up to rather more than it appeared to be. The fear might surface in gratuitous acts like the dismissal of the Athenian contingent at Ithome (c. 463). On this occasion Thucydides' narrative quite clearly points to aspects of the Athenian character (rather than particular suspicious acts) as the source of Spartan fear: "their daring and innovativeness" [τὸ τολμηρὸν καὶ [ἡ] νεωτεροποιία] (1. 102.3). This same general anxiety is implicit in the successful arguments of the Corinthians. For its precipitation into the specific fear of Athens which led to this war, specific catalytic acts and specific political processes were necessary, but the general fear itself seemed always to be available for conversion into specific fears and actions.

Presumably, it is because the fear depended on Sparta's own character that it was so entrenched and unalterable. The Spartan nation was like no other, with some of its customs antique and others wholly idiosyncratic. These differences might in themselves have made Sparta defensive, but were surely exacerbated by constant reference to them. It is not only the Athenians who point out how different the Spartan character is from that of all other Greeks (1.77); the Corinthians do, too (1.70 and 1.71). The continuous reminders of their difference led to a Spartan reaction of self-conscious conservatism, to a promotion of their difference to the status of old-fashioned virtue. No doubt all Greek states, in their modernity, constituted a kind of threat to the Spartans, but foremost among them, both in their modernism and in their democracy, were the Athenians. These would be the people most different from the Spartans, and no particular actions would be necessary for the Spartans nevertheless to perceive in them an implied threat.[4]

The Corinthians manipulate this fear brilliantly in their speech at the first Spartan congress. They omit almost entirely any mention of particular grievances they have with Athens and concentrate all their rhetorical efforts on the comparison of Spartan and Athenian characters (1.70–71) and on the maximization of the differences between them. It is a magnificent piece of hyperbole, in which Sparta is portrayed at every moment as overreached by the modern Athenians. The culmination comes in two parts: the summary of the comparison[5] and the Corinthians' threat at the end to desert Sparta for another alliance. Nothing we can imagine could have used this Spartan fear to greater advantage. Having maximized in all ways the alienness of Sparta from the modern world, they leave the Spartans face to face with the terror that must always have been just below the surface: that at a certain moment the entire world would outstrip Sparta and either leave it isolated or turn en masse against it. It is the rhetorical skill of the Corinthian speakers which calls our attention to this Spartan trait. To ignore particular grievances (the Spartans were rarely moved by the sufferings of others) and to concentrate on this general fear demonstrated a quite clear and even cynical understanding of the specific audience they were addressing. The peculiarity of ignoring the particular grievances makes this trait apparent to us. And we must understand this trait to understand other of Sparta's actions.

When Sparta has to be pushed into resuming the war with Athens (at the end of the seventeenth year), Alcibiades repeats the same argument. Counting on Sparta's constant fear of Athens, he gives a report of the Athenian program in which the Sicilian expedition is merely the first step toward eventually isolating the Peloponnese from all external aid, and then conquering it easily (6.90). This program must be Alcibiades' invention—it sounds characteristically hyperbolic, and we have no other confirmation that Athens had anywhere near so definite and extensive a design. Apparently, no Spartan notices or questions the hyperbole, something we may now understand as a natural result of their underlying and chronic fear. Sparta could always be convinced the Athenians were capable of anything, so different were they felt to be, and so little could Sparta understand them. Alcibiades had just the character to devise this plan, and also fit the Spartan image of what all Athenians were like. And in fact, Alcibiades was trying to create this image, for it would lend credence to his claim to be the person best able to aid the Spartans on this occasion.

It would be wrong to say that Sparta went to war again because of its old fear of Athens. Certainly it had a sufficient number of new fears and other reasons to do so. But the fear is an important factor in its decision to go to war in the first place, and the generalized fear, mistrust, and even awe that the Spartans constantly felt toward Athens must remain in the background as forces that influence every Spartan decision with respect to Athens throughout the course of the war. Strategic considerations alone will never explain the responses Sparta makes to Athenian actions. The necessities of Sparta's situation must always be considered in combination with this special attitude to understand why the Spartans act as they do at any given moment.

2. Speaker

Personality: Extrinsic Facts Concerning Speakers

In considering the speakers in debates from a rhetorical point of view, a distinction must be made between the *personality* of the speaker and his *character*. Within this distinction, character is what the speaker reveals of himself, or presents as himself, in the speech given. By personality, on the other hand, is meant the speaker as known by facts extrinsic to the speech, and often unincorporated into the speech. It is what an audience knows of a speaker before he even opens his mouth. The speaker's personality is who in fact he is, or is believed to be, and it is inescapable and unalterable. His character, however, may appear to change from one speech to the next, as different characters are relevant to different situations. In his speech, the speaker projects a character, or *ethos,* that is appropriate to the job at hand, appears to be capable of giving advice, and, therefore (the speaker hopes), is worthy of attention and agreement. The distinction is important because different weights or amounts of influence should be attributed to these two different ways in which a speaker may be known. Within the structure of rhetoric, character is always significant; personality is only occasionally so. Thucydides' practice with respect to the presentation of speakers is entirely consistent with this distinction, and not only reflects the rhetorical principles which underlie the history, but also demonstrates the care Thucydides has taken to provide the information necessary to judge the effect of these factors on particular deliberative occasions.

Thucydides displays a "double standard" in his treatment of speakers. In his representation of political speeches, he sometimes identifies the speaker by name and sometimes does not, contenting himself with a more general identification such as "the Athenians" or "the Corinthians." This apparent lack of consistency would seem to suggest either that he was sometimes ignorant of the names of the speakers or that he sometimes felt the names were insignificant. The former explanation seems unlikely, considering the importance of those occasions on which he contents himself with the general designations, and considering that on occasions of much lesser importance—and under more difficult circumstances—he is able to discover the names of all of the speakers. But the latter explanation, too, would be closed to us, were we not able to discover a rationale under which the names of certain speakers—even when known, and even when their speeches were of the utmost importance—could be called insignificant. In fact, the principle that directs the naming (or not) of speakers in Thucydides' history follows the distinction made in the preceding paragraph between character and personality, and makes possible the recovery of the appropriately different weights given these in rhetorical evaluations of deliberative situations.

We are aware that audiences, in responding to speeches urging them to one or another action, do not respond only to the logic of the arguments in support of the positions. Audiences respond, as well, to the speakers proposing the positions. In a theoretical, and also prudential, sense, it is not only a fact that audiences do this, it is quite proper that they do. Not every speaker is qualified (by intelligence, or by that political sympathy Greek politics called εὔνοια) to give advice; not every speaker is to be trusted as much as every other. Evaluation of the speaker becomes, then, a part of the calculus and practical logic of decisions. It is for this reason that most theories of rhetoric include sections on the proper presentation of oneself to ensure that one's arguments are given the sympathetic hearing one hopes for them. These sections outline, in fact, the procedures for presenting a character—an *ethos*—appropriate to the circumstances and to the advice to be given. The name given this is "ethical proof." A history written from a rhetorical point of view must, in turn, represent somehow the particular evaluations of the speakers on particular occasions, for these evaluations, too, were part of the cause of the event and must constitute part of its explanation.

Experience and the realities of actual deliberations, however, raise complications for the historian. Theories of rhetoric, written abstractly and with no particular audience or speaker in mind, provide guidelines for the sorts of statements to be made *in one's speech* in order to project one or another *ethos*. Were this abstract formulation the only rule operating in real situations, the historian's job would be simple. Since *ethos* in

this sense is demonstrated in the speech itself, a faithful repro-
duction of the speech would provide all the information necessary for understanding the audience's evaluation of the
speaker and for recovering this dimension of deliberative situations. But audiences also evaluate speakers on evidence *not*
included in their speeches. When speakers are famous—or
notorious—to their audiences, this fame or notoriety may influence the audience's evaluation of the speaker and so the
decision on the issue, quite apart from the statements of his
speech that delineate character. Under these circumstances, of
course, merely to reproduce the speech would not adequately
explain either the audience's reaction to the speaker or their
decision. That the speaker was well known, and what he was
well known for, must also be made known to us.

There will be times, then, when knowing the *personality* of
the speaker will be necessary for our understanding of a situation. There will also be occasions when—the speaker not being
known, or not so well known as to influence the audience with
extrinsic predispositions to him—personality will not be historically significant. On these latter occasions all that the audience knew of the speaker, in effect, was the character he
projected in his speech. For the history of these occasions the
representation of that character will be sufficient. Thucydides'
practice in the naming of speakers parallels exactly the different weights that must be assigned to personality and character under these differing rhetorical circumstances.

In this history, wherever the personality of a speaker may
have had some influence on the audience's evaluation of him,
that speaker is named. Where the audience would not have
been influenced by personal information known from any
other source outside the speech—that is, where the audience
would know the speaker only from the speech they heard, and
where, therefore, personality would not be significant, only
character in the rhetorical sense—the speaker is not named. In
the application of this rule, Thucydides is almost certainly
overcautious, on some occasions naming speakers when, in
fact, personal knowledge of them was probably not influential. But, of course, we would expect him to err in the direction
of inclusion rather than exclusion.

The rule can be, for the purpose of our exploration, overstated slightly to make a point. The personalities of speakers will be best known, naturally, to audiences in their own cities. When a speaker from one city, however, speaks in front of an audience of another city, we would not expect that audience to possess personal, extrinsic knowledge of the speaker in most cases, and we would think relevant only his character as it as presented in his speech. If we apply this distinction by *location* of the relevance of personality or character to the practice of naming speakers, we would expect to find the following two regularities: (1) that Thucydides will name every speaker speaking before an audience of his own citizens; (2) that Thucydides will not name speakers speaking before "foreign" audiences.

Indeed, these are almost exactly the practices we do find in the history. To the first of these rules there are no exceptions. Whenever a speaker is speaking at home or before fellow citizens, his name is given by Thucydides.[6] This may often be unnecessary. When Thucydides names both Cleon and Diodotus, it is surely only Cleon's name that is significant. He was the notorious one; of Diodotus we know nothing else. Yet both because it would seem strange to name one but not the other speaker in a debate, and because perhaps the Athenians knew something about Diodotus which influenced them, Thucydides includes both names.

To the second of the rules there are a few exceptions. There are indeed occasions where speakers are named although the speeches they gave were given to "foreigners." But the exceptions are few, and present no contradiction to the rhetorical principle behind the naming of speakers. We can see in the exceptions those infrequent cases in which a speaker was rather well known even outside his home city. On these occasions, therefore, his personality—in addition to his character as presented in his speech—may have had an effect on the audience. On these occasions too, therefore, Thucydides names the speakers. There are four exceptions. Two involve Hermocrates of Syracuse, speaking at Gela (4.59-64) and at Camarina (6.76-80).[7] Hermocrates himself was emphatic in his belief in the essential unity of the Sicilian population. At Gela (4.61.1) he says Sicily should really be considered as if it were one city. It is not unreasonable to assume that part of this de facto unity was manifested in a greater than usual awareness among the Sicilian population of politicians in many or all the Sicilian cities. Hermocrates may have been a famous figure throughout the island, and his personality may have been known in other cities. (Camarina, of course, is quite near Syracuse, and Hermocrates would be even more likely to be a known figure there.) A further exception is Brasidas speaking at Acanthus (4.85-87). His campaign in Thrace would have made him famous in that region, at least; further, he was called in by a faction in the city, to whom he would indeed be known. The last exception is Alcibiades speaking at Sparta (6.89-92). Again, of all Athenians he was probably the most notorious outside Athens. He himself makes reference to known personal facts, and it is not unlikely his personality did influence the Spartan audience. In addition, his family had been *proxenoi* for Sparta in Athens, and this, too, may have made him known in Sparta.[8]

These exceptions aside, we can see Thucydides following this practice: before a "home" audience the speaker is named; before a "foreign" one he is not. We can see strikingly consistent uses of this on two occasions. At the first Spartan congress neither the Corinthian nor Athenian speakers are named,[9] for both groups are speaking to an audience which does not know them personally, and for whom only what they hear will enter into their evaluation of the speakers. However, once the Spartans retire to their deliberations immediately after these two speeches, and Spartans are speaking to Spartans, the speakers are named. The second example has an odd twist, but is consistent. When the unnamed Plataeans plead for their lives they are speaking at home in Plataea. But they are speaking to Spartan judges, "foreigners" to whom they would be personally unknown. So they too remain unnamed.

Thucydides' practice throughout is consistent with what we would expect to be necessary to his rhetorical interpretation of events. Where speakers are unnamed we see an extraordinarily pure form of rhetorical analysis. In these instances Thucydides—even if he did know the names of the speakers—restricts the information he provides us to only that information which could have had an effect on the audience. For these speeches, since all the audience knew of the speaker was what it heard, this is all that Thucydides discloses. Where Thucydides does believe the person of the speaker may have had a rhetorical effect on the audience, he not only names the speaker, but often provides the specific extrinsic information we need to estimate the nature of the influence of his personality. Even where Thucydides does not indicate precisely what influence this or that personality had, his use of names on these occasions gives us warning that the personality of the speaker may well have had an independent effect on the audience.

Character: Intrinsic Qualities of Some Particular Speakers

In the cases of Pericles and Alcibiades, the influence of their personalities on the public decisions in which they participated was greater, perhaps, than in all others. On the basis of their known personae decisions were made which might otherwise be inexplicable, and in both cases Thucydides has reported to us information to take this into account. Without Pericles' extraordinary presence in Athenian deliberations, Athens might very well have ended the war at the outbreak of the plague. So, at least, it would appear Thucydides believed. But for Alcibiades' perceived untrustworthiness, Athens might yet have won the war. This Thucydides asserts at 6.15.

Much of the information we need to evaluate the impact of these men Thucydides provides directly in narrative. Yet, since both were striking and powerful speakers, their personalities do not remain only extrinsic to their speeches, but find concrete embodiment and expression in them. We can use these speeches as examples of the possibility of uncovering yet another dimension of deliberative situations through the rhetorical structure Thucydides represents. A character parallel to his actual personality is constructed (or projected) by each man in his speeches, and in the touches of their styles we can get a direct sense of some of the reasons for Pericles' unwavering control of Athenian politics and for Alcibiades' eventual failure.

Pericles' style is a strangely complex one, composed of about equal parts of disapproval of the *demos* and admiration for the institution of the democracy. Even while he lectured the people in the assembly he never despised them, and the equilibrium of these attitudes gave his substantive proposals an appearance of solidity, justice, and wisdom. He could berate the assembly for its fickleness (1.140.1 and 2.61.2) or its inappropriate love of rhetoric (2.35.2), but in the same speech would treat its powers of discernment with respect (in his presentation of arguments and alternatives) and even praise it (in the Funeral Oration). The evenhandedness of his criticisms seems to argue for their justice, and helps create the appearance of the character he claims for himself in his last speech (2.60.5): "inferior to no one both in knowing what is necessary and in getting this across, and a lover of the city, and above money." When Pericles says in this same speech that he is the same man he was (when he urged the beginning of the war), the statement seems true and full of content. It expresses a steadiness of purpose, policy, and consideration of the city's interest that makes Cleon's direct echo of the line (at 3.38.1) seem a hollow mockery. Every statement of Pericles' about the city, and the tone in which he delivers every argument for the adoption of a specific policy, gives the impression of integrity and thoughtfulness. The unexpected Athenian continuation of the war is only explicable because Pericles urged it, and because being who he was the Athenians accepted it.[10] Similarly, our understanding of how it was that Athens came to make this unexpected choice depends on our having been able to discern just how great an effect such an argument from *this man* would have on the assembly. It is in seeing how he handled his audiences, in hearing the tone and style of his rhetoric and public manner (in his two full speeches that precede the last one) that we can correctly gauge that effect.

Our recognition of Alcibiades' character and the effect that had on Athenian decisions is achieved in the same way, though our judgment is opposite. Although he first appears in the history in book 5 as a rather reckless member of the Athenian war party (5.43.2), it is through his first speech in book 6 that we are able to understand how the Athenians could admire him enough to undertake the Sicilian expedition with him in a position of authority, then cripple it by recalling him, and cripple their strategies during the Ionian War by rejecting his aid. In fact, it is because the question of his character is so important in deciding how to receive his advice that the debate on the Sicilian expedition contains the first direct personal attack of one orator on another (Nicias on Alcibiades). That he was a brilliant orator is evident from his speech during the Sicilian debate, but so are all his flaws of character. That he was utterly irresponsible and that he had only contempt for the *demos* is represented to us with the greatest force. His speech was successful, but only because it so perfectly touched the appropriate chord in Athenian desires and because his character seemed the right one to fulfill those desires.

It is strange how strongly we feel that Alcibiades does not believe a word of what he says to the assembly. Perhaps it is because his statements about the political necessities of the city (at 6.18) are mirror images of his personal necessities (at 6.16).[11] Perhaps it is because the dismal future he foresees for Athens if it does not undertake the Sicilian expedition is so obviously unreal and even hysterical, yet we cannot believe that Alcibiades would himself succumb to this hysteria (though we can believe he would manipulate it). The combination of the untrustworthiness of his advice with the contempt he shows the assembly in reducing the city's motivations to those of his own life (in defending his character against Nicias) creates a striking image. This was a successful speech, certainly, because his personal excesses were exactly what the city would need to tap as a resource to accomplish this campaign. But in this speech he reveals aspects of his character which must have been even more evident to the Athenians. Though a brilliant orator, what is clearest is his egotism and unreliability. Though we cannot be surprised that he is successful on this occasion (given Athenian attitudes at this moment), neither are we surprised when he defects to Sparta (though we know of no other instance of such an action by an Athenian), nor are we surprised by the distrust with which he is treated even while Athens uses his services during the Ionian War. The changing fortunes in Athens during the last phase of the war depend in great

measure on the characters of its politicians, not least on Alcibiades'. And we are prepared to understand some of these
changes through what is revealed of Alcibiades' character by
the style of his rhetoric, and prepared to understand Thucydides' judgment:

> In the public sphere he managed war business for the best,
> but everyone being vexed with his personal conduct, en-
> trusted [the war] to others, and in no great length of time
> overthrew the city. [6.15.4]

3. Speech

The Rhetoric of a Particular Occasion

If it is the case that in deliberative situations the nature of
the audience and of the speaker influences the decision made,
so too the very way in which arguments are formed and presented, as a rhetorical problem which must be solved for every
situation individually, has its effect in the final outcome.
Attention to the quality of the speech itself may provide facts
significant to the explanation of events.

The orator must find words, phrases, and a general tone
appropriate to what he is proposing, to what his audience will
readily receive, and to the particular situation subsisting
around this moment of decision. He must be able to decide
what it is possible for him to do, and he must have a sense of
how his audience is responding. The audience's character and
attitudes and the orator's personality are givens for any rhetorical situation, but in addition to these, as a part of the process of
persuasion and deliberation itself, there are all the technical
and practical aspects of political activity. An example of the
influence these can have on the decision-making process is the
failure of the Spartan peace offer to Athens in the seventh year
of the war (4.17-22). As a rhetorical problem, it is hard to see
how the Spartan speakers could have managed it worse.

I am not at all sure that any approach to the Athenians for an
end to the war could have been successful at this moment.
Athens had the Spartans over a barrel, and this happy circumstance had come about wholly unexpectedly. The boost this

gave to Athenian self-confidence was enormous, and in addition the war generally had been going quite well for them for the first time. They would certainly have driven a hard bargain for a peace, but perhaps the Spartans would have paid. We have indications that they may have been willing to make almost any concession the Athenians required, when at 4.22 Thucydides tells us that they did not reject the first, grossly inflated Athenian demands. Much of their failure here must be attributed to how badly they handled the rhetorical opportunity. If it were not that their speech embodies their rhetorical mistakes, we might find Athenian rejection of the peace offer merely perverse. This, apparently, is not the conclusion Thucydides wanted us to reach, and in showing us the whole of the Spartan speech and enabling us to understand how they set about to approach the Athenians on this matter, Thucydides makes it possible for us both to understand how it was that without perversity the Athenians were simply not persuaded, and to see a realistic dynamic within which there was little to expect beyond Athenian rejection.

The Spartan speech demonstrates an utter failure to grasp the necessities of this particular political situation. They mistake who their audience is and what its specific attitudes and feelings are at this moment; they utilize the wrong sorts of arguments for this audience and occasion; the entire tone of the speech—in a sense its style or diction—is inappropriate.[12] The key to this rhetorical debacle is that the Spartans imagine the Athenians must be as eager for peace as they are themselves, without realizing that the fact that Sparta had come to Athens to propose peace indicated in itself that the relations between the states had changed, and without considering that perhaps under these new circumstances Athens might be less willing to end the war. The Spartan failure was a practical one: they misjudged the particularity of the moment.

The general tone of their speech is wildly inappropriate. The speech is so measured, so calm and dignified, that it sounds as if it ought to have been given before the war began, and not at its hottest moment. In this seventh year of the war, the Athenians were feeling for the first time that they were winning it. The coolness and *amour-propre* of the Spartans could not have been less acceptable to this audience.

Understand this, by considering our present [mis-]fortunes,
who have come to you, though we have the greatest reputation among the Greeks, and though before we would
have thought ourselves better able to give what now we
have come to ask of you. And we have suffered this neither
from lack of power nor because we became arrogant through
increase of our power. We suffered in having erred in
our judgment of the existing circumstances, which can
happen to anyone. So you should not think because of the
present effective strength of your city and your additions
that the benefit of good luck, too, will always be on your
side. [4.18.1–3]

While things are still undecided, and while good repute
and our friendship are being given to you, and while
our misfortune is being moderately settled before anything
shameful happen, let us be reconciled. [4.20.2]

The Spartans were speaking as if they had not been at war
with the Athenians, and as if they were not now themselves in
the more difficult situation. To ask for reconciliation while
events were undecided would perhaps have been more appropriate in 432. Further, it is a most peculiar judgment of the
rhetorical situation to keep insisting that your enemies could at
any moment become your friends, since nothing very bad has
happened.

In addition to this general error of tone, the Spartans chose
the wrong arguments both for the circumstances and for their
audience. They urged moderation at a moment when the
Athenians would first have felt they might safely be immoder-
ate. Further, their supporting arguments were those piously
sententious ones for which the Athenians had most contempt
in political speeches:

Those wise men who prudently account their good fortune
as uncertain (and these same men are also more intelligent
in their dealings with misfortune) also understand that
war does not accompany someone only for that portion he
wishes to undertake, but rather as far as the fortunes lead.
[4.18.4]

And we believe that great enmities may be most securely

ended, not if someone taking up arms and having conquered the greater part in war and by compulsion encom-
passing his enemy with oaths shall make an illegitimate
peace, but if—though it were possible to do that—conquering him in decency and virtue (beyond what he
expected), so he shall moderately make a reconciliation.
[4.19.2]

Finally, having met with an unexpectedly fierce reaction to
their speech, the Spartans made a disastrous political blunder
in asking that the negotiations be conducted apart from the
assembly. Cleon said he would have none of this "secret"
dealing, and the situation fell apart completely.[13]

There is no question that the Athenians had the Spartans in
a difficult position and that the rhetorical opportunities remaining for the Spartans were severely limited. Nevertheless,
these were the wrong arguments to use at this time and to this
audience. The coolness of the Spartan tone would have been
inflammatory to the Athenians. Since the Athenians had the
Spartans over a barrel, they would want the Spartans to admit
it. Not to do so would amount to a continuing challenge to
increase the pressure until the Spartans finally did make the
admission. Similarly, if the Spartans wished to make the case
that it would be wiser for the Athenians to cut their possible
losses and to settle for what they had already achieved, they
should have searched for a way to make the case other than by
lecturing loftily about the vagaries of fortune. Such platitudes,
to an Athenian audience, could appear only as an admission
that the Spartans had no real arguments to bring. And, of
course, should they reach that conclusion, the Athenians
would be encouraged to try to wring further concessions from
Sparta.

One does not want to say that the Athenians were right to
react as they did. Nor ought one to suggest that the Spartans
had much else they could have said in these circumstances. But
the Spartans could well have made their argument more effectively. Political situations are not abstract occasions. They are
irreducibly concrete: particular circumstances, particular
audiences. Success in political rhetoric depends on being able
to work with the concrete particulars of the situation most

effectively. It is exactly in the realm of the particulars on this occasion that the Spartans failed. This failure becomes for us not only a historical fact, but part of the explanation of the outcome of this event.

It is important that we notice that the Spartan proposals are just and even extremely wise. In the abstract it is a generous and far-sighted offer that is made. Yet in the concrete the offer is so disastrously presented that it had to appear unacceptable to the Athenian audience, and may well have even seemed phony. When the Spartans asked for secret sessions, Athenian distrust of the offer was made complete. Had Thucydides merely reported to us that the Spartans offered the Athenians a peace on such and such lines, and that it was rejected, the decision might have remained unfathomable to us. But by representing this rhetorical disaster to us, Thucydides recreates for us (and thereby makes comprehensible) a concrete political situation within which natural processes of speech and response can—without malice or perversity—obscure the intelligence of a proposal and doom it to rejection.

General and Particular in Rhetorical Situations

Finally, attention to the technical problems of rhetorical situations makes possible the better observation of the particularities of the situations and (with a view to the writing of history) the better representation of these particularities. The sorts of problems a speaker will face in different circumstances can be roughly grouped and codified. Were this not possible, the teaching of rhetoric would itself be impossible. One gathers, in the writing of theories of rhetoric, rules to cover similar circumstances, and arranges advice concerning the arguments to use whether proposing a policy or dissuading from it. In practice, the possibility of making these rough groupings manifests itself in the fact that speeches written to similar purposes will display noticeable similarity in the kinds of arguments used. We have seen an instance of such similarity in the comparison of the Corinthian speech at the second Spartan congress and Pericles' first speech. In this case, both speeches are tactical evaluations and share a common structure.

Attentiveness to this fact of the practice of persuasion can enable the historian to discover (and later exhibit) the unique aspects of specific situations. For if speeches to similar purposes are similar, they are never identical. Knowledge of the technical necessities of rhetoric allows the historian to cancel out of the equation, as it were, those arguments the art of rhetoric abstractly demands. Those arguments which remain after this analysis constitute the irreducible effects of the specific situation in which the speech occurs. These arguments cannot be accounted for as necessary to the *general* rhetorical task at hand; they can only be accounted for as the result of *particular* needs of the particular occasion. They constitute, then, evidence of specific facts about specific historical moments. Accuracy in this discovery of particularity requires, however, a systematic consideration of the rhetorical elements of the situation. Otherwise, it is always possible that arguments which are present because of the generic rhetorical situation will be wrongly assigned to the particular historical one.

An instance of both the possibility of using the rhetorical frame to discover historical particulars and the possible dangers in ignoring the rhetorical frame can be found in a comparison of the speeches given by Archidamus at the first Spartan congress (1.80-85), and by Nicias on the occasion of the debate about the Sicilian expedition (6.9-14). Both of these speeches were given to perform an identical purpose. They are both speeches to dissuade an audience from going to war. Moreover, both speeches were given to audiences already more or less committed to going to war. Because of their identity of purpose, and, up to a point, the identity of the problems each must solve, the two speeches contain a considerable number of similar arguments. There are also, however, marked differences in the specific arguments and in the overall tone the speeches exhibit, and these differences are striking evidence of the specific political facts of the occasions on which they were given. The very similarity of the speeches makes possible the discovery of the differences, and recognition of the generic rhetorical necessities makes possible the discovery of those facts significant to the particular occasion.

The similarities that exist between the two speeches are entirely the result of the identity of their purposes. What arguments are there to be used in dissuading from war? One can claim that it is not in the nation's best interest to go to war. Both Archidamus and Nicias make this claim. One can claim that the supporters of the policy of war have not accurately evaluated the dangers, costs, forces. Both speakers do. One can claim that there is more to lose than to gain by going to war. Both do. One can claim that one's enemy is too well prepared to be defeated. Both do. One can claim that one does not have the material preparations to succeed. Both do. One can make the commonplace claim that war is always risky and that one would do better to preserve what one has. Both do. One will have to deny personal cowardice or timidity to make one's advice credible. Both do. And, because one is facing an audience already predisposed toward war, one must claim that important decisions must not be made hurriedly. Both do.

But while the list of similarities is long, it is crucial that we recognize that all of these similarities are the result of the generic rhetorical necessities and possibilities of the similar situation Archidamus and Nicias find themselves in, and of the generic arguments available for dealing with this situation. If we ask, "What can we find in these speeches *not* necessitated by the generic situation?" the two speeches begin suddenly to diverge in significant ways.[14]

The tones of the speeches are virtually opposite. Archidamus gives an extremely calm appraisal of the situation and makes his case with restraint. His calm is immediately emphasized when his speech is followed by the terse but emotionally charged speech of Sthenelaidas. By contrast, Nicias' speech is anything but calm. Dangers are everywhere, enemies are all around, the nation is even threatened from within. The difference in tone provides us with specific evidence about each speaker, and also, indirectly, with evidence about each audience on these two specific occasions. The Spartan audience was not, evidently, as calm as Archidamus. Yet neither could they have been hysterical or Archidamus would never have expected so restrained a speech to have succeeded. The Athenian audience, in turn (given the arguments they accept in Alcibiades' speech), could not be called calm. Rather, we would say, they found Nicias' speech, agitated as it was, *too* calm, and expressed in their decision an agitation even greater than Nicias'.

The arguments the two men use also differ significantly. Nicias speaks, throughout his speech, of the dangers and enemies of which Athens stands in peril. The nation, he says (6.13.1), is in the greatest danger it has ever faced. The Sicilian expedition risks the possible loss of all of Athens' power and possessions; it lays it open to all of its enemies, who wait only for the opportunity to pounce. It even exposes it to the possible subversion of the democracy itself (6.11.7). Alcibiades, in his turn, also speaks of danger, though of a more abstract kind than Nicias does. But this is surely significant. For the first time, all speakers in a debate at Athens seem driven by fear of something, and this is occurring, paradoxically, in a time of at least nominal peace. The audience does not choose between fear and confidence, but between two kinds of fear. At no previous time has there been such fear expressed in Athens, and in observing this we can find evidence of the new and desperate state of Athenian consciousness in this seventeenth year of the war.

By contrast, the greatest danger Archidamus foresees is that the war will be longer than intended and the honor of it lost. Significantly, nowhere does he even suggest the possibility that Sparta might lose the war. It is not that Archidamus sees no threat in Athens. He, too, feels that Athens must, at some time, be stopped or controlled. But though he shares the general Spartan fear of the eventual threat Athens poses, he never manifests any immediate fear that Sparta would be unable to defeat Athens. This too is a significant fact. Even the man dissuading from war in this debate had no ultimate fear of it. This confidence in an opponent of the war in 432 indirectly testifies to what must have been an even greater confidence in Spartan success held by those in favor of the war. Spartan fear of Athens (the *prophasis* of the war) originates in Spartan passivity. Once into action, it is characteristic of the Spartans to have nothing but confidence in their success. (The period between the loss at Pylos in 425 and the victory at Mantinea in 418 was a notable exception, and is treated as such by Thucydides. See 5.75.3.) Insofar as this might make them incline toward belligerency because they felt safer there, their confidence (wise or foolish) is as much a crucial factor in our understanding of the Spartan decision in 432 as the later Athenian fear is in that instance.

We might mention merely one other difference between the speeches that provides a significant datum in our comprehension of the specific decisions. There is in Nicias' speech an argument unparalleled in Archidamus', and uncalled for by rhetorical necessities. This is the personal attack on Alcibiades and his motives. In Archidamus' speech the only "trouble-makers" are Sparta's allies, urging war prematurely. In Nicias', however, the public interest is under attack even from its own citizens. Whether Nicias' attack implies a widespread breakdown of public spirit in Athens, or merely a particular fear of the person of Alcibiades, we are apprised by it of the disproportionate influence that the personality of Alcibiades had in this deliberation, and we are alerted to take this into account in evaluating the factors which went into creating the eventual decision.

These examples of facts deducible from the rhetorical details of the speeches not only could be multiplied, but should be, for Thucydides' history is able to provide us with two quite different orders of information, of which only one has been so far exploited. From the, as it were, grammatical analyses of the first four chapters—analyses of the parts of the history and of the deployment of the parts—we were able to discern Thucydides' interpretation and explanation of that single, continuous event, the Peloponnesian War. But it would also be possible to discover—from the analyses of the individual speeches or occasions, analyses directed now by an awareness of and alertness to the elements of rhetoric—quite profound but often obscured information concerning the nations and politicians engaged in the war, and information concerning the dynamics of the specific moments of decision in the war. This information would have its natural limits. We would not discover facts about the nations generally, but only in their role as deliberating bodies; we would not find information of enduring factuality by this method, but only information concerning the specific state of affairs at a given moment. Yet because even information limited in this way would be precious to us, such rhetorical analyses ought to be pursued. They would deepen (and perhaps modify) our understanding of the events of the Peloponnesian War, and they would, presumably, deepen our understanding of the nature of human action. They would be limited, of course, by Thucydides' selection of material for inclusion; the search for them, however, would be the most proper use of Thucydides' history.

7 The Human Thing

To subject the speeches of this history to a systematic rhetorical analysis would be a fruitful way of developing information about Greek political life, and would be of great significance to Thucydidean research. It would not, however, complete the particular inquiry upon which we have been engaged. Any and all of the information we could develop, as also the conclusions reached in the six examples of the last chapter, would remain specific facts about specific agents and moments in the Peloponnesian War. Our inquiry is rather different from that. We have been searching for that principle of regularity—embodied in, of course, every specific event—which can properly be seen as the explanation of Thucydides' τò ἀνθρώπινον, the source of the events of the Peloponnesian War, and, so Thucydides asserts, of events to come. We must, as far as we can, describe the principles which, in Thucydides' history of these events, are to be seen simultaneously as the causes of the events themselves and as the means by which these events can be explained and understood.

We should say, initially, that Thucydides has located the cause of events in the public deliberations of the bodies which were the agents of the events. We can continue by saying, further, that he has defined the forces that operate in these deliberations as the elements of deliberation when this is considered an essentially rhetorical activity. To recover the causes of events, and, therefore, to be able to explain them, requires
the recovery and display of the rhetorical elements of a delib-

erative occasion. At this point we can see that it is also necessary to conclude that for Thucydides the regularity which constitutes τὸ ἀνθρώπινον is a regularity of process rather than of result. That is, what occurs again and again for Thucydides are not specific events but a specific process of deliberation in which all actions are begun. The outcome of any action—its event, in the proper sense of the term—is dependent on other simultaneous, sometimes counter-, actions, and is also dependent on chance—that is, on factors which cannot be systematized. No one, therefore, can predict events with certainty. But what can be predicted and understood is that all actions are undertaken after and on account of a process of deliberation which is common to all groups and which has "rules" and necessities of its own. I think it would almost surely be a mistake to conclude that Thucydides (at 1.22.4) makes any claim to a recurrence of specific events: that actions of certain sorts are inevitably followed by results of certain sorts, or that nations of given natures have destinies proper to them. Nothing in the history gives any solid support to such recurrence; and, indeed, Thucydides' sensitivity to the particularity of specific situations would seem to argue against the likelihood of such recurrences. Between actions and their outcomes supervene the most complex and various sets of particular circumstances. To search for regularities of result under these conditions would seem vain. What does seem appropriate to Thucydides' statement at 1.22.4 is the notion of τὸ ἀνθρώπινον as something constant rather than something regularly recurrent. It is this constant, this manner of acting in all circumstances, which both causes all events and is revealed in a history of them.

We should also notice that while this process displays regularities, they are not of the nature of rules in the usual sense. That is, Thucydides neither sees nor provides conclusions of the order of "If such and such occurs in a deliberative or rhetorical situation, thus and so necessarily follows." To provide such rules would merely be to transfer to the realm of deliberation those "regularities of result" we have just claimed Thucydides avoided. Instead, the regularities by which Thucydides constructs his explanations of events are regularities of relations among elements in a situation. What the outcomes of specific deliberations will be is not predictable. But that within the deliberation certain regular elements will exert influences according to their regular relations with other elements of the process is the foundation of Thucydides' historical method. These regularities, while formal and contentless, are sufficient for our purposes, for they provide us with a structure within which it becomes possible to *understand* the origin and even the outcome of events. For example: there is no system of rhetoric that can predict whether the Spartans were to be successful in their peace offer (discussed in the fifth example, chapter 6); but the system of rhetoric gives us an instrument by means of which we can analyze that offer as a deliberative event and can understand the reasons for its failure.

We should go even further. As we consider the details of Thucydides' history, it becomes apparent that while this rhetorically structured process of deliberation is undergone on the occasion of every action, the process is itself subject to modification and distortion. The large-scale change in the nature of the war as a result of the "ideologization" of the grounds of conflict had consequences not only for the way in which the war was fought, but also for the very process of politics during the war. The introduction of ideology was itself a rhetorical and deliberate response to circumstances. Once introduced, it influences concrete policies, to be sure, but also casts a more abstract influence over the war that we can perceive in the new completeness with which oppositions were drawn and in the ease with which they could be justified as irreconcilable. This influence produced serious distortions in the style of rhetoric and the activity of deliberation. Of these, Thucydides' description of the *stasis* at Corcyra provides the most dramatic pictures, but by no means the only ones. As ideological grounds produced both more abstract and more violent oppositions, the very possibilities of deliberation were distorted and reduced. In slogans and in polarized partisanship the desire, the vocabulary, even the audience for rational deliberation was destroyed. Left was a cruel and mocking image of deliberation, in which attempts at communication could only reinforce the tendency toward fragmentation. The initial move to ideological interpretations has in it, apparently, something natural to rhetoric and deliberation under conditions of stress. We find our evidence for this in the fact that *both* sides responded in this way to similar—but not identical—circumstances at approximately the same moment in the war. In this case, it seems that for Thucydides something in the very process of rhetoric and deliberation is also the source of its stress and change.

Our awareness of Thucydides' interest in the process of deliberation as itself subject to change and development enables us to recognize a further peculiarity of the way in which he has conceived of and used rhetoric in the history. As an art of speaking, rhetoric considers each rhetorical occasion as static and instantaneous. That this is so is turned by Thucydides to his advantage, for it is this aspect of rhetoric that enables him to make use of it as a way of recovering and representing the particularity of occasions and decisions. But, in fact, occasions are not truly instantaneous and discrete. They are linked in relations of direct and indirect causality, though rhetoric per se is unable to take account of this linkage. It is in this respect that Thucydides has constituted for his own purposes an idiosyncratic use of rhetoric and a novel system of deliberation.

Thucydides has made use of rhetoric as it is usually conceived (static and instantaneous) as an instrument for the discovery of the individual operating factors on individual occasions. But to this usual conception of rhetoric he has added an extra dimension. He has put the notion of static rhetoric into motion, investigating deliberation not only in isolated occasions but in the relation of occasions to each other. The resulting historical method is firmly grounded in rhetoric, but is different from it. When we speak of rhetoric in Thucydides we must no longer limit our understanding of the term to its usual significances. We are not concerned, here, with the discovery of the means of persuasion, nor with using a system of the means of persuasion as a tool only for the discovery of isolated facts of a situation.[1] Thucydides has explored the elements and the relations of elements that exist *between* deliberative situations as well as the elements that exist within them. What are

looked for are the regular relations between deliberations
thought of as connected chains, in which there exists not only
the usual structure of interdependencies of audience, speaker,
and speech, but also new and complex structures of influences
(themselves the consequences of rhetorical acts) exerted by
earlier decisions and by limits imposed on the possibilities of
deliberation.

We might speak of Thucydides' extended use of rhetoric in
either of two ways. We could call it a science, or art, of politics
as it would be constituted by rhetoric. That is, where rhetoric is
static, and, in a sense, blind to consequence (in that it does not
consider how the success of an argument may affect later arguments and deliberations), Thucydides' new use of rhetoric
would precisely construct a structure of consequence among
the elements of rhetorical situations and among isolated
rhetorical situations themselves. Or we could speak of Thucydides' approach as the constitution of a new shape of rhetoric, in which the notion of deliberation is extended from that
of individual decisions to that of a continuous process of inter-
locking decisions. Within what is, essentially, a new definition
of the nature of deliberation, appropriately new determinations of the elements of rhetoric and their relations would be
made.

We can now make a statement about the content of τὸ
ἀνθρώπινον which, if necessarily formal, will seem satisfactory both to the requirements we have established in this
inquiry and to our experience of Thucydides' history. Tὸ ἀν -
θρώπινον is that process of deliberation which all men undertake in initiating action. It is a process which, since it involves
men as constituted in a public (the deliberating public being
the mediating body between the individuals in whom ultimate cause must be located and the national actions with
which this history is concerned), can be represented as and
understood by means of a version of rhetoric. The version of
rhetoric is one which structures not only the relations of public
(functionally divided as speaker and audience) to circumstance
in discrete situations, but also structures the relations of situation to situation, and comprises, therefore, a structure of past
to present circumstance and of public to itself over time.

Insofar as this process is, to Thucydides, universal, it is embodied in and directs events at all moments. Insofar as the process is known to us only as a structure of elements and relations, its universality guarantees only that we can predict the recurrence of the structure in all human attempts to deal corporately with the world. It cannot guarantee the predictable recurrence of any specific event. Insofar, however, as the process has a kind of shape and also a developmental structure of its own, it imparts a characteristic shape and development even to actions of quite disparate outcome. That τὸ ἀνθρώπινον which is, for Thucydides, both the cause, in the most general sense, of all events, and also what is to be learned by the study of his history, is this complex rhetorical structure through which—as Thucydides conceives it—men organize their individual existences into social actions.

This explanation of τὸ ἀνθρώπινον strikes, I believe, the proper balance between generality and particularity. It is, as a universal structure of concerted human action, necessarily general enough to account for all actions. Yet, as a flexible structure of elements for which individuated content is discovered occasion by occasion, it is naturally adapted to the particularities of specific actions. Explanations of τὸ ἀνθρώπινον which are too abstract, such as Hunter's "tragic warners" (see note 14, chap. 6) or the "ironic" relation Stahl sees between human action and human knowledge prove unsatisfactory in that they obscure the crucial individuation of specific historical events.[2] Explanations which are too specific, on the other hand, lose sight of the regularity Thucydides claims directs human actions. But our notion of a complex rhetorical structure of action is appropriately regular and specific.

The choice of a given principle (or set of principles) for the investigation and composition of history necessarily has the most profound consequences for the inclusion and exclusion of evidence and fact. The choice of the specifically rhetorical principles of this history is no exception. Two consequences especially must be singled out for examination, one concerning the nature of the evidence adduced in, and one the nature of the entities considered by, the history. The peculiarities of Thucydidean evidence and entities distinguish the character of the history and its significance with the greatest clarity.

Because the Thucydidean τὸ ἀνθρώπινον provides that the explanation of actions is to be found in an understanding of the deliberations of the publics whose actions they are, all relevant evidence for the understanding of the deliberations must itself be public. Where small groups or individuals have the authority to decide and implement policy, secret motives and factors may well influence their actions, and to understand these actions would require the recovery of these hidden motives and forces. But when publics are the deliberating bodies, secret evidence is irrelevant. The material about which the public deliberates, its motives, and the arguments it hears are all perforce public, too. Not only will the evidence be public, it must be public, for information concealed from the public by definition cannot influence the decision of the public. Thucydides recognized both the opportunity this presented (all information necessary to an explanation of events would be publicly available) and also the limitation it imposed (all proper explanations of events must restrict themselves only to public information), and the consistency with which he adhered to this structure of explanation can be indicated by the example of his treatment of Demosthenes' strategy for Pylos (book 4).

In explaining the invention of a strategy, there are two quite different moments a historian may choose for its presentation: he may present the strategy at the very moment of its conception or at the later moment that the plan was presented to the public. In the case of Demosthenes, Thucydides has chosen the later, public moment, and has done so for an essentially rhetorical reason. For Thucydides to withhold his presentation of this information until public receipt is not mere punctiliousness. Inasmuch as a public cannot react to or act on information or a plan until the moment it has been made known to it, proper understanding of the subsequent public action requires evaluating *when* the public learned something as well as what it learned. By presenting Demosthenes' plan at the moment it was made public, Thucydides makes easier the proper evaluation of the impact (and therefore the influence) of the information on the particular deliberative occasion at which it arose. In his sensitivity to this, Thucydides is clearly consistent with his concentration on the rhetorical explanation of events. In the case of Demosthenes' plan the relevance of all this is apparent.

That Demosthenes did have a plan for Pylos (possibly formulated during his temporary self-exile in Acharnania) is the only reasonable interpretation to be made from Thucydides' introduction to this episode (4.2–5). That Thucydides does not present the plan at the moment Demosthenes conceived it has led Hunter to speak of a "total lack of plan,"[3] but this seems wrong. Demosthenes asks (αὐτῷ δεηθέντι) to accompany the expedition of Eurymedon and Sophocles even though he was not a general at this time (ὄντι ἰδιώτῃ); he asks for, and receives, an unspecified grant of authority (εἶπον χρῆσθαι ταῖς ναυσί); he asserts, *in situ,* that the fortification of Pylos was his sole reason for accompanying the expedition ([εἶπε] ἐπὶ τοῦτο γὰρ ξυνεκπλεῦσαι). Why choose Pylos, why ask for authority, why desire to accompany this expedition, if not in the execution of a predetermined plan? Thucydides could, of course, have been explicit on this occasion, but the postponement of the presentation of Demosthenes' plan helps to explain two phenomena otherwise more obscure. In the first place, it explains the reluctance of Eurymedon and Sophocles to participate in what turns out to be a wonderfully successful and economical strategy. The plan was sprung on them as much as it is on us, and their reaction is not unreasonable considering that they were unprepared for it. If we had been told of this plan earlier, and thought it well known, we would probably misinterpret their rejection of it. Even more importantly, however, postponing the revelation of the plan until its execution helps to explain the reaction of the *Athenians* to the plan's success. Their actions are precisely those of the recipients of a windfall. They exhibit all the improvisation and lack of forethought of people surprised by an event and without a plan to deal with it. The excesses of the Athenians on this occasion (seen most vividly in their responses at 4.21–22 to the speech of the Spartans) certainly have their origin in the unexpectedness of Athens' good fortune. But had we been told of Demosthenes' plan at the moment of its conception we would assume (or be tempted to assume) its public knowledge, and the surprise of the Athenians would then be inexplicable. Postponement of the presentation of Demosthenes' strategy until its public presentation, however, embodies and emphasizes the fact that the Athenians had not participated in the formulation of this strategy, and makes it easier for us to understand their response and their subsequent deliberations.

Further examples of Thucydides' consistent concern only with public evidence can be found in his almost cavalier treatment of the motives of individual politicians and, indeed, of individuals generally, until quite late in the war. Woodhead[4] in essence judged Thucydides untrustworthy in personal judgments, and in a sense may well be right. Thucydides' statements about individuals are summary and usually unsupported by evidence. But if they are untrustworthy it is not for the reasons of political prejudice or blindness that are usually suggested. Rather, Thucydides' virtual disregard of evidence to support his judgments of persons is the result of the consistency of his historical principles. Within the rhetorical structure of τὸ ἀνθρώπινον, the motives of politicians are rarely relevant, and, if secret, are never relevant. In this rhetorical structure, publics act only on public influences. Why Cleon or another politician proposed a policy is, in Thucydides' explanation of events, of no importance unless by the motive being publicly known, it influenced public approval or disapproval of the policy. But since the motives of politicians are not often common knowledge (and, indeed, are sometimes concealed), for Thucydides the motives behind the action of individuals rarely carry any explanatory force. This said, we can see that Thucydides' judgments of individuals are most often by way of personal asides, and would be felt by the historian to be outside criticism since they would not be evidence used to explain an event. That is, it is because motives are rhetorically insignificant (and, let us add, because Thucydides felt the actions of individuals were easily understood) that Thucydides is nonchalant in his treatment of them.

Similarly, individuals as individuals tend to play a subordinate role in public deliberations. The person of the speaker is sometimes relevant (and, as we have said, when it is Thucydides gives us the requisite information), but is often not. In the later stages of the war, however, events became less and less the actions of the public and more and more the actions of small partisan groups or even the coups of individuals. Under these circumstances the importance of individuals and individual motives as explanations of events would necessarily increase relative to the declining importance of the public. And indeed, Thucydides' history reflects this. The increased numbers of individuals about whom we learn in the later books do not indicate a change in Thucydides' approach to historical explanation. They exhibit the employment of a consistent approach under changed historical conditions.

In addition to the deemphasis of individuals and the almost complete exclusion of motive as historically significant, we should recognize that the principled concentration on the *public* activity of deliberation makes necessary the exclusion of two other broad—and usually potent—areas of historical evidence. Insofar as publics act consciously and at determinate moments, no explanatory force can be given to factors which do not satisfy these criteria. Factors such as economics or culture, destiny or dialectics, must in most cases be excluded from the Thucydidean schema. As subterranean or unconscious forces they will mainly be excluded. Their appearances will be limited to those specific occasions on which they are explicitly appealed to, or to those occasions where their influence can be seen embodied in other explicit statements. But the notion of an invisible, impersonal, unconscious, and unmanipulable force behind events is obviously foreign to Thucydides' principles. This is one area of evidence (potent in modern histories) excluded by Thucydides. Even more startling (given the interests of the history) is the necessary exclusion from the history of any account of what we might call "politicking."

In this exclusion we find another indication of the individuality of Thucydides' notion of politics and of that political "science" which informs his history. That in addition to public acts of deliberation there also exist numberless private acts of intrigue, bargaining, agreement, and influence is so central to our usual understanding of the political process that we cannot conceive of politics occurring without them. Yet, in the main, such private acts go unrepresented in Thucydides' history, for the most part for reasons akin to the spotty representation of information concerning individual politicians. The principle involved is straightforward. Since the agent in all instances is a public, the intrigues or private bargains which bring one or another policy to the public cannot truly explain the public event which ultimately occurred. In the final analysis, for Thucydides, the *public* had to choose the action deliberately. Such a choice cannot be explained by nonpublic arrangements from which—necessarily—the public had been excluded and by which, therefore, it could not have been influenced. For this reason evidence to explain public action is restricted to public evidence, and private actions are for the most part omitted.

We are probably more willing in the case of Thucydides' history to accept this drastic exclusion of what we would usually consider political fact than we would be under other circumstances. The character of the political entities with which Thucydides deals has much to do with that willingness. In the case of direct—that is, nonrepresentative—"democracies"[5] and of publics that are, essentially, politically unorganized (in terms of formal parties or pressure groups) it is more reasonable to restrict evidence to public factors than in the case of modern, representative, highly organized polities. In our determination of the fitness of this restriction the size of the deliberating body plays a large role. Beyond a certain size an unorganized body can, practically speaking, only be influenced wholesale—that is, by public appeal and persuasion. Under a certain size it is conceivable that the body can be swayed by personal agreements or by, for example, bribery. The smaller the body the more important we would feel it was to consider "politicking" in the explanation of events.[6] The larger the body, the more acceptable we would find a history which restricted its evidence to public deliberation. As regards Thucydides' history, it is most likely the immediacy of *all* Greek political activity which causes us to believe that despite the history's overwhelming interest in the activity of politics, it is not fatally incomplete in omitting consideration of the politicking which must certainly have surrounded the occasions of public deliberation that are recorded.

These restrictions on the kind of evidence adduced constitute one consequence of the rhetorical orientation of Thucydides' history. There occurs as well, however, a second consequence no less critical in the shaping of the character of this history. There is manifested throughout the history an entirely rhetorical notion of what social entities are to be considered the agents in the war, and this rhetorical notion influences the kinds of explanation the history provides.

Within a rhetorical analysis of action, the agent is an *audience* persuaded to undertake a specific act. Within a rhetorical analysis of persuasion, every audience is *generically* alike. Of course, every individual audience is in fact different from every other audience. This, indeed, is one of the most important lessons taught by any adequate theory of rhetoric. Even the same body constitutes a different audience on different occasions, as it is under the influence of one or another emotion, for example. But audiences, in this regard, are different *specifically*. They are alike generically insofar as they are all audiences.

This distinction turns out to be critical. In saying that individual audiences are specific variations within a single genus, audience, we bind ourselves to the consequence that audiences differ from one another only according to those differentiae proper to their genus. This limitation of the differentiae of the groups which are the agents of the Peloponnesian War to only those differentiae appropriate to audiences has a profound effect on the nature of historical explanation in this history. Certain qualities of nations—because qualities of audiences— become essential to an explanation of the actions of the war; other qualities, although known facts about the nations, are rendered irrelevant because they are not qualities of audiences considered rhetorically. Rhetorically, audiences are composed of individuals who act under the influence of individual motivations (passions, goals, habits). (That rhetoric considers audiences as composed of individuals is in fact what makes rhetoric useful—to the historian—as the intermediary between individuals and social action.) Audiences are identified and distinguished by differences in those individual motivations or by qualities which implicate differences in motivation.

As an example of the first, angry audiences are different from calm ones; they are distinguished by the difference of their emotions. We should note that this difference is, at base, a difference which resides in individuals (passion). As an example of the second, audiences composed of the old are different from those composed of the young; they are distinguished by a quality (age) which brings with it differential emotional responses to identical situations and differential methods of dealing with circumstances. Again, we should notice that the differentia (age) resides in individuals.

When this rhetorical orientation is applied to deliberative bodies, the aspects of them that it selects as important (and also those it rejects as irrelevant) give the nature of its explanations a characteristic and unusual cast. An example remote from the Peloponnesian War may make the shape of this analysis (and its consequences for the writing of history) clear. Were one to examine the United States Senate from the standpoint of rhetoric—that is, as a body constituting an audience for persuasion—one would want to determine certain sorts of facts to suggest how to move it to action or to explain why it acted as it did. One would be interested in the average age of the members (the old act differently from the young); one would be interested in their wealth (the rich have different goals, perhaps, from the poor); one would want to know their previous occupations (lawyers, no doubt, approach action differently than laborers); one might want to know whether they had previously lived in urban or rural areas; one would certainly want to know their party affiliation. All of these facts (and many more like them) would differentiate this body as an audience from other bodies as audiences, and would form materials for use in persuasion or, more to our purpose, elements of the explanation of its action. But all of these facts, we must note, would be facts concerning the individuals who belong to this body. Not one of these facts concerns the nature of the body as a body. To put this another way: one might, according to a rhetorical analysis, explain an action of the Senate as a result of the character of senators as a group older, richer, and more lawyerly than most groups. But one would not—rhetorically—explain the action as a result of the senators being the members of an institution called the Senate and constituted according to organizational rules and procedures of its own.

Rhetorical analysis is essentially subinstitutional, and it is in this way that all audiences are seen as generically the same. Groups, in rhetoric, are differentiated by the different qualities of their members (these are the specific differentiae of audiences), not by differences between the groups *as groups*.[7] Rhetorically, and for Thucydides, any group which acts and which is to be persuaded before it acts, is essentially the same as any other such group, regardless of differences of size or of function or of the rules of order according to which it operates. As long as it has authority to act and deliberates in deciding upon its action, any group is generically identical to any other. In Thucydides we can see this rhetorical characteristic in three striking ways. First, we can see it in his representation of the activity of deliberation as identical even in quite dissimilar situations. Deliberation appears to proceed in exactly the same fashion whether the location is Athens, or Sparta, whether the group addressed is numerous (as the Athenian assembly) or limited (the Spartan judges at Plataea). This homogeneity of treatment has sometimes been criticized as unrealistic, but follows the principle of the functional identity of all audiences. Insofar as the essential structure of persuasion is always the same, one can represent an unchanging and universal *structure* of deliberation. The homogeneity remains, nevertheless, only at the generic level. At the individual level all audiences in Thucydides are distinguished, and if the shape of persuasion is ever the same, the content of persuasion is ever different.

Secondly, we can see the rhetorical conception of the nature of group agents in Thucydides' consistent application of the rhetorical model of deliberation to all groups which act, even where the application seems bizarre to us. In this particular instance I am referring to Thucydides' representation of the actions of armies as deliberative actions. That armies should be *persuaded* to take the field, or to follow a certain tactical plan, is foreign to our experience. Yet it is thus that Thucydides does present them, even the Spartan army. The Spartan example may be taken as evidence of the consistency of Thucydides' practice, for he is equally aware of the routine discipline of the Spartan army, ascribing to this discipline its dramatic success in the battle of Mantinea (5.66.2-4, 5.70). Yet insofar as an army is a group of men and a group which must act, armies too are treated by Thucydides within the schema of rhetorical analysis. I believe we are meant to accept the speeches of generals not only as convenient narrative devices for informing us of intentions and tactics, but as, for Thucydides, an essential part of the process of bringing the army into action. In this practice, however, we see the deemphasis of all those characteristics—discipline and chain-of-command, for example— which render armies institutionally different from groups of other sorts. We see, rather, a concentration on precisely those characteristics which armies have in common with every other acting group of individuals.

Finally, we can see the characteristic shape of the rhetorical conception of action in Thucydides' almost total silence on the institutional details of the nations and groups involved in the war. As much as we would have been grateful for information concerning the institutional structure of the political bodies of the nations and alliances, we cannot find such information in this history. Nor can we explain Thucydides' silence away by pretending that he felt such information was so well known to his contemporary readers that its inclusion would be otiose. Thucydides shows hardly any confidence in the breadth of knowledge of his readers, to judge from his comments at 1.20.1 and 1.20.3. If he felt that most Greeks did not know how many votes the Spartan kings had (1.20.3), we can hardly expect that he believed them to have known very much about far more complicated institutional arrangements. Our explanation must be found, simply, in the fact that, from a rhetorical point of view, institutional rules or rules of procedure are of significance only when they change in some way the shape of deliberation.[8] Under all other circumstances they are irrelevant, not being proper differentiae of the *audience* to which persuasion is addressed and by which deliberation is carried out.

As in the case of the first of our consequences—that the

rhetorical analysis of action restricted evidence to public evidence—here, too, the rhetorical nature of Thucydides' history delimits and distinguishes the kind of history this is. If rhetoric as a system indicates to us those facts of a historical situation which are significant to explain an event, it also excludes all other facts as insignificant. The public dimension of rhetoric excludes from consideration impersonal, "underground" forces, and also private political activity. The generic identity of audiences from the point of view of rhetoric excludes consideration of all differentiae of groups which are not also differentiae of audiences. The most important effect of this is to exclude institutional explanations of events. In our consideration of those factors of action included by rhetoric and of those factors excluded can emerge the precise and idiosyncratic conception of action which constitutes the principle according to which actions occur ($\tau\grave{o}$ $\grave{\alpha}\nu\theta\rho\acute{\omega}\pi\iota\nu o\nu$), the principle according to which actions must be understood, and the principle according to which Thucydides has composed his history of the Peloponnesian War.

At the beginning of this inquiry, in chapter 5, it was agreed that three benefits would accrue to us from making explicit the principles of Thucydides' history. First, our acquisition of these principles—that is, our understanding of the lessons of the history—could only be improved. Second, knowledge of the principles would make apparent the areas of strength (and weakness) of the history, and thereby guide us to the proper use of the history. Third, we would be able to judge the value of the principles as principles of history more easily when they were stated abstractly and explicitly than when they remained embodied in the events of the history. At this point in our inquiry we are in a position to be able to reap these benefits which have served as the goals toward which the inquiry was directed. Our approach to the benefits can be restated as questions: In what way is our understanding advanced? What is the proper use of this history? What is the value of the history? Our answers to these questions must necessarily be summary, corresponding to the very formal discussion we have developed of the principles. Yet our answers can direct further inquiry as more material statements of Thucydides' principles are eventually made.

The first question is most easily answered, at least in the brief form all of these answers will take. Our understanding of the meaning of Thucydides' history of the Peloponnesian War is advanced and perfected by our explicit recognition of the rhetorical principles of the history, and our understanding of the nature of action is broadened (should we decide, ultimately, to accept these principles) to encompass Thucydides' rhetorical structure of action. In considering the events of the war and their explanations, our attention is now directed to those aspects of Thucydides' narrative demonstrably relevant to these principles—that is, to those statements in the narrative which relate to or provide explanation of the rhetorical factors as they might influence the actions of the war. Without knowledge of the principles it would be possible to misconstrue the elements of the narrative by not seeing their relation to essentially rhetorical forces, entities, and necessities. Knowing the principles, all details are organized as elements of a rhetorical explanation of action. In some cases we can only now become aware of the relevance of details, as, for instance, those whose lack of material influence on the war makes their inclusion in the history seem gratuitous may yet be seen as having a significant influence on one or another aspect of the rhetorical structure of deliberation. In other cases details known to be significant will now be given univocal significance as we can see that for Thucydides their essential significance is to be found in their relation to rhetorical factors and processes. The discovery of the proper significance of all details and the reduction of ambiguity to univocal meaning are precisely the advancement and perfection of the understanding of a document, in this case Thucydides' history. In the advancement of our understanding of action, explicit statement of the principles enables us to apply them outside the single context of the Peloponnesian War. (Stated abstractly they are indeed abstracted from the events of this war, and made available for use elsewhere.) Their application to other actions, of course, will give those actions structure and intelligibility along these rhetorical lines and will broaden our awareness of the forces operative in action generally.

Our ability to make an explicit statement about the nature of Thucydides' principles also allows us to indicate the proper and improper uses of the history. The proper use of a history, of course, is one that exploits the history in the areas of its strength and that does not ask of it information that by principle it cannot provide. In our consideration of the uses to which we can put the history, we should probably distinguish two different levels of use. We should ask, ''What uses can one properly make of the history in the understanding of fifth-century Greece, and also, in the understanding of those regularities which underlie all human action?''

The extreme individuality of Thucydides' analysis of action immediately indicates some uses of the history as fruitful and others as vain and improper. The concentration of the history on the process of public deliberation makes the history necessarily weak on all those facts which do not comprise elements not only of deliberation but of Thucydides' special conception of deliberation. To expect the history to provide systematic information about Greek economics or Greek social classes or Greek culture is a foolish hope; to fault Thucydides for not providing this information an unfair criticism; to use the history as a source for this information a practice to be undertaken with the greatest caution. It is not that Thucydides is entirely silent on these sorts of subjects. Were he entirely silent the issue would probably not arise. But these subjects appear fitfully in the history, as they occasionally become material for or influences on specific deliberations. One cannot expect that these subjects will appear with any consistency. Worse (from the standpoint of historians of these matters), when they do appear, the subjects appear only in the guises they naturally take in rhetoric, that is, as alleged evidence in partisan arguments. It is for this reason that even the appearances of these subjects must be treated with caution. We must constantly be aware of the possibility that statements on these matters have been systematically distorted (by habit, prejudice, art, or malice) for their use in rhetorical situations. It may yet be possible to make use of these statements, but to do so will require constant evaluation of the rhetorical circumstances in which the statements appear.

If in general Thucydides must be considered a bad source for evidence for all of the nondeliberate factors we believe may operate in history, he is, conversely, precisely useful as a source for information in respect of all of the elements of a deliberative situation conceived of rhetorically. We would make proper use of the history in the determination of details of fifth-century political life and practice, although even here we must recognize limits. We will learn little of the institutional aspects of Greek politics; we will learn little of informal politics "behind the scenes." But of politics as a public activity of the citizens of the Greek states, Thucydides must be the premier source. In addition to information about the specific practices of politics we can also properly use the history to discover facts about the citizens who composed the politically active elements of the cities. Again, we must recognize limits. Rhetoric is interested in only certain circumscribed aspects of the people who attend deliberations. We cannot expect to learn too many facts about the Athenians, for example, who composed the audience at the assembly, for many of their characteristics do not appear in the schema of rhetoric. On the other hand, we can learn details about these audiences which —although confined to those characteristics of groups *qua* audiences—are of an intimacy and depth we might otherwise find startling. We can use Thucydides to discover facts about the different emotions and active habits of the different nations and of the same nations on different occasions. This, too, would be a proper use of the history.

At the level of the regularities of action (rather than of specific facts about Greece) we find similar uses and limitations. We must not look to Thucydides for laws of economics or culture or institutions or for laws of the influence these sectors have on action. Nor should we expect to find rules of the form, "If such and such happens, such and such else will happen." The analytical principles by which Thucydides has written his history are simultaneously contentless so as to avoid such determinate laws, and adapted to particularity so as to render unlikely such regularity. With the sensitivity to the manifold of influences that operate on each occasion that one develops through rhetorical analysis, regularity of outcome is rare. Rather, the regularities one finds are regularities of the way in which politics and action are carried out, and it is laws of the conduct of politics and of the structure of concerted human action that we can properly try to discover in Thucydides' history.

The strengths and uses of the history are so hedged round with weaknesses and limits that we might fear our initial abstract judgment of its value ought to be equivocal. We cannot ask of the history questions about institutions, economics, culture. It is a political history, yet we cannot find in it consistent information about those informal political acts we know form part of any political event. Action is reduced, in Thucydides, not only to political causes, but to a very limited notion of what constitutes political causes. If we consider the almost excessive limitation on the nature of political explanation that Thucydides exhibits, and compare the *abstract* statement of this principle to our modern beliefs about the complexity of action and (therefore) of the explanation of action, our first impulse might be to judge Thucydides' principles deficient and even naïve.

If there was ever a time at which action was believed to be adequately explained by any narrow rhetorical conception of deliberation, the time has long passed, and Thucydides has borne the brunt of criticism directed from positions established by and grounded in other principles of action. First in time in this century the efficacy of economic forces was admitted to the explanation of action, and, whether the economics was liberal or Marxist, Thucydides was faulted for ignoring the influence of this element. More recently, we have expanded our notions of the originating and shaping factors of action to include social, psychological, and cultural forces whose content and influence are still being debated, but whose operation is now felt to be significant. To all of these factors Thucydides, as we have said, pays only fitful attention, and then only as they appear in rhetorical shapes. Oddly, Herodotus, whom Thucydides no doubt felt to be gullible or fanciful for his admission of a multiplicity of causes (rather than the ''scientific'' reduction of causes to Thucydidean simplicity), comes closer in many respects to our modern notions of the complexity of factors in action than Thucydides does. (And, perhaps, recently reawakened interest in Herodotus as a serious historian reflects this belief in the need for complex and often indirect explanations of the causes of events.)

Yet, if on the abstract level there appears to be a deficiency in Thucydides' principle of history, it is rare that we feel any such deficiency in the concrete experience of reading this history. Far from seeming excessively reductionist or naïve, Thucydides' narrative seems both complex and convincing. Throughout the history we are struck by the prudence of the explanations and judgments Thucydides tenders. Insofar as we believe prudence is precisely not the result of the reduction of the scope of one's analysis but of its expansiveness, our judgment of Thucydides' prudence and our concrete approval of the history suggests we reconsider the abstract evaluation we have made of its principles, to discover in them an authentic source of their actual complexity and multidimensionality.

Deliberation can be conceived of as little more than rational calculation. When this is the case, no one will feel that deliberation alone can adequately account for the actions humans undertake, nor could a history of deliberation provide an adequate explanation of these actions. But it is evident that Thucydides holds no such limited conception of deliberation, nor so narrow a conception of rhetoric as to limit it only to the presentation of policy. From the standpoint of rhetoric, deliberation is far more than calculation. There enters into rhetoric not only reason but also the entire range of subtle extrarational elements with which we have dealt in the preceding chapter. Deliberation becomes, under this schema, a complete human activity, involving both the rational and emotive life of the participants. Insofar as the audience, once persuaded, has come to agreement and concord (or its opposite), deliberation becomes a process of communication, community building, and community reinforcement (or their opposites). Insofar as deliberation in this model requires concert of ends as well as means, it comes also to include values as well as facts.

In the treatment Thucydides has given it is not the case that action has been "reduced" to politics. Were this so, our initial equivocal judgment would be proper, perhaps even too kind. In fact, however, Thucydides has come to his treatment of action with a conception in which politics has been generalized into a structure of human communication, interaction, and action. The structure is not one restricted solely to the political arena as it is usually demarcated, but one by which all human action takes place insofar as actions involving more than one person always require a form of persuasion for their accomplishment. It is this extensiveness of conception, this notion of rhetoric as a form of communication and action that gives to Thucydides' history the depth and complexity in the concrete which seem to be missing in a curt expression of the principle. It is the universality of communication and persuasion that guarantees the fitness of Thucydides' representation of the experience of human action, and it is also their universality which makes it proper that the principle of regularity at the heart of these processes be called the human thing.

List of Abbreviations

Journal abbreviations are in the form used in *L'Année philologique*.

AClass	*Acta classica*
BICS	*Bulletin of the Institute of Classical Studies*
BRL	*Bulletin of the John Rylands Library*
CPh	*Classical Philology*
CQ	*Classical Quarterly*
GRBS	*Greek, Roman, and Byzantine Studies*
JHS	*Journal of Hellenic Studies*
PCPhS	*Proceedings of the Cambridge Philological Society*
QS	*Quaderni di Storia*
REA	*Revue des Etudes Anciennes*
REG	*Revue des Etudes Grecques*
TAPhA	*Transactions and Proceedings of the American Philological Association*
YClS	*Yale Classical Studies*

Notes

Introduction

1. "The Speeches in Thucydides and the Mytilene Debate," *YCIS* 24 (1975): 71-94, esp. pp. 71-79. See also Donald Lateiner, "The Speech of Teutiaplus (Thuc. 3.30)," *GRBS* 16 (1975): 175-84, esp. pp. 180-81.

2. See also Kagan, "The Speeches in Thucydides," p. 76.

3. "Speeches and Course of Events in Books Six and Seven of Thucydides," in *The Speeches in Thucydides* (hereafter *SIT*), ed. Philip A. Stadter (Chapel Hill: University of North Carolina Press, 1973), pp. 60-77, esp. p. 61.

4. As Kagan has also argued, "The Speeches in Thucydides," p. 78.

5. Kagan, p. 79.

Chapter One

1. For this date, the date of this debate, and of events up to the outbreak of the war, I have relied on A. W. Gomme, *A Historical Commentary on Thucydides* 5 vols. (Oxford: the Clarendon Press, 1945-) 1: 196-98 and 424-25.

2. Herein I differ with G. E. M. de Ste. Croix, *The Origins of the Peloponnesian War* (Ithaca: Cornell University Press, 1972). De Ste. Croix speaks (pp. 57-58) about justifiable and unjustifiable αἰτίαι, and at p. 72 speaks of Corinthian arguments which have "some validity" against a full offensive and defensive alliance, but "none whatever" against a merely defensive alliance (as was concluded after this debate). He does not take full account of two serious points: first, Thucydides makes no such distinction between justifiable and

unjustifiable αἰτίαι. In the *political* processes at work, such a distinction is futile, for justifiable or not, nations do allege these events as αἰτίαι, and so act upon them. Second, with respect to the validity of Corinthian arguments, the Corinthians make no distinction between a defensive alliance and full offensive and defensive alliance. They declare that *any* Athenian aid to Corcyra will be interpreted as a hostile act. That a defensive might literally be considered different— in law—from a full alliance is no doubt true. But in the face of the Corinthian statements this distinction is specifically denied, and for our purposes rendered irrelevant.

3. Τὸ μέλλον τοῦ πολέμου: a striking rhetorical play on the Corcyreans' "the coming war" (τὸν μέλλοντα πόλεμον).

4. See Donald Kagan, *The Outbreak of the Peloponnesian War* (Ithaca: Cornell University Press, 1969), p. 242.

5. This, to my mind, is the explanation of Thucydides' omission of any Athenian speeches in the deliberation following this debate (see Kagan, *Outbreak,* pp. 237, 370). The meaning of the event had been rendered absolutely unequivocal and unambiguous by the terms of the Corinthian speech. Though we may regret losing the information about Athenian politics such speeches would have provided, for Thucydides' account of the war no Athenian speeches were necessary.

6. Insofar as wars do not suddenly occur, but come into being step by step as any political process does, so their causes do not operate simply on an "off/on" basis. The need for steps to turn even an existing, underlying hostility into an actual war explains the coexistence, in Thucydides, of two different kinds of cause. Their relation will be dealt with extensively in chapters 4 and 5. We need not attribute them to different moments of composition, as A. Andrewes, "Thucydides on the Causes of the War," *CQ* n.s. 9 (1959): 223–39, esp. pp. 227–31, and Raphael Sealey, "The Causes of the Peloponnesian War," *CPh* 70 (1975): 89–109.

7. See also Kagan, p. 278.

8. As Andrewes claims ("Thucydides on the Causes of the War," p. 234), thus demonstrating that revenge is the motive that comes most quickly to mind here. It is no doubt because of the naturalness of assuming revenge that Thucydides is careful to explain that it was not the motive.

9. As Thucydides himself indicates at 1.66, in introducing this conference: "Nevertheless, the war itself did not yet break out, but there was still a ceasefire. For the Corinthians did these things on their own account."

10. Also Kagan, p. 289.

11. See Kagan, pp. 290–91, though I believe it is rhetorical formalism that we see here rather than his speculative indictment of a particular party in Spartan politics.

12. Examples are: (1) of inappropriate description: 1.70.2, "they are innovators who both make their plans quickly and accomplish in deeds what they conceive" (but almost all Athenian speakers claim that love of debate precisely retards the speedy execution of policy—a claim common to all democracies) and 1.70.8, "and so they weary themselves with every kind of toil and risk throughout their whole lives; and they least of all enjoy what they have at any given moment because of their continual acquiring of more; and they believe in no other holiday than the accomplishment of what is necessary, and they think inactive quietness is no less a misfortune than toilsome business is" (which not only is contradicted by Pericles in the Funeral Oration, but, as description, might more properly apply to the constant Spartan military preparation); (2) of telling only part of the story: 1.70.4, "they are always away from home in comparison to you [the Spartans] who will never leave it; for they think that by absence they can acquire something, while you think your leaving will injure what you already have" (but the Athenians must be "away from home" because that is where their commerce is, and the Spartans "stay at home" not because of flaws of character, but from the fear—quite real to them—of Helot rebellion); (3) of elegance overwhelming sense: 1.70.6, "and further, to do something on their nation's behalf, they use their bodies like foreigners' but their minds like natives' " (which is surely magnificent, but difficult to refer to any particular actions).

13. See Kagan, pp. 285, 290–91.

14. Thucydides himself notes that this is the reason the peace was broken, at 1.88: "And the Spartans voted that the truce had been broken, and that there must be war; not so much because they were persuaded by the speeches of their allies, as because they were afraid of the Athenians (lest they become even more powerful)."

15. See also Kagan, p. 233.

16. The only rhetorical mistake they make in this argument is in their brutally candid discussion of the nature of power over others (chapter 1.76). This discussion probably made the Corinthian picture of their character that much more plausible to the Spartan audience.

17. I cannot agree with de Ste. Croix's statements (*Origins,* pp. 12–13) that the Athenian speech as recorded in Thucydides could not faithfully reflect the actual speech because its tone is wrong and

because it thus could not have been accepted by the Spartans. Indeed, its tone is wrong for the occasion (though in a very characteristically Athenian way), and that is no doubt one of the reasons the Spartans in fact did not accept the speech. I think it very likely that the Athenians did make this rhetorical mistake (a similar mistake in tone is made by the Spartans in their peace offer of 425—recorded in Thucydides' history on its occasion at 4.17-20—with the same result that it, too, is rejected by its audience), either because of their character and characteristic way of speaking about foreign affairs (a way not likely to be congenial to the Spartans) or as a sort of gamble, believing they had little to lose, and hoping to shock the Spartans into reconsidering their decision.

18. Indeed, without the losing speeches to these first two debates, the beginning of the war would acquire a strange insubstantiality. The Athenians would appear to have had no choice; the Spartans likewise. The war would seem to come about as the only possible result of some unknown forces. This would provide a sense of the inevitability of the war, to be sure, but one at wide variance with Thucydides' continuing portrayal of events as initiated wholly by the intentions of the combatants.

19. Nor should we worry whether the intent of his speech is simply to delay the declaration of war—as he maintains—or, by delay, to oppose the whole idea of war, for his arguments are all given as if delay alone were intended.

20. See also Kagan, p. 302.

21. De Ste. Croix, too (pp. 124-51, esp. p. 143), has noted that the overriding of Archidamus' advice demonstrates the exceptional circumstances and exceptionally high emotions of this deliberation and decision.

22. See also Stahl, "Speeches and Course of Events," p. 70. Thucydides testifies, by the order of his composition, to this narrative connection: in 1.88 he states that the Spartans were convinced to declare war because of a fear they already had; and at 1.89 he begins the account of the Pentecontaetia—that is, of the source of this fear.

23. J. de Romilly, struck by the similarities of the speeches, has gone so far as to call them virtually an extended dialogue or debate (*Thucydides and Athenian Imperialism*, trans. Philip Thody [New York: Barnes and Noble, 1963], pp. 27-32). Their close relation does not require that we conclude Thucydides invented these speeches for this occasion and mock debate. The similarities in structure and subject of the two speeches would quite naturally be the result of the parallelisms of occasion and the rhetorical necessities of

touching on certain subjects in any speech seriously presenting strategic designs and describing the expected consequences of those
designs. Under the circumstances it is likely that the speeches would
appear so similar. See Kagan, pp. 331-32.

24. De Ste. Croix, pp. 104-24.

25. The latter levies were not accomplished. See Donald Kagan,
The Archidamian War (Ithaca, N.Y.: Cornell University Press,
1974), pp. 22-23.

26. How actively the Corinthians meant to pursue imperial revolts
is not clear. Archidamus proposed encouraging them (1.81.3), but
saw that to do this the Peloponnesians required a navy they did not
possess. The Corinthians here are much vaguer about the need to
encourage revolts. In this I believe we see their essentially traditional
approach to the war. See also Gomme, *Commentary* 1: 418. In the
actions actually undertaken by the Peloponnesians we do not see
them going beyond traditional strategies at these early moments of
the war. No fort is established in Attica until 413. And it is only with
the Mytilene episode in 428 (and reaching a kind of apogee with
Brasidas' campaigns in the north) that we see the Peloponnesians
recognizing the strategic importance of an active campaign among
the Athenian allies. This, when we come to it, will mark an important change in Peloponnesian military policy.

27. It is striking, though, that faced with the war almost afoot,
Pericles specifically cautions against using it as an opportunity for
imperial expansion.

28. There is considerable controversy about whether this truly was
the Athenian strategy. That it was is denied by A. W. Gomme,
"Four Passages in Thucydides," *JHS* 71 (1951): 70-80, esp. pp.
76-78; A. G. Woodhead, "Thucydides' Portrait of Cleon,"
Mnemosyne iv 13 (1960): 289-317, esp. p. 311; and B. X. de Wet,
"The So-Called Defensive Policy of Pericles," *AClass* 12 (1969):
103-19. But see de Ste. Croix, p. 208; P. A. Brunt, "Spartan Policy
and Strategy in the Archidamian War," *Phoenix* 19 (1965): 255-80,
esp. pp. 255-58; and George Cawkwell, "Thucydides' Judgment of
Periclean Strategy," *YCIS* 24 (1975): 53-70, esp. pp. 54-56 and
68-70 in support of the interpretation that a purely defensive strategy would bring concrete benefits to Athens by way of a serious
weakening of Spartan hegemony were Sparta forced to sue for peace.
It is this result, I believe, that formed the basis of Pericles' strategy.
See also V. Ehrenberg, "Polypragmosyne: A Study in Greek Politics," *JHS* 67 (1947): 46-67, p. 49. For our purposes, however, the
question is much simpler. Once one distinguishes the exegetical

question (of Thucydides' text) from the historical question (of the actuality of Athenian policy) it is clear that, whatever our ultimate conclusion as to the historical policy of Athens, Thucydides is here insistent that Pericles' strategy was essentially passive. It is this conclusion that is relevant to our inquiry.

29. That this is a fair argument can be seen in later Peloponnesian attitudes toward the start of the war. When Sparta recommenced hostilities against Athens eighteen years from this moment (7.18), Thucydides specifically refers to Spartan feelings of guilt over having refused arbitration before the beginning of the war.

30. See also Calkwell, "Thucydides' Judgment of Periclean Strategy," p. 53. And, of course, the abandonment of this strategy in the years after Pericles' death—the result in part also of new pressures— shows the unhappiness of the Athenians with the strategy.

31. I do not believe that anyone has commented previously on the full relevance of this chapter—an archaeological study of a single city unparalleled in Thucydides' history—to the events of the narrative. Gomme, in his own expanded archaeological study of the chapter (*Commentary* 2: 48–61), certainly does not. V. J. Hunter (*Thucydides, the Artful Reporter* [Toronto: Hakkert, 1973], p. 14), while understanding that the chapter makes vivid the extent of the sacrifice the abandonment of the farms and villages demanded, relates it only to Archidamus' plans, and not to the rhetorical solution Pericles proposed in the Funeral Oration. Its relevance, however, is not hard to see. At chapter 14 Thucydides says the removal of the countrymen to the city occasioned great hardships. Chapter 15 supplies the proof of this by providing a story of the country districts which explains their antiquity and thereby enables us to understand how the country-dwellers could feel as strongly about the outlying towns as about Athens itself. Chapter 16 emphasizes the emotional hardship involved in leaving the towns, while chapter 17 describes the material hardships of resettling in Athens. Chapters 18 and 19 bring the Peloponnesian army to the borders of the towns; chapter 20 informs us of Archidamus' hope that the townsmen would obstruct the defense of Athens (quoted above). Chapter 21 describes the political uproar caused by the destruction of the suburbs. In this narrative chapter 15 is vital to our evaluation of the political pressures on Pericles at this moment. Chapter 22 gives an account of the immediate political moves that Pericles took to deal with this crisis (a token attack on the Peloponnesians and the prevention of any assembly which might reverse his stategy). It is only with the Funeral Oration, however, that Pericles undertakes the construction of a set of political

principles (or "philosophy") to which the Athenians can appeal to sustain themselves, in the long term, against the material losses which any passive military strategy necessarily entails.

32. J. de Romilly has also noticed the critical importance of Pericles himself (as a sort of human event in the history) to Athens' successful and safe prosecution of the war at this time. See her "Les intentions d'Archidamos," *REA* 64 (1962): 287-99.

33. Pericles uses the empire as a carrot—as well as a stick—and this, too, distinguishes him from the later Athenian speakers. If he says that the allied cities will take revenge on the Athenians, this is the stick, for he must convince them that surrender is not a simple solution. Alcibiades and Euphemus (and, presumably, the Athenians themselves) remembered this aspect of the speech, but forgot the carrot. For Pericles can also still say that the empire is the foundation of the unique lives the Athenians lead and want to lead. That the empire provides any benefits for the Athenians (indeed, anything other than anxiety) is a sentiment wholly missing from Athenian political rhetoric in the latter part of the war.

34. The city seems to have been ruled as an oligarchy (certainly only oligarchs negotiate for it here) which, although not forbidden in the empire, was rare, and denoted a more confident and independent position within it. See Thucydides 3.27 and R. P. Legon, "Megara and Mytilene," *Phoenix* 22 (1968): 200-225.

35. Though it is worth noting that in the Mytilenean case we see a stage of development rather than the completed process of strategic change. The Peloponnesians did not go looking for a Mytilene, the Mytileneans had to take the initiative. The moment at which the Peloponnesians themselves would initiate revolts still lies in the future. The older, more passive, Peloponnesian attitude toward the empire retains its influence here.

36. The word used by Herodotus is actually ὁμότροπα, which we would expect to have a different meaning. But Herodotus never uses ὁμοιότροπος, and Thucydides never uses ὁμότροπος. For the two historians, I believe, the words are synonyms Ὁμότροπα is used in two passages in Herodotus, of which the most often cited is at 8.144. There, the Athenians respond indignantly to a Spartan suggestion that perhaps the Athenians have considered an alliance with Xerxes. Even had they *wanted* to do so (the Athenians say), they are utterly prevented from doing so because of, first, the destruction of the Greek temples—which must be avenged; second, the kinship of the Greeks in all things, blood, language, religion, and character [αὖτις δὲ τὸ Ἑλληνικὸν ἐὸν ὅμαιμόν τε καὶ ὁμόγλωσσον καὶ θεῶν

ἱδρύματά τε κοινὰ καὶ θυσίαι ἤθεά τε ὁμότροπα . . .]. Herodotus' other use of the word, at 2.49, although not as dramatic, is no less definite in its implication that there is a *natural* Greek character (in his proof that a certain religious observance is of Egyptian origin by showing that even in Greece it is not celebrated in the Greek manner). Naturally, feelings of pan-Hellenism would come under stress during the oppositions of Athens and Sparta. But what we can detail in Thucydides' history is more than stress: we can see the invention of opposing systems of beliefs invested with authority and emotion great enough to insist that the differences among Greeks were even more important than the similarities.

37. And, moreover, summarized by words (two special -τρόπος compounds) which imply either natural kinship or, at the least, an already reified and fixed pattern of behavior rather than mere circumstantial agreement.

Chapter Two

1. See Louis Bodin, "Diodote contre Cléon," in *Mélanges offerts à Georges Radet, REA* 42 (1940): 36-52, and R. P. Winnington-Ingram, "τὰ δέοντα εἰπεῖν: Cleon and Diodotus," *BICS* 12 (1965): 70-82.

2. Whose speech is the conservative one is a crucial point. If, as many suggest, it is Diodotus', then we have a picture of an older Athenian decency only barely holding its own against a growing brutality. If the conservative speech is Cleon's, we may see in Diodotus' a new Athenian direction. D. Kagan (*Archidamian War,* pp. 158, 160) and B. X. de Wet ("Periclean Imperial Policy and the Mytilenean Debate," *AClass* 6 [1963]: 106-24) would have Diodotus, rather than Cleon, the conservative and heir to Pericles. But their conclusion depends on the identification of Diodotus and Pericles solely on the basis of their moderation, as compared to Cleon's immoderation. Diodotus is, certainly, the more moderate of the two speakers in the debate, and Cleon's immoderation makes a shocking contrast to previous statements by Pericles. But we should not confuse moderation of tone with identity of principles. (Nor should we be carried away in thinking Diodotus moderate: his moderate solution kills one thousand prisoners.) Gomme ("Four Passages," p. 78) has seen the similarity of Cleon's language to that of Pericles. See also A. Andrewes, "The Mytilene Debate: Thucydides 3.36-49," *Phoenix* 16 (1962): 64-85, esp. p. 76. Even more important than consonance of language, however, is consonance of principles. On the

identity of Cleon's principles with Pericles', see Bodin, "Diodote contre Cléon," pp. 44, 47, and H. D. Westlake, *Individuals in Thucydides* (Cambridge: Cambridge University Press, 1968), p. 65. In Cleon's immoderation we can see how the stresses of war impose distortions on policy. Under Pericles the early principles of the Athenians tended toward moderation. After five years of war these same principles can, given the psychological changes war produces, be used to justify harsh and cruel measures. Moderation has disappeared not because Cleon has substituted new principles, but because war has eroded that reserve of confidence and decency upon which moderation depends.

3. Cleon here virtually echoes the statement made by the Mytilenean ambassadors to the Peloponnesian League (3.11.2), and we can take this agreement as another indication of the currency of Cleon's principles. That is, we can find them held even in other cities. This, therefore, is another indication that the defeat of these principles would mark a departure from earlier policies.

4. That this is so may also explain the lack of an articulated policy toward the allies before this moment. See p. 56. Diodotus, of course, disagrees with Cleon about the utility of deliberation. Andrewes, "Mytilene Debate," p. 75, rightly points out that in this instance Diodotus holds views similar to Pericles. But this similarity is on the procedure of politics. As far as the principles that govern the substance of politics is concerned, it is Cleon who most resembles Pericles.

5. Bodin, pp. 50, 52.

6. "Regulations for Erythrai: (?) 453-2 B. C.," in *A Selection of Greek Historical Inscriptions to the End of the Fifth Century B.C.,* ed. Russell Meiggs and David Lewis (Oxford: the Clarendon Press, 1969), *ML* 40, pp. 89-94; "Athenian Treaty with Samos: 439-8 B.C.," *ML* 56, pp. 151-54; see also Thucydides 1.115.2-3. Democracies may also have been established at Colophon (*ML* 47, pp. 121-25) and Chalkis (*ML* 52, pp. 138-44), but this is by no means certain.

7. [Xenophon], *Constitution of the Athenians*, 1.14, 3.10-11, indeed suggests that it was a policy. Given the uniformly partisan exaggeration of the "Old Oligarch," however, it is hard to base any secure conclusions on his testimony. (Were we to take him at his word at 1.19-20, for example, we would have to believe that every Athenian was a sailor.) What may have occurred on an ad hoc basis in a few cases could easily be blown up by him into a general policy. Moreover, other of his statements may be seen to contradict his assertion that this was a policy. At 1.18 he seems to suggest either

that the allied cities as a whole hated and feared the Athenians (thus contradicting the notion of allied democratic sympathy for the Athenian *demos*) or that the "better" people (who did have grounds for fearing Athens, according to him) were in control of the governmental actions and trade of the cities (contradicting the notion of democracies in power in all the allied states). At 3.11 he draws our attention to occasions when the Athenians supported oligarchies, despite his earlier general assertion that they never did. In its partisanship the pamphlet comes close to being scurrilous, yet even if one assumes its strict factual accuracy, the most likely date of its composition renders its statements about Athenian political policy inconclusive. If the work was written before the Peloponnesian War (as Hartvig Frisch, *The Constitution of the Athenians* [Copenhagen: Gyldendalske Boghandel, 1942], p. 62) it may indeed describe an ideological Athenian foreign policy in operation before 427 (always assuming the factuality of its statements). But if, as now seems to be more widely agreed, the date of composition be placed at or near 424 (as de Ste. Croix, pp. 308-10; Harold B. Mattingly, "The Athenian Coinage Decree," *Historia* 10 [1961]: 148-88, p. 179—Russell Meiggs, *The Athenian Empire* [Oxford: the Clarendon Press, 1972], pp. 390-91 places the composition at some moment during the war), the policy—if it be such—to which the author is referring may in fact be one which began in 427 yet which, because of its popularity and pervasiveness, seemed to have been in effect for a much longer time.

8. Notably Miletus, 449, see Meiggs, *Athenian Empire,* p. 115, 562-65, and possibly Colophon and Chalkis. (The establishment of a democracy at Colophon can only be conjectural, as it rests on the substantial reconstruction of an inscription [*ML* 47, pp. 121-23].)

9. Mytilene, Chios, Samos and Miletus before their revolts, and Corcyra come quickly to mind. See Meiggs, pp. 208-10; *ML* p. 143; Benjamin Dean Meritt, H. T. Wade-Gery, Malcolm Francis McGregor, *The Athenian Tribute Lists* 4 vols. (Cambridge, Mass. and Princeton, N.J.: Harvard University Press and the American School of Classical Studies at Athens, 1939-53) 3: 149-54, "Democracy in the Allied Cities." There would, of course, be sound political reasons for not pursuing "democratization" as a policy: it would tend toward *unsettling* many cities. As long as an oligarchy would remain quietly in the empire it would hardly be worth the upheaval of changing its government.

10. Corcyra (3.70-85), Megara (4.66-74), Boeotia (4.76.2), and, during the Peace of Nicias, Argos, Elis, and Mantinea (5.47, 5.76, 5.82). Thucydides' interest in the ideological basis of actions relating

to Athenian allies is limited primarily to the defections of Torone (4.110.1) and Mende (4.123.2) during Brasidas' campaign.

11. Insofar as questions about the Peloponnesian War itself and about Thucydides' interpretation of the war constitute two distinct inquiries demanding rather different evidence, we must leave open the possibility that Thucydides could be wrong on certain matters, for which, then, we would have different answers to these sets of questions. Evidence for Thucydides' interpretation is only to be found directly in his narrative, and in its structure there can be no doubt, I believe, that Thucydides saw this debate as the occasion of an Athenian innovation. Although this is the only properly authoritative evidence of Thucydides' interpretation, it is far from the only evidence, and in fact the "external" evidence itself provides some support to Thucydides. While evidence does exist of Athenian support before 427 for democracies in the empire, evidence also exists of Athenian indifference to the governments of its subjects (as long as they remained quiet). It would be wrong, then, to conclude that there existed any Athenian *policy* with regard to democracies prior to this moment. Further, and most important, this is the first moment at which we can see the Athenians use an ideological interpretation of events to articulate a policy that could extend to governments of cities *not* their subjects.

12. Cleon, in fact, specifically denies that the distinction has any significance (3.39.6), as he would have to in order to remain consistent with his principles.

13. Whether these sympathies existed or not touches on the question of the "popularity" of the empire. Without attempting to treat this problem directly, the following observations should be made here: (1) Diodotus may well be expressing an Athenian opinion (or hope) concerning allied democratic support, whether the allies themselves felt at all sympathetic to Athens or not; (2) as long as the Athenians believe this, true or not, it could shape their policy, and they would have been unwise not to try to manipulate or generate whatever sympathy they could. Therefore, Diodotus could propose such a policy as a way of *creating* sympathy (and new allies) for Athens. Diodotus himself recognizes this in his statement (3.47.4) that Athens should always speak of the democrats as allies, even when their actions have not warranted it, for fear of losing their only possible supporters.

From this position we need not conclude with Gomme (*Commentary* 2:322) that the apparent contradiction between Diodotus' assertion of allied support and Thucydides' statement at 2.8.5 of universal hostility to Athens indicates that the passages were written at different stages of Thucydides' thought about the war. The contradiction may be explained by (1) a difference between Diodotus' opinion and the true feelings of the allies, or by (2) rhetorical and political needs at Athens which led Diodotus to propose his policy in order to woo the allied democrats. It is also possible, of course, that opinion had changed within the imperial cities since the start of the war. This would not imply that Thucydides had changed *his* opinion. T. J. Quinn ("Political Groups at Chios, 412 B.C.," *Historia* 18 [1969]: 22–30) also points out that the possibility of a decisive victory over one's political enemies could create an authentic tie between Athens and the democrats in allied cities that was independent of the question of popularity.

14. The events of the fifth year of war are treated at disproportionate length. In addition, they include four speeches, all in debates. Such treatment is accorded only two other occasions of the war: its beginning (book 1) and the Sicilian expedition (book 6).

15. As John H. Finley, Jr., *Thucydides* (Cambridge, Mass.: Harvard University Press, 1942), pp. 177–80; F. M. Wassermann, "Post-Periclean Democracy in Action: the Mytilenean Debate (Thuc. III 37–48)," *TAPhA* 87 (1956): 27–41, esp. pp. 28–29, 34.

16. As Gomme, *Commentary* 2: 354–55, who also hints at a general slide toward accepting brutality.

17. The Athenians act either better, as at Mende (4.130.7) and Lesbos and Clazomene (8.23.6), or worse, as at Torone (5.3.4) and Scione (5.32.1). Gomme suggests (*Commentary* 3: 362) that the Toronean sentence was mitigated, in which case it was treated much better than Mytilene.

18. To speak of ideology in the world of the fifth century may justifiably cause some uneasiness. Certainly we can find no evidence of ideological positions or conflicts which come anywhere close to mirroring the overwhelming political importance and organization that ideologies have acquired in our own age. Nevertheless, prototypical forms of ideology have always existed. Racism is an example. Under the stress of conflict and the need to develop ways of distinguishing oneself from one's enemies and of attributing value to freedom and independence, new symbols are created which, too, acquire the characteristics of ideologies. Again, in early circumstances, these may be cultural (or political masquerading as cultural): Medism and Hellenism. Eventually, low-level but continuing political conflict may create new distinctions which can become

symbols and ideologies if need be to justify a sudden intensification of political oppositions. The political slogans which belong to the opposition of democracy and oligarchy (of which some are recorded by Thucydides in conjunction with the *stasis* in Corcyra, 3.82.4–7) are of this nature.

As I intend to use the word "ideology" (and also its abstract nouns and verbs like "ideologizing," etc.) rather extensively, a note here on the meaning I attribute to it will avoid later confusion. I do not specifically mean "ideology" in its modern, sophisticated, and somewhat dogmatic usage, although I am not certain that such a usage would be as anachronistic for fifth-century Greece as it might at first appear. If I say "ideological interpretation" I mean merely the explanation of actions or events by their attribution to forces which are at once abstract, symbolic, simple, and greater-than-human. In the materialistic interpretation, the explanation of events is found in the size and motions of states. In an ideological explanation, events are the result of the influence and activity of nonmaterial forces on states and men. Ideologies are intellectual constructs, but with the power to cause events. Ideologies take many forms, and are either naïve or sophisticated. (They may be as complex as the institutional arrangements—and the value-systems they create—called "capitalism" and "communism"; they may be as simple, but evocative, as the statement, "All Germans are Huns.") In all cases, however, they provide a simple but universal explanation of the origins of actions. The explanation claims the existence of nonmaterial and invisible forces. Events are seen as the actualizations of these intellectual forces: as the forces effecting material consequences by their embodiment in men and states who act on these beliefs. Further, ideologies have a tendency to come in at least pairs. In the twentieth century we have seen explanations of events based on the opposition of capitalism and communism; in Thucydides' history the ideological oppositions which he represents as having exercised power over the actions and deliberations of men are aristocracy-democracy, Hellenism-Atticism, and Dorian-Ionian.

19. That on this early occasion the Spartans were unwilling to encourage this revolt may either (depending on its date) indicate Spartan indifference to ideological distinctions before 428–27 or perhaps simply a reluctance to break the terms of the Thirty Years' Peace.

20. See also Gomme, Dover, and Andrewes, *Commentary* 4: 57–61, which, in addition, gives evidence of the toleration of democratic

governments within the Peloponnesian League, and therefore of the lack of ideological discriminations, at first, among the Peloponnesians too.

21. Even after the Athenian defeat at Syracuse the power of ideology can be seen to operate in ways which simply did not exist before 427. At the beginning of the war Thucydides asserts (2.8.4) that every city was sympathetic to the Spartans and hoped to be freed by them. Yet by 411 we can see that once support had crystallized around the ideological distinctions of 427 it remained so. Speaking of Thasos' revolt from the empire (8.64.4–5), Thucydides makes the direct assertion that the democrats would have opposed defection from the empire, but that Pisander's installation of an oligarchy in Athens removed the last obstacle to Thasian rebellion. Here we see democrats willing to accept the loss of some autonomy if complete national independence meant domination by their local oligarchs.

22. The feelings of the democratic party on this occasion, too, are revealing of the depth of ideological hatreds. The democrats felt that delivering the city to the Athenians (including, presumably, the possible loss of the city's autonomy) was a lesser price to pay than accepting the return of the oligarchic exiles, and the probable overthrow of the democracy (4.66.3). We can see the same priorities within the empire after 427 at Mende (4.123.2), Chios (at least at the beginning of the revolt, 8.9.3, 8.14.2, 8.38.3), Samos (8.47.2, 8.76), and Thasos (8.64.4).

23. "The Thebans feared . . . lest the Spartans give in at all (μή . . . τι ἐνδῶσι)," 3.60. The true vehemence of Theban hatred for Plataea is described here by Thucydides. The Thebans will not admit even the slightest mitigation of the judgment on the captives. On the other hand, the phrase shows the readiness of the Spartans to accept the Theban argument. Having heard it, the Spartans do indeed become unwilling even to make the slightest concession—not of innocence, for the Plataeans do not ask for that—but of mercy.

24. At 3.55.4 they also argue that in any case they are not to blame for their actions: "So, whichever of you [Athenians or Spartans] is leading your allies, it is not the followers who are responsible if anything ill be done, but those who commanded the incorrect acts." That this would most likely not have been an effective argument I believe we can see from the Theban speech, in which this argument is used three times, in contradictory senses. At 3.62.4 the Thebans use it to exculpate themselves from having fought with the Persians; at 3.63.2 they deny the application of the argument and insist the

Plataeans should have revolted from Athens; and at 3.65.2 they again invoke the argument to demonstrate that the Plataeans were wrong in opposing the Theban attack of 431 (this time even paraphrasing the Plataean words). To have the Thebans unself-consciously use the argument in contradictory cases seems to me to throw the gravest doubt on the credibility and effectiveness of any such *remotio criminis* at this point in the war. If anything, it shows the emptiness of the trope, and indicates that the argument was so little listened to that it could be applied in opposite senses without anyone objecting. It therefore suggests the futility of employing such an argument in the Plataeans' situation.

25. The Plataeans first mention Medism at 3.54.3, and then again at 3.56.4-5, 3.57.2-3.58.1, 3.58.4-5, and 3.59.2.

26. *Hell.* 1.6.13; 6.3.14. Xenophon also appears to be the first to use the terms Laconize and Laconism in the parallel sense of "siding with" (rather than "imitating") the Spartans. As he uses these terms they are merely descriptive.

27. Testimony to the existence of an actual crime called Atticism is found in an Athenian inscription (*IG* ii²33, dated c. 385) honoring Thasians who were prosecuted for the crime of Atticism. The inscription is cited in H. W. Pleket, "Thasos and the Popularity of the Athenian Empire," *Historia* 12 (1963): 70-77.

28. This is not to say that politically ideological perceptions were lacking among the Peloponnesians. We can find numerous cases in which Peloponnesian ideologizing of the war took an explicitly political form: though a minor case, Brasidas' general's speech (4.126); more significantly, Boeotian and Megarian abstention from the Argive alliance (5.31.6); and the alliance of the Argive oligarchs with Sparta as a means of suppressing the democracy (5.76). Yet oligarchs are less likely to use direct political appeals—the constitutional form claims to be, at root, antipolitical—and their political sentiments tend to find expression in slogans heavily laced with "morality": the "best" people, the "ancestral" constitution, the "mob." Although Brasidas, in the speech cited above, makes a political distinction, it is cast almost entirely in the light of these moral sentiments. Consequently, without denying that the Peloponnesians, too, saw the confrontation of oligarchies and democracies in the war, and that they likewise saw that democracy was an essential part of what they called Atticism, I believe that the slogan "Atticism" is a more accurate symbol or emblem for the way the ideological character of the war appeared to the Peloponnesians than

any bald political representation. Further, "Atticism" had an extensiveness more appropriate to the threat as perceived by the Peloponnesians. Within any single city the conflict between democrats and oligarchs proceeded in a straightforwardly political manner. Examples of the entirely political slogans which were employed in these circumstances are given by Thucydides at 3.82.8. But by this fifth year of the war the political conflicts between parties were no longer simply domestic disorders. On the basis of these new interpretations, both parties could appeal to the appropriate great power for support in their internecine warfare. Consequently, an "international" aspect of democracy as a force emerged, and demanded its own tag to identify it. Insofar as this international threat to oligarchs was centered (or was felt to be centered) in Athens, "Atticism" was coined as the sloganistic description of the threat. The word covered both the aggressive characteristics of the Athenians (by its formal similarity to Medism) and the democratic content of this aggression (through Athens' known identification with democracy). The word was, moreover, both in its form and content, more appropriate for the expression of the generalized fears of oligarchs in *many* cities than were the more particular political slogans they would normally utilize at home.

29. In this light we can see Lysander as the final executor of this interpretation. His general means of liberation and pacification was the installation of oligarchic regimes, and this was his key, too, to the final defeat and pacification of Athens in 404. Plutarch, *Lysander* 5.5, 8.1–3, 13.5–14.2, 15.6, 21.3; Diodorus Siculus 13.70.4, 14.3.4–5, 14.10.1, 14.13.1; Xenophon, *Hell.* 2.3.2–3, 2.3.13–14, 2.4.28–29.

30. Kagan argues persuasively (*Archidamian War,* pp. 220–23) that the choice was deliberate on the part of Demosthenes, one of the Athenian commanders and perhaps the best strategic thinker at Athens during the entire war. The lack of support for this plan from the other two Athenian generals with him, however, indicates that the plan was not initially considered to be of any special importance. Hunter (*Thucydides, the Artful Reporter,* pp. 61–83) argues that there was in fact no plan. Thucydides' narrative (4.2–5), however, seems to indicate planning on Demosthenes' part. This question is discussed in greater detail in chapter 7.

31. That this was Thucydides' interpretation of Pericles' position is discussed in relation to Pericles' first speech, at pp. 36–39. Kagan (*Archidamian War,* p. 232) admits that this is Thucydides' interpretation, though he and Gomme (*More Essays in Greek History and*

Literature, ed. David A. Campbell [Oxford: Basil Blackwell, 1962], pp. 105–7) believe Thucydides was wrong. Their arguments depend primarily on the discovery of good reasons for Athens to reject this offer, and they therefore deny Thucydides' statement that the Athenians rejected the offer merely ''because they were hungry for more'' (4.21.2). For the purpose of this inquiry it is sufficient to establish Thucydides' interpretation without worrying whether it is correct or not. But it is worth noting that even if good reasons exist for doing something (in this case rejecting a peace offer)—though I do not feel that this is established beyond question by Kagan and Gomme—the fact that the action was accomplished does not mean that it was done for those good reasons. I see no reason to doubt Thucydides' judgment of the motives for which the Athenians rejected the offer, even if there were other conceivable motives for doing so. They may have been unaware of the good reasons, or may even have ignored them, acting as they did for stupid ones.

32. The narrative of this first venture into Sicily must be reconstructed from the fragments of it that Thucydides has stitched around the longer pieces of narrative dealing with Greece proper: 3:86, 88, 90, 99, 103, 115; 4.1, 2, 24, 25, 46, 47.

33. A part, moreover, strikingly like that played by the debate in Syracuse at 6.33–41. That debate, too, appears inconsequential, and yet it marks a moment at which the course of events changed direction radically, as does this speech here. Both changes, indeed, were initiated by Hermocrates, and the far-sightedness of his policies here prepares us to accept the influence he would have on later events in Syracuse.

34. I do not mean to imply that Thucydides has tampered in any way with the order of events. But by his choice of which events to emphasize and how they are to be emphasized, he has managed to replicate in his composition the way in which the progress of the war was perceived in Athens and in the rest of Greece. The decision at Gela was far from enough to drive the Athenians to conclude a peace. The *series* of disappointments (which constitutes the narrative from this moment onwards), and especially the success of Brasidas with the Athenian allies in the north, was. The Athenians, no doubt, fixed a beginning point to this trend, and the beginning point (if not the most important point) is here, in Sicily.

35. See Kagan, *Archidamian War,* pp. 291–93.

36. It is significant that he admits (4.85.1–2) that the Peloponnesians have been able to fulfill this promise only with the new policy of an aggressive campaign to encourage Athenian allies to revolt. The

initial Peloponnesian military policy was a failure.

37. The language Thucydides uses, however, is quite uncompromising with regard to both the paradox and the cynicism. Brasidas' phrase is τοὺς μὴ βουλομένους ἐλευθεροῦν, "to liberate those who do not wish it." That this is not simply a straightforward statement that he would take the Acanthians out of the empire can be seen in two ways. First, of course, is the μὴ βουλομένους, "those who are unwilling." It might be possible to call removal, even forcible removal, from the empire "liberation." But the "unwillingly" sticks. One cannot free someone who does not wish it. Moreover, the ἐλευθεροῦν, "liberate," is a self-serving euphemism. This can be seen by comparison to the phrase Thucydides uses himself (i.e., not the phrase of some speaker to one side of a case) on the occasion of the actual occurrence of such a forcible liberation. At 5.33 the Spartans attack the Parrhasians, and remove them from Mantinea's influence. The phrase there (5.33.3) is αὐτονόμους ποιήσαντες, "making autonomous." This is the straightforward statement, for αὐτονόμους contains no judgment on the form of government nor any promise as to the condition of the citizens. Brasidas' phrase is the propaganda equivalent of this, full of promise. But it is exactly with the promise inherent in ἐλευθεροῦν ("liberate") that the μὴ βουλόμενους ("against their will") jars.

38. That the city which could prevent the enslavement of others, but stands quietly by, is the true enslaver was a trope used in political oratory throughout this war. The Corinthians used it at the first Spartan congress, and Hermocrates, as we will see, used it at Camarina (6.80.2). But what constituted "standing by" might be different on different occasions. So, for the Corinthians, "not to stand by" required active military opposition to the Athenians. But, appropriate to the ideological interpretation of the war, Brasidas does not require military support from the Acanthians, merely a public demonstration of allegiance to the Peloponnesians. (On the other hand, though they need not actively fight, they must actively declare sides. If the ideological interpretation frees states from the necessity of military engagement, it also compels them to another kind of involvement.)

Chapter Three

1. Finley, *Thucydides,* pp. 208–12.

2. As examples from the vast literature on this debate: A. Andrewes, "The Melian Dialogue and the Last Speech of Pericles,"

PCPS 186 (1960): 1–10, and his general comment on this dialogue in *Commentary* 4: 182–88; F. M. Cornford, *Thucydides Mythistoricus* (London: Routledge and Kegan Paul, 1965), pp. 174–87; Georges Méautis, "Le dialogue des Athéniens et les Méliens," *REG* 48 (1935): 250–78; Meiggs, *Athenian Empire,* chap. 21, "Fifth Century Judgements," pp. 375–96; F. Wassermann, "The Melian Dialogue," *TAPhA* 78 (1947): 18–36.

3. W. Liebeschuetz, "The Structure and Function of the Melian Dialogue," *JHS* 88 (1968): 73–77.

4. See M. Amit, "The Melian Dialogue and History," *Athenaeum* 46 (1968): 216–35.

5. To assume that it is, as Andrewes, Meiggs, and Wassermann do, makes it perforce impossible for us to perceive that any difference does exist. If we can see no difference, then of course it is difficult to see the dialogue as an event. But insofar as we can perceive a difference, we can restore its historical importance to the dialogue: it can inform us of a moment of change, and in its change is itself an event.

6. We should also remember that the same penalty was contemplated—indeed, voted—for the Mytileneans in 427, more than ten years before this moment. In addition, in the year before this Melian campaign, the Peloponnesians had executed all the free males of Hysiai (5.83.2), but this, too, passes without comment from Thucydides. It is not the fact of the killing that makes Melos shocking or interesting to him.

7. De Ste. Croix, *Origins,* p. 14 and Amit, "Melian Dialogue," p. 217 are the only commentators to have given this fact the attention it deserves in the development of any interpretation of the dialogue. See also a note of Gomme's in *Commentary* 4: 191. He does not, however, draw any conclusion as to how this affects our understanding of Thucydides' purposes in recording the debate.

8. Compare to: "These were the charges and differences on both sides before the war, which began with the events at Epidamnus and Corcyra. Nevertheless, they continued to deal with each other, and went back and forth to each other without heralds, but not without suspicion. For these events were the ruin of the peace and the cause of their going to war" (1.146).

9. The novelty of this fear of their own empire has also been recognized by C. W. Macleod, "Form and Meaning in the Melian Dialogue," *Historia* 23 (1974): 385–400, esp. p. 392.

10. To emphasize the novelty of this anxiety, it is worth quickly canvassing the earlier attitudes concerning the security of the empire. At the beginning of the war Archidamus saw that the only true

chance of Peloponnesian success depended upon encouraging the revolt of the Athenian allies (1.81.4). Pericles' first statement on this matter (in his first speech) dismissed Archidamus' hope, and, indeed, turned the matter wholly around. At 1.143.5 he stated that the Athenians should only fear being defeated, for then they would lose the empire *which is their strength*. Later, pressed by war and plague, Pericles (in his third speech) called Athens a tyrant city (2.63.2), but was unwavering in his confidence in the security of the empire. Danger could come from the empire only in releasing the hold on it, not from continuing to hold it. The danger exists only in a loss of will by the Athenians. As long as their will remains firm, so does their possession of the empire, which is, again, their greatest strength (2.62.1-3). When Mytilene revolted, both Diodotus and Cleon were certain that Athens could easily retain control of the empire. They disagreed only on how to do so. For neither was the empire a source of fear: it was merely a problem with which to deal. At Melos, however, the new fear was first made apparent. Meiggs (*Athenian Empire*, p. 389) and Liebeschuetz ("Structure and Function," p. 74) note the absence of any ideological appeal to the democratic faction of Melos in the arguments of the Athenians. This can be attributed partly, of course, to the fact that the Melian rulers deliberately kept the Athenians from addressing the *demos*. But the absence of an ideological appeal also seems a further indication of the change in Athenian attitudes. Diodotus had indeed laid down a policy—ten years before—to insure a continued secure hold over the empire by means of ideological bonds. But even that notion of a new-model empire, and the sense of safety it created are now seen to have disappeared as the war entered its third, most anxious phase. A further attenuation of the ideological interpretation by this new Athenian anxiety can be seen in the failure of an ideological appeal when it was used by Nicias in the debate on the Sicilian expedition (6.11.7).

The question of the "popularity" of the empire does not truly enter into this situation. I would believe that in a very limited sense the empire was more "popular" in the period between Diodotus' speech and the Melian dialogue than at any other time. Considering that the empire could never have been wholly popular with the allied cities, the moment of its greatest popularity must surely have come during this period when the Athenians were willing to render direct political assistance to the democrats in the imperial cities. Further, these cities did remain strikingly loyal during this period, and even during the Sicilian expedition. Nevertheless, we must distinguish between the "objective" loyalty of the allies and Athenian attitudes and beliefs concerning their loyalty or disloyalty. It is in this respect that we must rule the question of popularity irrelevant here. As revealed by Athenian statements here, in the debate on the Sicilian expedition, and at Camarina, the Athenians themselves did not—despite the "objective" evidence which should have convinced them to the contrary—believe in the loyalty or trustworthiness of the allies. See also Macleod, "Form and Meaning in the Melian Dialogue," p. 392. This distrust, I believe, was part of a more general war anxiety which developed during the Peace of Nicias, and which came to characterize Athenian activities in this third phase of the war.

11. See Amit, pp. 232 and 234.

12. See Westlake, *Individuals,* p. 171.

13. K. J. Dover, in *Commentary* 4: 229, has seen both the lying and its basic irrelevance to our understanding of the event, and has put both pointedly: "No statement or prediction or factual implication in these speeches can be taken at its face value; everything is coloured; everything is exaggeration, insinuation, or half-truth. . . . Much has been said about the 'real motives' of the Sicilian Expedition . . . but the mechanism of 'real motives' does not always receive the scrutiny which it deserves. No project, however economically desirable to one class or another, could be put into effect until the assembly had been presented with what seemed to it an adequate reason; but any reason which was accepted by the assembly can be the real and only reason, and there is no justification for looking behind or beyond it without positive evidence."

14. Nicias' maximization of the Spartan threat includes a very special appeal which one would expect to have received an immediate and strong response. At 6.11.7 he raises directly the conflict of democracies and oligarchies: "So that, if we are wise, we will not claim our struggle concerns barbarians in Sicily; rather, it is how we may best protect ourselves against the city [Sparta] which is even now laying oligarchic plots." There was even some support for this in Spartan plots against the democracy in Argos (5.76.2; 5.78; 5.83.1; 5.116.1; 6.7.1), and against Athenian control in Thrace (5.80.2; 6.7.4). That such a direct appeal to a previously potent source of concern was utterly ignored by the Athenian audience should alert us to the fact that something has changed in the attitudes of the Athenians. Further, the failure of this appeal is emblematic of the change that is exhibited in this cluster of speeches (including the Melian dialogue): *away* from simple ideological interpretations, and *toward* (anticipating Alcibiades and Euphemus) a starker, more desperate

view of the war as having evolved into nothing less than a life-or-death struggle.

15. A basis from which to see the exaggeration and desperation inherent in this statement (whether it represents Alcibiades' own feelings on the subject or represents what the Athenians were willing to hear) can be supplied by comparison to a statement of Pericles' which bears a superficial resemblance to Alcibiades'.

Pericles, 2.64.3: "If, indeed, we should succumb (for everything that grows must decay), the memory [of our power] will remain behind. . . ."

Alcibiades, 6.18.6: "Consider that a city, if it remains quiet, will wear itself away on itself, just like anything else. . . ."

For Pericles the use of the quasi-philosophical "For everything . . ." is simply homiletic: "for it would be foolish to think the empire could last forever." Consequently, there is no direct relation between this maxim and the possible destruction of the empire. That, if it comes, is for very particular reasons: "if we succumb in this war (at this moment when our fortunes appear worst)" ($\mathring{\eta}\nu$ $\kappa\alpha\grave{\iota}$ $\nu\mathring{\upsilon}\nu$ $\mathring{\upsilon}\pi\epsilon\nu\delta\mathring{\omega}\mu\epsilon\nu$).

In Alcibiades' statement, however, the maxim is in fact the source of the destruction of the city. At this moment there were no immediate dangers to Athens' existence. The danger is now believed to be located in the efficacy of this apparently biological or philosophical principle. Decay is now seen as inherent in the city simply as something that exists (which Pericles in no wise implied in his statement), and the condition of rest (whether $\mathring{\eta}\sigma\upsilon\chi\acute{\alpha}\zeta\eta$ means simply "at rest," and $\tau\rho\acute{\iota}\psi\epsilon\sigma\theta\alpha\iota$ therefore only "wear out" or "erode" or "decay"; or whether $\mathring{\eta}\sigma\upsilon\chi\acute{\alpha}\zeta\eta$ has a more concrete meaning—"not engaging in foreign conquests"—and $\tau\rho\acute{\iota}\psi\epsilon\sigma\theta\alpha\iota$ means the friction of politician against politician and faction against faction) is seen as a pathological state. Such an attitude is itself pathological in politics. On this pathological exaggeration of Periclean attitudes, see also C. W. Macleod, "Rhetoric and History (Thucydides, VI, 16-18)," *QS* 2 (1975): 39-62, esp. pp. 56-57.

16. See A. E. Raubitschek, "The Speech of the Athenians at Sparta," in *SIT,* pp. 32-48, esp. pp. 37-38, on the consonance of the arguments of the Athenians at Melos, of Alcibiades here, and of Euphemus at Camarina (6.82-87) and the radical difference between the attitudes embodied in these arguments and earlier Athenian attitudes. Also, Macleod, "Form and Meaning in the Melian Dialogue," p. 392.

17. For all the surface similarities of Alcibiades' statements with

those of Pericles' third speech (primarily at 2.63), the two politicians mean quite different things. Pericles is responding to an actual period of danger; Alcibiades is not. Pericles sees the danger coming from the allies; Alcibiades sees it in the nature of the city itself. For Pericles, the surrender of the empire would be dangerous because of the real grievances the allies would try to avenge; for Alcibiades the danger is abstract, even metaphysical: not to rule is to be ruled, not to expand is to collapse. For Pericles, one assumes the burden of controlling the empire for the sake of the quiet life that exists apart from imperial concerns (at 2.63.3: "For quietness is not secure unless ranged with activity"); for Alcibiades, there is never any quiet: one struggles with the empire, not for the sake of any good, but of necessity—the alternative is decay, perhaps death. For Pericles, the only necessity is holding the empire; for Alcibiades, holding the empire necessitates getting more. It is in the abstractness of Alcibiades' imperatives that we can see his argument as the generalization of the attitudes expressed in the Melian dialogue. The Athenians there denied the existence of neutrality. Generalized, this implies that there exist in the world Athens and its empire at the center, and Athens' enemies on the outside, nothing more. Life, in this model, is a constant struggle: one overcomes or is overcome. When this is made into a theory, the theory asserts that only decay exists as an alternative to growth—as true for states as for living things.

18. The distinction of fact and fantasy is meant in a different sense than that of Stahl, "Speeches and Course of Events," p. 72. That an assembly will sometimes make decisions without being in possession of the facts of a situation is (as Stahl makes poignantly clear elsewhere in this article) characteristic of human events. Often an assembly has no choice but to do so. This debate is such a circumstance. While the flamboyance of Alcibiades' arguments make manifest their disconnection from reality, we should recognize that Nicias' arguments are no less speculative. Their later apparent confirmation is misleading, for the errors Nicias is responsible for are instrumental in making events turn out as they did. Another general, avoiding these mistakes, might well have "refuted" Nicias' arguments at this debate. What Nicias' arguments do have is a specious concreteness which is the result of choosing familiar enemies as the source of one's alleged dangers. It is along these lines that one can reasonably speak of fantasy in the arguments the Athenians accept. While the danger Nicias alleges is as hyperbolic in its fearsomeness as the one Alcibiades does (and perhaps it is a significant datum that for the first time in a debate both Athenian speakers claim that fear is the appropriate

emotion for the circumstances), it is located differently. Sparta and oligarchic partisans constitute authentic and concrete enemies, even if not the imminent danger Nicias asserts. When Alcibiades locates the danger in the Athenians themselves and in their city, he evokes something most like a nightmare—an abstract phantasm existing nowhere but in their own minds. Athenian belief in the efficacy and fearsomeness of this phantasm is indeed a substitution of fantasy for reality.

19. This is reflected in Thucydides' explanation (6.6) of the motives involved in undertaking the Sicilian expedition. Greed is there (6.6.1), but so is fear. The Segestans, who called the Athenians into Sicily, did so on the basis of an argument that if the Syracusans were not punished for having defeated an Athenian ally there, they would immediately conquer all the other Athenian allies, and then set their sights on the destruction of the entire empire. The Athenians seem to respond favorably to this patent exaggeration.

20. See Daniel P. Tompkins, "Stylistic Characterization in Thucydides: Nicias and Alcibiades," *YCIS* 22 (1972): 181–214.

21. This is even more striking in that it is not the case for Thucydides' accounts of the actions of the Peloponnesians (so that we cannot say that he simply became more interested in personalities at the time he wrote book 8) despite the fact that personalities played a large part in, say, Hermocrates' being exiled (8.85.3), and despite the fact that Thucydides himself was still in exile at this moment (so that the names of Peloponnesian personalities would have been comparatively easier, and Athenian names comparatively harder, for him to acquire). The key to the importance individuals acquire at this time is surely that the political community at Athens began to come apart at the seams. Thucydides himself, of course, alluded to this in his criticism of the post-Periclean politicians (2.65.10–11). Gomme, in "Four Passages," has good comments on the degeneration of Athenian politicians, and at p. 78 makes some especially appropriate observations on Alcibiades' argument identifying individuals and cities in terms of their appetites. Gomme exhibits this as a debased form of imitation of earlier, Periclean, political virtues. J. de Romilly, "Thucydides and the Cities of the Athenian Empire," *BICS* 13 (1966): 1–12 (see esp. p. 8) and "Les problèmes de politique intérieure dans l'oeuvre de Thucydide," *Historiographia Antiqua, Symbolae* A 6 (1977): 77–93 (esp. pp. 79–80), also attributes the emergence of individuals in the history to a radical change in the political situation. This, it seems to me, is a more appropriate explanation of the greater numbers of individuals who appear than West-

lake's thesis of greater interest in individuals on Thucydides' part (see *Individuals*, pp. 15, 319). That individuals and their personalities become more important in the second half of the history is indubitable. But this, I believe, is merely Thucydides' recognition and treatment of a change in the nature of politics in the second half of the war.

22. This apparent inconsequentiality has led commentators, again, to treat these debates epideictically, either as exemplary of issues supposed to be generally interesting or as exemplary of political types. E.g., of the former, de Romilly, ed., *La Guerre du Péloponnèse, Livres VI et VII*, pp. xii, xiv, and Meiggs, *Athenian Empire*, p. 380; of the latter, K. J. Dover, *Commentary* 4: 301.

23. At 6.17.3–4 and 6.17.6, Alcibiades argues emphatically that *stasis* within Syracuse and hatred of Syracuse among the other cities of Sicily and Italy will make the military part of the campaign easy.

24. Although it is also possible that he was not, and that Athenagoras' characterization of him is altogether slanderous. So Dover, *Commentary* 4: 296–97.

25. Despite Dover's judgment on this plan (*Commentary* 4: 299), I believe it offered at least as reasonable a chance of success as the simple defense of Syracuse which was actually chosen. Consequently, I believe—against Dover citing Westlake—that Hermocrates indeed expected the plan to be taken seriously, and not merely that its rashness would awaken the Syracusans to the danger that confronted them. Whether the Syracusan navy could have defeated the Athenian is certainly arguable either way (it did, after all, defeat it later). Surprise and maneuverability were on the Syracusan side, and the effect of others' daring on the Athenians (who never expected it from others)—and especially on Nicias—should not be underestimated. Moreover, to repel such an attack, the Athenians would have had to act with the same dispatch by which, had they been willing to employ it on their arrival in Sicily, they could have beaten the Syracusans on land and sea at the city itself. As they were unable to act with that dispatch once they had reached Sicily, I see no reason for assuming they could have shown it before.

26. And it is this irrelevance, most likely, that has led Dover (*Commentary* 4: 301) to interpret this speech epideictically ("The speech...is valuable in that it contains an explicit theoretical defence of democracy and illustrates...the technique and language of political attack"), rather than historically, as valuable because it illuminates a historical event.

27. Most strikingly reminiscent of Thucydides' description of the

brutal distortion of deliberation and justice at Corcyra (3.82) is Athenagoras' bloodthirsty appeal (at 6.38.4) for "punishing plotters [i.e. oligarchs] not only for the things they are caught doing (for that is hard to accomplish) but also for what they want to do but cannot (for one must retaliate beforehand against an enemy not only for what he has done, but also for what he is thinking of doing—if, indeed, one is to strike first and not be forestalled)."

28. In this respect I feel Stahl ("Speeches and Course of Events," pp. 60–77) is, despite the perceptiveness of many of his particular interpretations, wrong in principle in his general thesis that the narrative of the Syracusan expedition demonstrates the irrationality of all Athenian expectations besides Nicias', and that the triumph of irrationality in debate and the counterblow of reality in events is what constitutes τὸ ἀνθρώπινον for Thucydides. If one looks at the beginning and then at the end of the campaign (but nothing in between), then yes, it appears as Stahl states it. But what happened at the end no one, certainly not Nicias, could have foreseen. Alcibiades was not behaving irrationally in suggesting that Sicilian resistance might collapse because of *stasis*. This debate shows us just how real that possibility was. It did not occur, but before this debate no one could have known that. Nicias' belief that it would not occur was no better grounded than Alcibiades' belief that it would. Athens might have picked up important allies in Sicily, as Alcibiades proposed as the strategy for the campaign (6.48). Although it did not, the next debate shows that it might have, and again, Nicias' pessimism is no more realistic than Alcibiades' optimism. All of these events are particular, and their outcome depends on particular circumstances and agents. Thucydides' treatment of these debates demonstrates his respect for their particularity, and his avoidance of any abstract interpretation of the relation of speech and action.

29. This debate presents to us information about the existence of the possibility of *stasis* in Syracuse at the moment at which it is relevant to our understanding of the development of the campaign in Sicily. There is also, however, corroboration of it elsewhere in the narrative. At 6.103.3-4 Thucydides mentions the existence of an Athenian faction inside Syracuse and informs us of its dealings with Nicias. At 7.48.2 these dealings are said to have been a part of Nicias' general strategic design. And at 7.86.4 we see the most dramatic evidence of the seriousness of this faction, for it arranges the executions of Nicias and Demosthenes—against the wishes of Gylippus—to ensure that the two Athenian commanders cannot betray those Syracusans who dealt with the Athenians.

30. A more detailed analysis of this progression (and of Thucydides' construction of his account of the Sicilian expedition) can be found in J. de Romilly, *Histoire et raison chez Thucydide* (Paris: Société d'Edition "Les Belles Lettres," 1956), ch. 1.

31. Camarina had been one of the allies of the Leontinoi, who had asked for Athenian aid in 427 (3.86.2).

32. Westlake ("The Settings of Thucydidean Speeches," in *SIT,* pp. 90–108, esp. p. 95) underestimates the importance of this debate. Camarina is not merely part of a trend, it is an extreme case, and its security in, essentially, defying the Athenians in fact started a landslide in the other direction. Similarly, Stahl ("Speeches and Course of Events," p. 68) understates the dynamic aspect of this situation by speaking of this moment simply as one of equilibrium. Materially, of course, it was a moment of equilibrium, but insofar as Camarina was the city Athens ought most easily to have brought over to its side, the rejection of Athens here has an even greater effect than the mere tipping of the balance of power.

33. In 6.76.2 Hermocrates demonstrates that the racial argument has no real foundation by admitting that the Athenians subjugate or aid cities regardless of ethnic background. Yet, in 6.77.1 and 6.80.3, he appeals to racial solidarity and racial hatred. In this respect his argument is self-contradictory. But his use of the argument, despite his admission of the shakiness of its foundation, is, I believe, revealing. It suggests that, despite the contradictions involved in claiming a racial basis for the war, the racial appeal was desirable rhetorically for its clarity and urgency. It reflects profound hatred or fear of the Athenians—a fear no longer in need of rational explanation (or for which rational explanation was insufficient). It also reflects a desperate need for allies and the groping for a rhetorical foundation (which itself transcends reasons) for asking for allies. Further discussion of the question of the rhetorical use of racial arguments can be found below.

34. Within a year the Camarineans were overtly on the Syracusan side, and, indeed, Thucydides can say: "By this time nearly all of Sicily (except for the Agrigentines, who were on neither side)—all the rest, who had previously merely looked on, banded together and aided the Syracusans against the Athenians" (7.33.2).

35. In much the same way as the Peloponnesians found an appropriateness in the belief in an Attic threat parallel in kind to that of the Persians.

36. The questions of how to take these racial arguments and of the falsity of Euphemus' account of the acquisition of the empire are

related. It is of great importance to see that Euphemus' explanation of the empire is distorted (in comparison to Thucydides' earlier narrative of it), and that it is not, as Meiggs (*Athenian Empire*, p. 380) and others have suggested, simply a reiteration of other Athenian justifications. There are, of course, similarities between this speech and earlier Athenian statements. Yet the differences are even more striking, and reveal to us changes that have occurred not only in Athenian attitudes toward the empire, but also in their attitudes toward the war and the cities which opposed them.

Central to the changed attitudes is the racial question, for this debate marks, in Thucydides' history, the first serious use of such arguments. Let us be quite clear about this: to Thucydides, the racial explanation of the causes of the Peloponnesian War is a late invention by the participants, and is only that, an invention. The first αἰτία of the war, the Corcyrean-Epidamnian affiar, was a quarrel initially involving only Dorians. Athens entered the war wholly blind to race. Further, the Dorian Corcyreans remained allies of the Ionian Athenians throughout the war. Evidence at a much later date again shows the unreality of any ethnic undercurrent in the war: Thucydides' list (7.57) of the Athenian allies at the Sicilian expedition, when broken down into racial groups (see Dover, *Commentary* 4: 432–40), includes so many exceptions to the alleged Ionian-Dorian split that a racial explanation of the war would not survive objective examination. Thucydides himself points out throughout this chapter those cities which violated any simple racial division of the sides. The participants to this war did not fight for racial reasons, nor did they choose their allies because of racial affinity. The racial explanation came late, capitalizing on the indisputable fact that the greater number of Athenian allies were Ionians (and Peloponnesian allies Dorians), but answering to different, more abstract needs.

On the rhetorical side, too, the use of racial arguments began in earnest only quite late. The Corinthians waved the racial flag once— in their speech at the second Spartan congress, 1.124.1—as did Brasidas, at 5.9.1, to his troops before Amphipolis. In both cases the remarks were made to wholly Dorian audiences, and were exhortations touching on a traditional commonplace of Dorian bravery and Ionian cowardice. That is, they were morale-boosters rather than serious political statements or explanations. At the beginning of Athenian interest in Sicily the racial argument was used explicitly as a pretext (3.86.3–4). But it is in book 6 that the racial appeals become insistent and concrete (see, for example, the Athenian appeal to the Rhegians, 6.44.3). (See also de Romilly, *Thucydides and Athenian*

Imperialism, p. 244. De Romilly sees both the novelty and the objective falsity of the racial argument. That Hermocrates also uses it shows its attractiveness despite its falsity, and we must inquire why it was suddenly so attractive.)

It is no accident that the racial appeals became useful in connection with the Sicilian campaign, for both sides were hurriedly trying to assemble allies in Italy and Sicily. If the hearers were willing to allow it, the racial argument could be most effective, for it was another way of denying the possibility of neutrality: it insisted that all nations were *already* on one side or the other, by birth. The Rhegians did not allow the argument, nor do the Camarineans here. Yet the Syracusans and Athenians continued to advance it. The explanation for its invention lies, as I have suggested, in the urgent need for allies felt by both sides, and in the conciseness of the racial argument as an emblem or symbol of the depth of fear and irreconcilability of hatred existing between both blocs.

37. See Raubitschek, "The Speech of the Athenians at Sparta," pp. 36–38.

38. For the meaning and use of πολυπραγμοσύνη, the reader should consult Victor Ehrenberg, "Polypragmosyne, a Study of Greek Politics," *JHS* 67 (1947): 46–67, and A. W. H. Adkins, "*Polupragmosune* and 'Minding One's Own Business': A Study in Greek Social and Political Values," *CPh* 71 (1976): 301–27. There is, however, a further observation to make about this term, relevant to our inquiry. Although Ehrenberg does not make this observation, his section on Thucydidean uses provides ample evidence for it. The observation is this: Euphemus' use of this word is the only occasion in Thucydides that this very rhetorically charged word appears. To my mind it is not accidental that the word first appears in this place and in the mouth of an Athenian. It was most definitely not a neutral term of description, and with its clear suggestion of real excess could be used in only two ways: in denunciation of Athenian actions, or, conversely, in a cynical Athenian boast about these actions. We see the latter use here. But why here and nowhere else? The appropriate place for the term as denunciation would have been the Corinthian speech at the first Spartan congress. The Corinthians do not use the word on that occasion (although they use its opposite adjective, ἀπράγμων, 1.70.8), but I believe we can follow Ehrenberg in concluding (p. 47) that the Corinthians opt for a graphic description of Athenian πολυπραγμοσύνη without employing the word itself.

On the Athenian side—that is, pride in their πολυπραγμοσύνη —the absence of the word is suggestive indeed. The Athenians not only do not use the word before Euphemus does, they avoid it. (Adkins' analysis, both of the meanings associated with it and of the persons for whom it would have its strongest pejorative force—and these would include all of our Athenian speakers in this history—provides a concrete explanation for avoiding it.) The opportunities for employing the word are fairly numerous but on every occasion declined. Pericles uses ἀπράγμων in the Funeral Oration (2.40.2), but couples it with ἀχρεῖος, and ignores πολυπράγμων entirely. In his third speech the avoidance is even clearer. He scorns ἀπραγμο-σύνη (2.63.2), but contrasts τὸ ἄπραγμον not with τὸ πολυπράγ-μον, but with τὸ δραστήριον. Even Alcibiades shies from using πολυπράγμων, and calls Athens instead a πόλις μὴ ἀπράγμων (6.18.7).

What can we make of Athenian recourse to euphemism and pe-riphrasis about this word? *Polypragmosyne* could not be acceptably used by the Athenians until such time as a policy of excess would justify pride in being πολυπράγμων. One could be proud of not being ἀπράγμων, for it, too, was a form of excess (as also Adkins, "*Polupragmosune*," p. 315). But one did not freely call oneself πολυπράγμων. Even Alcibiades, in proposing a policy of continual activity, did not use the word, for he could not yet know that such a policy would be acceptable. But with its acceptance in the decision of the assembly, the psychological way was clear for the employment of this term as one of self-congratulation. In a period in which Athe-nians believed that only constant activity could ensure their survival, πολυπραγμοσύνη could become yet another of these "hard-headed" or "realistic" descriptions of the foundation of power and of political life. The word could be used, as here, for boasting that the Athenians recognized this "truth" of politics, and did not shrink from calling it by its true name, however much opprobrium common usage attached to it.

39. Dover's long and extremely clear discussion of this episode in *Commentary* 4: 264–88 suggests how this religious act could become entangled with political sentiment.

40. Rivalry among Spartan commanders is seen to lead to contra-dictory (and therefore counterproductive) military decisions at 8.12.2 and 8.17.2. A specific personal animosity between Tissaph-ernes and Hermocrates is said to have serious consequences for the Peloponnesian forces in Ionia, 8.85.2.

41. And we should recognize that this is a new development. For all that Thucydides attributed personal motives to Cleon, he never accused him of the sorts of betrayal of the city we now see occurring. If Cleon was ambitious, his ambition depended on the security of

the city so that he would have a powerful political entity of which to be leader. But for this latest set of Athenian politicians, the safety of the city is of less importance than their personal safety and success.

42. That on this occasion Thucydides believed a single speech sufficient for explaining the recommencement of the war embodies his belief in the real—though not apparent—continuity of the war through all its twenty-seven years (5.26.2). That is, the initial outbreak of the war, since it required a *change* from peace to war, required also some *pairs* of speeches for its explanation. Insofar as Thucydides does not believe the Peace of Nicias a real peace, there is no more than a diplomatic change occurring here (from covert to open war), and therefore, as with all previous policy elaborations (but not changes), only a single speech is needed to explain its direction.

43. That Alcibiades himself saw Carthage as an objective is the conclusion of Thucydides (6.15.2). But Alcibiades did not mention it in his speech in the Sicilian debate, nor did Nicias attack him for it (as we should expect he would have, had he known it, since it would make the magnitude of the campaign and its risks even larger), nor is it mentioned elsewhere. Athenian relations with Carthage at the time were amicable. Thucydides mentions a friendly embassy to Carthage during the Sicilian expedition (6.88.6; there is also a later treaty between Athens and Carthage, *ML* 92, pp. 280-83). The inference we must make is that the conquest of Carthage was an Alcibiadean dream, not an Athenian policy. De Ste. Croix, too (*Origins*, p. 223), believes this grand strategy is more Alcibiadean than Athenian, and also notes that it nevertheless probably had an electrifying effect on the Spartans.

44. In his appendix 4 to *Origins,* de Ste. Croix compiles a list of the decisions in this history very similar to ours. His list, however, is either too long or too short. Too long in that he includes decisions not accompanied by speeches; too short in that if one begins to admit decisions unaccompanied by speeches, the list might well be made longer. I believe our list is to be preferred since in the case of our seventeen decisions Thucydides has unequivocally marked them as important by exhibiting the speeches according to which they were taken and are to be understood.

Chapter Four

1. The naval battle at Naupactus, 2.86-92, provides an example of how a pair of generals' speeches can illuminate the confusing events of a battle in progress. For an example of how a general's

speech can also alert us to the concrete significance of chance or accident, see Brasidas' march through Macedonia, 4.125-28.

2. Another mark of how persuasively Thucydides has manipulated his material, especially in terms of the passage of time, is this: we have no doubt, while reading his history, that the entire stretch of twenty-seven years comprises one single war, *the* Peloponnesian War. Yet this apparently was not felt to be the case by his contemporaries (see Andocides, *On the Peace with Sparta,* 8-9). To someone living through these times, the period between the Peace of Nicias and the Sicilian expedition was quite long enough to make it appear that the Sicilian campaign was unrelated to the earlier war, and that the subsequent outbreak of war with the Peloponnese was the beginning of a new war, rather than the resumption of the earlier one. Yet in Thucydides' telescoping of the events of this interval, it seems impossible, to us, to consider the war as anything other than a single extended event.

3. Lionel Pearson's suggestion (most recently in "Prophasis: A Clarification," *TAPhA* 103 [1972]: 381-94) that neither πρόφασις nor αἰτία truly means "cause" in this passage, while persuasively argued on linguistic grounds and attractive as a way of cutting the Gordian knot of interpretation, cannot actually be followed. Pearson would have Thucydides say, essentially, "This is what the parties claimed as *grievances.* The truest *explanation,* however, was the growth of Athenian power and Spartan fear." It is true, as Pearson states (p. 383), that the uses of "cause" and "explanation" are close, especially in translation, but this is not merely a linguistic closeness, it is a natural one. When a historian asserts that one thing is the "explanation" of the existence or occurrence of another, what else can he be saying than that the first is the cause of the second? (There are "explanations" which are not causes, but these are explanations of, for example, the significance of something, not of its existence.) Thucydides' use of the Pentecontaetia assigns to πρό-φασις the sense of cause. The account of the growth of the Athenian empire begins at 1.89, immediately after the account of the Spartan congress and the decision that the Peace had been broken. It is introduced by a chapter (1.88) explaining why the Spartans decided as they did. The language recalls Thucydides' own distinction at 1.23 vividly: "The Spartans voted that the Peace had been broken and war should be waged, not so much because they had been persuaded by the speeches of their allies, as because they were afraid that the Athenians would grow even more powerful. . . ." At this point the narrative of the Fifty Years begins to explain the origin of the Spartan

fear. But in this passage at 1.88, the fear is not simply an explanation, it is actually the cause of an action, and "explanation" could be used as a translation of πρόφασις here only if it was used in the sense of "cause." Were one to ask, "Why did the Spartans vote as they did?" the answer would be, "Fear, not the speeches," and this answer would be a naming of the *cause* of their action—that is, the cause of their vote.

Similarly, αἰτία must also retain its sense of "cause." Of course, it does mean "what one alleges as a grievance," but nations tend to act on grievances, and insofar as they do, the grievances are causes, even if there may simultaneously be other causes in operation, and even if other causes may be called, in some sense, "truer." Considering the political process of the Spartan congress, were we to ask a Spartan why he voted as he did, he would have said, "Because of the allies." Nor would he, according to Thucydides, have been lying. The majority of the speeches at the congress (1.67) apparently concerned αἰτίαι (in the sense of "grievances"), and Sthenelaidas' winning speech to the Spartans (1.86) is almost wholly concerned with the injustices done to the allies of Sparta. Insofar as the Spartans were persuaded by Sthenelaidas' speech, we must also say that the αἰτίαι were causes of the final vote.

In Thucydides' initial statement at 1.23 and in its echoes at 1.88, both πρόφασις and αἰτία provide answers to the question "Why?" In some sense, then, both express genuine notions of cause. What is specifically Thucydidean is the explanation of events in terms of two different natures of cause. Rather than worry about the appropriate meanings of each in isolation, we must examine the interrelation between these two words for cause to discover how both may be causes and yet one be "truest."

4. The Peloponnesian decision to declare war would then have appeared as a simple, defensive reaction. A reaction which, moreover, would appear not only sensible but necessary, given the impressiveness of the Athenian empire—of which impressiveness we, too, would have had some indirect experience through Thucydides' extended treatment of the empire in the Pentecontaetia.

5. Indeed, the whole purpose of the first Spartan congress, and of the Corinthian speech at that congress, was to persuade the Spartans that the conflicts with Athens must not be regarded as private, but as involving the entire Peloponnesian League. (And, attempting to minimize the force of the Corinthian arguments, Archidamus in fact characterizes all the grievances of the allies as "private matters," 1.82.6.)

6. Archidamus prudently believed otherwise (1.81.6), and suggested the postponement of hostilities in order to allow for extraordinary preparations. He was ignored.

7. Although the largest Peloponnesian force in the field (and in one year the entire force) was deployed against this small city, the siege dragged on for five years (tying up an immense amount of Peloponnesian resources) and was, until the end, continually frustrated by the ingenuity of the defenders.

8. Insofar as we are interested in Athenian attitudes toward the empire and the war as Thucydides represented them, it is possible for us to sidestep the controversy over the "popularity" of the empire and over whether the good will Diodotus claimed actually existed. Whether Diodotus' proposal made the imperial cities trustworthier subjects or not, the Athenians accepted the proposal and acted upon it. Again, whether by the end of the Peace of Nicias the Athenians had more reason to fear the allies or not, fear them they did (as represented by statements in the Melian dialogue, Alcibiades' speech on the Sicilian expedition, and Euphemus' speech) in a new and desperate way. The Athenians may well have been mistaken in their judgment on either of these occasions, but for the sole purpose of this inquiry their judgment and consequent decisions are the data with which we must deal, rather than with what in fact were the feelings of the cities toward Athens.

9. Nor, apparently, did the democrats for Athens. See Legon, "Megara and Mytilene," pp. 209–10.

10. We can see two especially cynical uses of the trope, "oligarchs are never to be trusted," in the manipulation of democratic mistrust to reject (1) Spartan peace proposals (by Cleon, 4.22.2, in 425, the seventh year of the war) and (2) Spartan negotiations for the settlement of remaining disputes during the Peace of Nicias (by Alcibiades, 5.45.4, in 420, the twelfth year of war).

11. Being oligarchs by tradition, they would not find as fertile a ground for political slogans and emotion in the conflict of the institutions of democracy and oligarchy. Oligarchic political thought— or, at least, its rhetoric—tends to be noninstitutional (the slogan, "the rule of the best men," attaches little significance to procedure). Democratic politics do give great emphasis to institutions and procedures, with the result that democratic slogans and formulations tend to be overtly political, whereas oligarchic slogans and formulations tend, in the first instance, to be moral or ethical (or, at least, to cover political concerns with a moral vocabulary).

12. Atticism, in fact, came to be, during this war, even more

pejorative than Medism. In addition to the general moral opprobrium which attached to being likened to the Persians, since Athenian conquests almost inevitably encouraged democratic revolutions
in the conquered cities, a special political fear was added. The democratic attribute of Atticism also played an important part both in the
establishment of Atticism as a kind of political crime and ideology,
and in the development of a Peloponnesian policy to deal with it.

13. The Athenians, by contrast, did not come to this conclusion
until the next phase of the war. As far as they were concerned,
democracies and oligarchies had coexisted for years, and there was no
reason to believe the war could not reach some appropriate resolution
in which both forms had some place. But for the Peloponnesians, as
there could be no place at all for Medism in the Greek world, neither
could there be one for Atticism.

14. Thucydides makes this frighteningly clear at 3.82.4–5. Every
word had a special meaning, and therefore a sentence made out of
words attempting to offer some advice midway between the parties
underwent grotesque distortions, and came out a party statement in
spite of the intention of the speaker. Even words which normally
denote moderation itself became party slogans: "forward-looking
caution" became "specious cowardice," etc. In Thucydides' description of it, it was literally impossible to say something which
avoided partisan meanings, since whatever was said could only be
heard in its partisan senses. This distortion of language, and with it
the decay of the possibilities of deliberation, is a subject which can be
traced throughout Thucydides' history. See also Westlake, *Individuals,* p. 227, on Thucydides' interest in the debasement of political
language.

15. A modern example of such an extended conflict which,
through its ideological foundation, acquires the unity of a single
"war" is the Cold War of the 1940s and 1950s, in which, although
apparently discrete events take place over the widest expanses of time
and space, the ultimate grounds of hostility (and the origins of the
events) remain the same. It is in this form that the Peloponnesian
War, too, forms a unified whole.

16. Indeed, the ideological interpretation continued to the end of
the war, as evidenced by Lysander's policies of liberation and pacification, involving changes of constitution. See n. 29, p. 272 above.

17. H. D. Westlake, in "Thucydides and the Uneasy Peace: A
Study in Political Incompetence," *CQ* 21 (1971): 315–25, is quite
correct in asserting that Thucydides' account of the Peace of Nicias is
not a disorderly account of insignificant events, but is, in fact, an

emphatic account of significant diplomatic failure. Yet I think we might prefer to attribute the cause of this failure not so much to incompetence and timidity (though they may have played their part, too) as to the endurance of underlying ideological pressures and the fear and suspicion that these would naturally occasion.

18. All of the alliances established during the Peace were formed along ideological lines. This was true of both sides, and the constant emphasis of a serious ideological opposition between Athens and the members of the Peloponnesian League made it impossible for anyone to defuse ideological perceptions and antagonisms, exacerbated already existing fears, and gave reality to the notion that there was a *natural* or *necessary* ideological conflict which would eventually lead to war between the two blocs. Even the fact that certain states switched sides during the Peace (as Argos did) clarified rather than confused the ideological underpinnings of the war, for the switching of sides was always the result of a revolution, whether oligarchic or democratic. It is worth sketching the major diplomatic moves of the Peace to exhibit this. In the first year of the Peace, the democracies of Argos, Elis, and Mantinea (all Peloponnesian states) concluded an alliance. Significantly, Boeotia and Megara, although at odds with Sparta and shopping around for another alliance, did not join this Argive group, for they felt they would come out the worse for it—themselves being oligarchies and the Argive group democracies (5.31.6). Also in the first year of the Peace, Parrhasia (a Mantinean subject state) defected to Sparta following an outbreak of factional conflict. In the second year of the Peace, the Argive bloc concluded an alliance with Athens, again with ideological reasons figuring prominently (5.44-47). Almost immediately, this caused the Corinthians to drift back to Sparta's side, though they, too, had initially been disaffected with Sparta. By the fourth year of the Peace, Thucydides can make the general statement: "The Spartans, seeing that . . . of the other places in the Peloponnese, some had already revolted, and others were not doing well, and considering that, if they did not quickly forestall it, these things were bound to advance even farther, marshaled all their forces and the Helots. . ." (5.57.1). In addition to the indirect effect the ideological nature of these alignments had on the war, the Athenian-Argive bloc directly worsened tensions by initiating campaigns against other cities of the Peloponnese and Arcadia, creating for the Peloponnesians not merely the picture of a democratic bloc, but of an *aggressive* democratic bloc.

19. As, indeed, was true. Two processes were at work. On the one hand, in bypassing those cities which were not hostile, Athens ex-

tended its influence at all points until it encountered resistance. Thus, necessarily, at each of its extremities (of control) there were enemies. On the other hand, the sight of an apparently unstoppable Athens brought cities together in resistance which would normally remain aloof (as in Sicily). Thucydides twice portrays (in book 4 and in books 6 and 7) how Athenian successes created so much fear that nearly universal resistance to Athens was the result.

20. There were, of course, cities which remained neutral even at this time. But it was felt by the major blocs that no cities *ought* to be neutral. Those which remained neutral were able to do so only because circumstances allowed them: neither bloc was able—at the crucial moment—to compel them to take sides. Nevertheless, the concept of neutrality as a reasonable and justifiable political choice was destroyed.

21. It is worth noting that all of these changes are also characteristic of a condition of *stasis* within a single city. This is not to say that one ought to say, or that Thucydides is saying, that Greece at this time was like a city in *stasis*. Rather, the *causes* of these changes during a war are identical to the causes of these changes during a *stasis*. In both cases it is the coincidence of a belief that differences are irrevocable and a belief that defeat spells annihilation which drives men to these extremes.

22. Plato's tyrant is enslaved by desires as well as fears. Both exert their compulsion upon him. This sort of compulsion, too, may well have been felt by the Athenians, and one could probably construct a plausible account of the desires which were compelling the Athenian democracy (including, no doubt, the Sicilian expedition as one of these desires run amok). At this point, however, I wish merely to emphasize the compulsion felt because of the fear the Athenians had of being surrounded by enemies. The analogy with Plato is drawn from the ninth book of the *Republic,* from which the following citation can be made (from the Shorey translation): "Then it is the truth, though some may deny it, that the real tyrant is really enslaved to cringings and servitudes beyond compare, a flatterer of the basest men, and that, so far from finding even the least satisfaction for his desires, he is in need of most things, and is a poor man in very truth . . .; and throughout his life he teems with terrors and is full of convulsions and pains. . . ." (579d-e). For a similar reflection on Thucydides and *Republic*, book 8, see J. de Romilly, "La notion de nécessité dans l'histoire de Thucydide," in *Science et Conscience de la Société* 2 vols. (Paris: Calmann-Lévy, 1971) 1: 109–28, esp. pp. 127–28.

23. Book 7 contains two lengthy generals' speeches to prepare our understanding of the decisive battles in the harbor of Syracuse, and also contains Nicias' letter to the Athenian assembly (7.11-15). A word should be said about this letter. The letter—both in form and function—falls midway between a political speech and a general's speech. It performs a little of the function of each, though I believe it to be more like a general's speech (that is, tied quite closely to the immediate narrative of military events) than a political one. Throughout book 6 and the beginning of book 7, we have seen, Thucydides constructs a narrative of the gradual loss of Athenian initiative and the erosion of tactical position in Sicily. Nicias' letter is in fact a compact expression of exactly this decay of military opportunities, and also demonstrates that Nicias himself was aware of how badly the situation had deteriorated. The letter, therefore, in this respect forms a perfect summary of this process: a sort of general's speech after the fact, making clear the significant outlines and trend of the particular actions which have occurred. In its quasi-political aspect the letter demonstrates that despite the deterioration of the Athenian position in Sicily, the Athenian assembly *consciously* chose to continue the expedition. This is an important fact for us to know in following the history of the political processes of the war. That the letter was read in Athens demonstrates that the Athenians continued the expedition not because they were ignorant or misinformed, but because they were wrong. Thucydides has included the letter because it is important for him that there be no doubt about this matter. Nevertheless, the letter is not a political speech, for Nicias does not attempt to persuade the assembly of any position, he merely reports information and asks for instructions.

24. Compare, for instance, the shamefacedness and tentativeness with which Archidamus treated this topic at the first Spartan congress (1.82.1).

Chapter Five

1. J. de Romilly, *Histoire et raison chez Thucydide,* pp. 123-24.
2. See also Lateiner, ''The Speech of Teutiaplus,'' pp. 175-84.
3. That human actions are free may put them outside the range of science. Whether free actions can be the subject matter of a science is itself, however, a question to which multiple answers would be given, depending upon different philosophical positions as to the nature and canons of science. (Aristotle, for example, conceives science as capable of dealing not only with phenomena which always

and necessarily occur, but also with phenomena which occur "for the most part" [*An. Post.* 87b20; *Metaphys.* 1027a21—Aristotle's distinction of science from art depends not on the distinction "necessary/for the most part," but on the distinctions "universal/particular" and "speculative/practical"]. That there could be, for him, sciences of human action is a consequence of this conception, and, indeed, he classifies his *Ethics* and *Politics* as sciences. History, however, because of its particularity, would be at best an art rather than a science, though it would depend on the sciences of human action as, for example, medicine does on biology.) Our present discussion does not require a prior decision on the epistemological status of history, whether science or art (or even knack). Insofar as it is pursued deliberately (and of course it is), it is pursued according to some principles. And the difficulty of discriminating these principles is not the result of the ambiguity of the status of history but of the complexity of the subject matter.

4. Most criticism of histories—as also of Thucydides—proceeds by claiming either that the historian has ignored some specific influence or has improperly proportioned the force of different influences.

5. For, indeed, although we have so far considered prudence in its relation to general truths of action, it is also the case that the more prudent the historian the more satisfactory we will deem the account given of specific events—believing that the prudent person possesses acuter skills of observation and interpretation in the field of action.

6. There also occurs a third use, at 3.84.2. The authenticity of this chapter has long been doubted, but the relevant passage reads: "And when on this opportunity normal life was disordered in the cities, and the laws were too, and human nature [ἀνθρωπεία φύσις]—wont to do wrong even in the face of the law—had taken control, then gladly it revealed itself weaker than appetite, stronger than justice, and an enemy to any superior."

7. See, for example, *Leviathan* 1.6 and 1.13.

8. Whether this identification was also common among other cities is not so clear. The Corinthians certainly make use of it in their speech at the first Spartan congress. The Mytileneans make use of it in their speech at Olympia (3.10.1). Hermocrates does, too, in his speech at Gela (4.61.5-6; 4.62.3-4), yet other instances are not so straightforward. Perhaps the analogy was initially a sophistic trope, and found primarily in those cities which had some extensive contact with these "unorthodox" educational doctrines and techniques.

9. For example, Woodhead, "Thucydides' Portrait of Cleon," pp. 297-98.

10. It is worth noting as well that Thucydides is consistent in his usage of certain terms related to the distinction we are investigating. Where—in addition to the places already cited—Thucydides uses the word "nature" ($\phi\acute{v}\sigma\iota s$) in his own narrative (1.138.3; 3.74.1; 4.3.2), it retains its literal sense. It denotes the physical or biological nature present in all natural individuals—but not artificial entities, such as nations. On the other hand, on the one other occasion where Thucydides constructs a substantive from the adjective, human (in this case, 5.68.2, $\tau\grave{o}\,\mathring{a}\nu\theta\rho\acute{\omega}\pi\epsilon\iota o\nu$ rather than $\tau\grave{o}\,\mathring{a}\nu\theta\rho\acute{\omega}\pi\iota\nu o\nu$), the resulting concept refers to a human trait, but not necessarily a natural nor an individual one. It is far more likely that the exaggeration he speaks of in this place is a social phenomenon with a social cause, rather than a personal action resulting from natural causes.

11. So that Westlake ("The Subjectivity of Thucydides: His Treatment of the Four Hundred at Athens," *BRL* 56 [1973]: 193–218, esp. p. 208) is wrong in seeing this—and the collapse of morality—as new and as the object of Thucydides' concern in this section of the history. The crimes are old or ageless. What is new is a condition under which the conduct of politics and deliberation (without which there can be no restraint of these crimes) becomes impossible. This is a new development, and this is the subject of Thucydides' analysis.

Chapter Six

1. I continue to stress the extrarational aspects in this place only because the specifically rational ones have been dealt with extensively in their proper places in chapters 1–3.

2. One consequence of this is their willingness to hear themselves abused as irresponsible by their orators (for were this criticism unwelcome, we would not have the record of so much of it). Perhaps they even approved this abuse as a demonstration of the orator's realism: he expected they would act as badly as possible.

3. It is again worth noting that in these circumstances it is the appearance that is more important than the reality. Alcibiades was being both abstract and rather far-fetched. Yet his arguments *sounded* more realistic, most likely because they were more cynical. For all their professed realpolitik, the Athenian assembly was not above simple elegance and even great abstraction. But it was the style of talk that captured them more than the coincidence of the style and the content. By comparison Nicias' arguments sound empty and platitudinous, whatever their truth may have been.

4. This is true even for Archidamus, for all that he appears more

intelligent than other Spartans. His statements advising new kinds of military preparations of course testify to the lack of these in Sparta, hence to its backwardness in matters of military technology. More importantly, his assumption (1.82.1) that the Athenians lie in wait for Sparta shows that he, too, experiences this general fear.

5. "And so, as we have just made clear, your practices are, in comparison with theirs, outmoded. And it must be that what is newer—just as in the arts—will prevail" (1.71.2–3).

6. I add the qualification, "or before fellow citizens," to account for an entire class of speeches which take place away from the speaker's own city, yet before his fellow citizens—that is, the generals' speeches. In every instance, Thucydides reports the name of the general who spoke. This may be for reasons other than those we have developed. Yet we can also see in this practice a consistent extension of the principle enunciated here. Since generals are never strangers to their troops, their personalities are often more than casually known. How soldiers respond to the appeals made of them may in some cases be influenced by their extrinsic opinions of their commanders. Knowing the name of the general who spoke may then be significant in understanding the actions of the army.

7. Euphemus, also speaking at Camarina, is surely named because Hermocrates was (as Diodotus was for Cleon).

8. The speech of Teutiaplus (3.30) probably falls under the rubric of the generals' speeches: he would be personally known to his coleaders on this expedition. The various conversations of Archidamus (2.11 and 2.71–74) are again instances where someone is apparently fairly well known outside his home city. The Plataeans address him directly as if they expected him to act rather better than their other enemies.

9. And let us not be trapped into thinking Thucydides did not know their names. For the historian who could discover that it was Euphemus who spoke opposite Hermocrates at Camarina, the discovery of the Athenian speakers at this critical debate would hardly have been insuperable.

10. For further discussion of the importance of Pericles himself in this instance, see de Romilly, "Les intentions d'Archidamos" (cited n. 32, p. 263 above).

11. For discussion of the replacement of political virtues by personal excesses in Alcibiades' rhetoric, see Gomme, "Four Passages in Thucydides" (cited p. 261 above), and Westlake, *Individuals,* pp. 225–26. See also my discussion of this, pp. 99–100, and of his personal rhetoric in the speech at Sparta, pp. 114–16.

12. One must also point out that the Athenians, too, made as

complete a misjudgment of the rhetorical situation in their speech to the Spartan congress. They too failed to fit words to occasion and to audience. As possibly accurate as their assessment was in a theoretical sense, in the concrete practical situation in which they made it, it could hardly have been less appropriate. And it, too, was rejected by the audience which heard it.

13. Spartan motives here are unclear. They may have requested a confidential hearing to avoid the Athenian assembly, or simply to avoid speaking publicly about concessions *they* were willing to make but knew would be unpopular with their allies. In either case, given the realities of the specific political and deliberative situation, to make the request was a mistake.

14. To ask this question requires that we be able to assign certain arguments to rhetorical—rather than historical—necessities, and this requires a determination on our part to examine the rhetorical aspects of deliberations. V. Hunter (*Thucydides, the Artful Reporter*, pp. 123–35), having made an extremely detailed study of the similar arguments in the two speeches, stops at that point, and finds in the two men a model of action she calls "the tragic warners." The model lacks, however, historical specificity, for the similarity of the arguments is rhetorically determined. The similarity does not, therefore, imply or indicate any specific historical facts. The traces of the specific facts of the specific occasions must be found in those arguments *not* determined by the rhetorical necessities, that is, in those arguments by which the speeches of Archidamus and Nicias *differ*.

Chapter Seven

1. As we have seen previously, these two uses of rhetoric are coordinate. From the standpoint of the orator, knowing the facts of the situation one searches for the means of persuasion through the system of rhetoric. From the standpoint of the historian, the system of rhetoric is used analytically on the finished speech (something constructed to be persuasive) in order to discover the facts of the situation. We do, indeed, make use of rhetoric in this latter mode in the reading of Thucydides, just as, we believe, Thucydides made use of it in the composition of his history. But this is not the only use to which rhetoric is put in the history.

2. "Ironic" is my description, not Stahl's, but is, I believe, not inappropriate as shorthand to indicate the relation Stahl stresses ("Speeches and Course of Events," pp. 69–77) between human action in ignorance and the "facts" as they are revealed by events. We should notice, however, that irony is inappropriate here because

as a principle it reduces and obliterates the particularity of specific decisions. Stahl's concentration on the irony of the Sicilian expedition blinds him to the fact that Nicias' assessment of the situation, while more concrete, is no less erroneous (at least, no less speculative) than Alcibiades'. Nicias has no more evidence for his case than Alcibiades had, and if Nicias' dire prediction of the result of the expedition comes about, it is largely because of his own actions and mistakes. The alleged unity of the Sicilians was not a known fact, nor a particularly dependable one, as the debate at Syracuse shows (as does the evidence of a pro-Athenian party within the city). The disastrous military result of the expedition could not be predicted, and might well not have occurred with another commander. We see this in that every other Athenian general urges a course of action different from Nicias', and each of these courses would seem to have had a more fortunate result, had it been put into action, than Nicias'. It is Nicias' timidity that keeps him from aborting the expedition in good time; it is his superstition that fatally delays the withdrawal of the troops. If Nicias' prediction is prophecy, it is mainly self-fulfilling. But since irony would require that Nicias be farsighted yet ignored, it is thus that Stahl reads his Nicias, quite contrary, I believe, to the evidence in Thucydides.

3. V. Hunter, *Thucydides, the Artful Reporter*, p. 70. J. B. Wilson, *Pylos 425 B.C.* (Warminster, Wilts.: Aris and Phillips, 1979), p. 62 gives convincing explanations of both Demosthenes' deliberateness and his companions' hesitation.

4. Woodhead, "Thucydides' Portrait of Cleon."

5. Oligarchies are included in this designation of "democracy" as long as their citizen bodies are numerous even if not universal. For an enfranchised citizen of an oligarchy political participation would be as direct and unmediated as it would be for a citizen in a wider democracy.

6. Certain procedural arrangements may also influence our decision. For example, each house of the United States Congress is itself numerous, yet the committee structure through which legislation is brought to the floors of the Congress makes the actually authoritative deliberating bodies quite small indeed. The committee system would explain the greater importance given to politicking—rather than "public" address and persuasion—in the Congress.

7. We may also notice that while classical theories distinguish the different places in which speeches are given (assembly, law courts, festivals, or ceremonies), the different functions of the hearers (deliberation, judgment, praise), and sometimes the different roles of the hearers (deliberators, judges, spectators), they never make these

distinctions on the basis of institutional considerations.

8. As, for example, in the case of the Melian dialogue. That the procedures of this debate were quite different from normal (a fact upon which Thucydides insists, 5.84.3) did influence the nature of the discussion. The directness and even brutality of expression that de Romilly (*Thucydides and Athenian Imperialism*, p. 274) and Meiggs (*Athenian Empire*, pp. 388–89) condemn as unrealistic and therefore impossible are probably attributable to the particular procedural circumstances under which the "debate" took place. Such brutality of expression would indeed be inappropriate before a large, potentially volatile audience. But directness is a virtue, even a necessity, in discussions with small executive boards, and it was with just such a group that the Athenians were to treat. Notice, however, that even here the peculiarity of the rhetoric on this occasion is reducible to the composition of the audience according to differentiae of audiences, rather than to any institutional characteristic.

Index